Register for Free Membership to

solutions@syngress.com

Over the last few years, Syngress has published many best-selling and critically acclaimed books, including Tom S[...]'s Configuring ISA Server 2004, Brian Caswell and Jay Beale's [...] Detection, and Angela Orebaugh and Gilb[...] Packet Sniffing. One of the reasons for the [...] is been our unique **solutions@syngress.com** [...] site, we've been able to provide readers a real time extension to the printed book.

As a registered owner of this book, you will qualify for free access to our members-only solutions@syngress.com program. Once you have registered, you will enjoy several benefits, including:

- Four downloadable e-booklets on topics related to the book. Each booklet is approximately 20-30 pages in Adobe PDF format. They have been selected by our editors from other best-selling Syngress books as providing topic coverage that is directly related to the coverage in this book.

- A comprehensive FAQ page that consolidates all of the key points of this book into an easy-to-search web page, providing you with the concise, easy-to-access data you need to perform your job.

- A "From the Author" Forum that allows the authors of this book to post timely updates and links to related sites, or additional topic coverage that may have been requested by readers.

Just visit us at **www.syngress.com/solutions** and follow the simple registration process. You will need to have this book with you when you register.

Thank you for giving us the opportunity to serve your needs. And be sure to let us know if there is anything else we can do to make your job easier.

SYNGRESS®

How to Cheat at Managing
Windows Server
Update Services

Tony Piltzecker

Susan Snedaker

Chad Todd

Kirk Vigil

David E. Williams

Brian Barber   Technical Editor

FOREWORD
BY BRIEN M. POSEY

KEY	SERIAL NUMBER
001	HJIRTCV764
002	PO9873D5FG
003	829KM8NJH2
004	GHLPOMCCXX
005	CVPLQ6WQ23
006	VBP965T5T5
007	HJJJ863WD3E
008	2987GVTWMK
009	629MP5SDJT
010	IMWQ295T6T

PUBLISHED BY
Syngress Publishing, Inc.
800 Hingham Street
Rockland, MA 02370

How to Cheat at Managing Windows Server Update Services

Printed in Canada
1 2 3 4 5 6 7 8 9 0
ISBN: 1-59749-027-X

Publisher: Andrew Williams   Page Layout and Art: Patricia Lupien
Acquisitions Editor: Gary Byrne   Copy Editor: Judy Eby
Technical Editor: Brian Barber   Indexer: Nara Wood
Cover Designer: Michael Kavish

Distributed by O'Reilly Media, Inc. in the United States and Canada.
For information on rights, translations, and bulk sales, contact Matt Pedersen, Director of Sales and Rights, at Syngress Publishing; email matt@syngress.com or fax to 781-681-3585.

Acknowledgments

Syngress would like to acknowledge the following people for their kindness and support in making this book possible.

Syngress books are now distributed in the United States and Canada by O'Reilly Media, Inc. The enthusiasm and work ethic at O'Reilly are incredible, and we would like to thank everyone there for their time and efforts to bring Syngress books to market: Tim O'Reilly, Laura Baldwin, Mark Brokering, Mike Leonard, Donna Selenko, Bonnie Sheehan, Cindy Davis, Grant Kikkert, Opol Matsutaro, Steve Hazelwood, Mark Wilson, Rick Brown, Tim Hinton, Kyle Hart, Sara Winge, Peter Pardo, Leslie Crandell, Regina Aggio Wilkinson, Pascal Honscher, Preston Paull, Susan Thompson, Bruce Stewart, Laura Schmier, Sue Willing, Mark Jacobsen, Betsy Waliszewski, Kathryn Barrett, John Chodacki, Rob Bullington, Kerry Beck, and Karen Montgomery.

The incredibly hardworking team at Elsevier Science, including Jonathan Bunkell, Ian Seager, Duncan Enright, David Burton, Rosanna Ramacciotti, Robert Fairbrother, Miguel Sanchez, Klaus Beran, Emma Wyatt, Chris Hossack, Krista Leppiko, Marcel Koppes, Judy Chappell, Radek Janousek, and Chris Reinders for making certain that our vision remains worldwide in scope.

David Buckland, Marie Chieng, Lucy Chong, Leslie Lim, Audrey Gan, Pang Ai Hua, Joseph Chan, and Siti Zuraidah Ahmad of STP Distributors for the enthusiasm with which they receive our books.

David Scott, Tricia Wilden, Marilla Burgess, Annette Scott, Andrew Swaffer, Stephen O'Donoghue, Bec Lowe, Mark Langley, and Anyo Geddes of Woodslane for distributing our books throughout Australia, New Zealand, Papua New Guinea, Fiji, Tonga, Solomon Islands, and the Cook Islands.

Technical Editor and Lead Author

Brian Barber (MCSE, MCP+I, MCNE, CNE-5, CNE-4, CNA-3, CNA-GW) is coauthor of Syngress Publishing's *Configuring Exchange 2000 Server* (ISBN: 1-928994-25-3), *Configuring and Troubleshooting Windows XP Professional* (ISBN: 1-928994-80-6), and two study guides for the MSCE on Windows Server 2003 track (exams 70-296 [ISBN: 1-932266-57-7] and 70-297 [ISBN: 1-932266-54-2]). He is a Senior Technology Consultant with Sierra Systems Consultants Inc. in Ottawa, Canada. He specializes in IT service management and technical and infrastructure architecture, focusing on systems management, multiplatform integration, directory services, and messaging. In the past he has held the positions of Senior Technical Analyst at MetLife Canada and Senior Technical Coordinator at the LGS Group Inc. (now a part of IBM Global Services).

Contributing Authors

Jonathan Hassell is an author, consultant, and speaker residing in Charlotte, NC. Jonathan's previous published works include *RADIUS* and *Learning Windows Server 2003* for O'Reilly Media and *Hardening Windows* for Apress. His work is seen regularly in popular periodicals, such as Microsoft's *TechNet Magazine*, *PC Pro*, *SecurityFocus*, and *Windows IT Pro Magazine*. He speaks around the world on topics such as networking, security, and Windows administration.

Tony Piltzecker (CISSP, MCSE, CCNA, CCVP, Check Point CCSA, Citrix CCA), author and technical editor of Syngress Publishing's *MCSE Exam 70-296 Study Guide and DVD Training System* and the upcoming *How to Cheat at Managing Microsoft Operations Manager 2005*, is a Consulting Engineer for Networked Information Systems in Woburn, MA.

Tony's specialties include network security design, Microsoft operating system and applications architecture, as well as Cisco IP Telephony implementations. Tony's background includes positions as IT Manager for SynQor Inc., Network Architect for Planning Systems, Inc., and Senior Networking Consultant with Integrated Information Systems. Along with his various certifications, Tony holds a bachelor's degree in business administration. Tony currently resides in Leominster, MA, with his wife, Melanie, and his daughters, Kaitlyn and Noelle.

Susan Snedaker (MBA, BA, MCSE, MCT, PM) is Principal Consultant and founder of Virtual Team Consulting, LLC, a consulting firm specializing in start-ups and companies in transition. The company works with technology start-ups to develop viable business plans in preparation for debt/equity funding or due diligence with venture capital firms. VirtualTeam Consulting also provides IT consulting, design, and implementation services to companies of all sizes. The firm assists companies with strategic planning, operations improvement, and project management. Through its team of subject matter experts, VirtualTeam Consulting also offers financial, change management, and operations improvement services to targeted companies.

Prior to founding VirtualTeam in May 2000, Susan held various executive and technical positions with companies such as Microsoft, Honeywell, Keane, and Apta Software. As Director of Service Delivery for Keane, she managed more than 1,200 technical support staff, delivering phone and e-mail support for various Microsoft products, including Windows Server operating systems. She has contributed technical chapters to six Syngress Publishing books on

Windows and security technologies and has written and edited technical content for a variety of publications. She is the primary author of *How to Cheat at IT Project Management* (Syngress, 1-59749-037-7). Susan has also developed and delivered technical content from security to telephony and TCP/IP to Wi-Fi.

Susan holds a master's degree in business administration and a bachelor's degree in management from the University of Phoenix; she also holds a certificate in project management from Stanford University. She is a member of the Information Technology Association of Southern Arizona (ITASA).

Chad Todd (MCSE:Security, MCSE:Messaging, MCT, CEH, CEI, CNE) is co-owner and Chief Technical Officer for Training Concepts, a consulting and training company in Columbia, SC. He manages the Microsoft, CompTIA, Citrix, Novell, and Certified Ethical Hacking training programs. He also serves as the project manager and lead engineer for the dozens of Windows and Exchange migrations performed by Training Concepts every year.

Chad also spends a good amount of time in the classroom, where he focuses on security, Windows 2003, Exchange 2003, and ISA 2004 classes. He has been a Microsoft Certified Trainer for more than six years. He has taught hundreds of classes and thousands of students.

When he is not training or consulting, Chad enjoys technical writing. He has authored three other books on topics such as Windows XP, Windows 2000 Security, and Windows Server 2003. In addition to writing books, Chad frequently writes magazine articles for *Redmond Magazine* (formerly *Microsoft Certified Professional Magazine*). Chad can be reached on the Web at www.trainingconcepts.com.

Chad would like to thank his grandmother, Louise Richardson, for always serving as the perfect role model for his family, and his wife, Sarah, for her never-ending support and encouragement.

Kirk Vigil (MCSE, MCSA), coauthor of *MCSA/MSCE Exam 70-291: Implementing, Managing, and Maintaining a Windows Server 2003 Network Infrastructure,* is a senior systems consultant for NetBank, Inc. in Columbia, SC. He has worked in the IT integration industry for more than 13 years, specializing in Microsoft messaging and network operating system infrastructures. Kirk began working with Microsoft Exchange at its inception and continues to focus on its design and support as his core technology.

Kirk holds a bachelor's degree from the University of South Carolina. He also works as an independent consultant for a privately owned integration company, lending technical direction to local business practices. He is a contributing author for the monthly technical subscription *Redmond Magazine* (formerly *Microsoft Certified Professional Magazine*). Kirk would first like to thank God. Kirk also wants to thank his wonderful girlfriend, Kimberly Wells, for her complete support, understanding, love, and compassion during the many isolated hours that went into creating this book. He could not have done it without her. Secondly, thanks so very much to his family for their continuous support, prayers, and unconditional love. Lastly, Kirk is grateful to the owners, editors, and writers of Syngress Publishing for the opportunity to continue working and writing with them.

Kirk would like to dedicate this book to his loving Auntie Ri-Ri.

David E. Williams works as an Infrastructure Manager for the John H. Harland Company in Atlanta, GA. Harland is one of the leading software companies focused on financial institutions, one of the largest check printers in the country, and the leader in testing and assessment solutions for the education market. In addition to managing IT resources, he is also a senior architect and an advisory engineer, providing technical direction and advice to Harland's management team in long-range planning for new or projected areas of enterprise projects.

He is also a principal at Williams & Garcia, LLC, a consulting practice specializing in delivering effective enterprise infrastructure solutions. He specializes in the development of advanced solutions based on Microsoft technologies and strategic infrastructure designs. David studied Music Engineering Technology at the University of Miami, and he holds MCSE, MCDBA, VCP, and CCNA certifications.

When not rearchitecting corporate infrastructures, he spends his time with his wife and three children.

Foreword Contributor

Brien M. Posey is Relevant Technologies' Vice President of Research and Development (*http://www.relevanttechnologies.com*). Brien has previously served as the Director of Information Systems for a large nationwide chain of healthcare facilities and as the Department of Defense's senior network engineer at Fort Knox. He has also served as Editor in Chief of several technical publications and also as a network administrator for one of the country's largest insurance companies.

Brien is an award-winning technology author, a Microsoft Certified Systems Engineer (MCSE), and a Microsoft MVP. He has written or contributed material to 28 books and published more than 3,000 articles for a variety of Web sites and printed publications, including CNET, Jupiter Media, Microsoft's *TechNet Magazine*, *Windows Magazine*, Windows Networking, TechTarget, and ZDNet.

Contents

Foreword

I will never forget the first time that I ever had to deploy a service pack. It was Service Pack 1 for Windows NT Workstation. Although I had read about the upcoming service pack and knew that it was important, I was totally unprepared to actually install it. The installation itself wasn't difficult, but the service pack consisted of a stack of floppy disks that had to be manually loaded in sequence into each machine to which the service pack was being applied. The process took slightly more than two hours per machine to complete, and our company had more than 1,000 workstations.

At first, I adopted a technique in which as soon as disk 1 finished loading, I would insert disk 2 and then start running disk 1 on another workstation. That accelerated the process, but not to the extent that I would have liked. I considered placing the service pack onto a distribution point on the network and installing it over the wire, but disk space on the servers was tight, network bandwidth was limited, and I knew that my boss would blow a gasket if I tried it. Ultimately, I made about 20 different copies of the service pack disks and managed to use those copies to get the service pack deployed to all of the workstations over the course of a couple of weekends. The process was long, boring, and tedious to say the least, and I couldn't imagine ever having to install another service pack again for as long as I live.

Well, roughly 12 or 13 years have gone by, and Microsoft has released countless service packs, hot fixes, and patches since my first experience. In fact, hardly a week goes by that Microsoft doesn't release some kind of patch. Because so many patches are being released, it would be nearly impossible for a medium-sized or a large organization to manually deploy patches and to keep track of which patches have been applied to which machines.

To make matters worse, time is of the essence when applying patches. On average, it takes about four days from the time that a security vulnerability is discovered until a hacking technique, a virus, or a worm is created that exploits that vulnerability. Consequently, getting patches applied as soon as they become available is critically important. My old technique of waiting until the weekend to deploy patches is simply unacceptable in today's world.

Thankfully, Microsoft has automated patch management through a product named Windows Server Update Services (WSUS). WSUS is the successor to the Software Update Services (SUS) utility that was used to keep Windows up-to-date. The main difference between the two products is that SUS focused its attention solely on Windows, but WSUS can keep a wide variety of Microsoft products up-to-date (with the notable exception of Microsoft Flight Simulator ☺).

Because of the importance of patch management, I tend to think of WSUS as being one of the most critical applications for any Windows network that does not rely on third-party patch management products. That being the case, it amazes me that Microsoft has chosen to give us WSUS for free. All an administrator has to do to stay up-to-date with all the latest patches for Microsoft products is to download WSUS and spend a little time configuring it and learning how it works. That's where this book is helpful. It will teach you all of the ins and outs of deploying, configuring, and managing WSUS.

Happy patching!

—*Brien M. Posey*
Vice President of Research and
Development, Relevant Technologies
http://www.relevanttechnologies.com

Chapter 1

Windows Server Update Services Essentials

Solutions in this chapter:

- **Patch Management for the Enterprise**

- **Introducing Microsoft Windows Server Update Services**

- **Software Update Services vs. Windows Server Update Services**

☑ **Summary**

☑ **Solutions Fast Track**

☑ **Frequently Asked Questions**

Introduction

Microsoft Windows Server Update Services (WSUS) is the answer to all of your problems as long as they are centered on *patch management*. Patch management is the systematic application of updated code to operating systems and certain Microsoft applications, to repair a defect until the next version of the operating system or application is released. WSUS is the updated version of Software Update Services (SUS), and can be used to manage the download, approval, scheduling, targeting, and deployment of updates to recent versions of Windows and a range of Microsoft desktop and server applications.

Patch Management for the Enterprise

Picture this. You are the network administrator for *weneedpatchmanagement.com*. It is a beautiful Tuesday morning. The sun is shining. There is a spring in your step as you go to work. Latté in hand, you take your seat at your desk, flip your calendar, and break into a cold sweat. Reality hits you like a freight train. This is not just any Tuesday; this is the second Tuesday of the month, what we in the business call "Terrible Tuesday." It is the day that Microsoft releases its monthly batch of operating system, application, and device driver security hotfixes and updates.

The problem is that *weneedpatchmanagement.com* does not have a systematic way to deploy these updates consistently across its user base. Once these updates are released, some users religiously apply all of them, some apply some of them, and some ignore all of them. The random pattern of updating takes place, and results in different levels of security preparedness and stability in the software running on users' desktops and laptops, and company servers. Multiply the randomness for as many months as this has happened, and this network administrator has a real mess on his or her hands.

Microsoft released SUS to bring a system in-house to update the Windows family of operating systems. It allowed network administrators to enforce the application of updates on network-connected, Windows-based workstations and servers. In 2005, Microsoft replaced SUS with WSUS to update not just Windows, but Office, Structured Query Language (SQL) Server and, Exchange, among other additional functionality. With WSUS, Microsoft has brought the ability to keep the spectrum of Microsoft products up-to-date in a controlled manner, with relatively little management overhead.

The following chapters cover everything you need to know to install, upgrade, deploy, manage, secure, and troubleshoot WSUS. In short, by the end of this book, you should know enough to be fully prepared to administer patch management for your organization. The chapters build on each other as you progress through the book; however, each chapter also stands on its own in case you need to perform specific tasks such as upgrading from SUS to WSUS (see Chapter 4). This chapter begins with a definition of patch management and what it means for your organization. It then moves on to a description of WSUS features, and finishes with a brief comparison of SUS and WSUS.

BEST PRACTICES ACCORDING TO MICROSOFT

When Microsoft introduced SUS, it offered the following compelling arguments for determining the value of patch management in terms of the negative impact on your environment if you decide that you do not need patch management or that you should not devote a lot of time to it (from www.microsoft.com/technet/itsolutions/cits/mo/swdist/pmsus/pmsus251.mspx):

- **Downtime** What is the cost of computer downtime in your environment? What if critical business systems are interrupted? Determine the cost of lost end-user productivity, missing transactions on critical systems, and lost business during an incident. Downtime is caused by most attacks, either by the attack itself or by the corresponding remediation required when recovering.

- **Remediation Time** What is the cost of fixing a wide-ranging problem in your environment? How much does it cost to reinstall a computer? What if you had to reinstall all your computers? Many security attacks require a complete reinstallation to be certain that back doors (permitting future exploits) were not left by the attack.

- **Questionable Data Integrity** In the event that an attack damages data integrity, what is the cost of recovering that data from the last known backup, or confirming data correctness with customers and partners?

- **Lost Credibility** What does it cost if you lose credibility with your customers? How much does it cost if you lose one or more customers?

- **Negative Public Relations** What is the impact to your organization from negative public relations? How much could your stock price or company valuation fall if you are seen as an unreliable company to do business with? What would be the impact of failing to protect your customer's personal information, such as credit card numbers?

- **Legal Defenses** What would it cost to defend your organization from others taking legal action after an attack? Organizations providing important services to others have had their patch-management process (or lack of one) put on trial.

- **Stolen Intellectual Property** What is the cost if any of your organization's intellectual property is stolen or destroyed?

What Is Patch Management?

Before discussing patch management, we should define the "patch" aspect of the term. In Information Technology (IT), we understand a patch to be an update to an operating system or application; however, un-patched systems were exploited to propagate the attack and attack other systems. We have been led to believe that patches are the ultimate solution—*patches are not the ultimate solution*.

SOME INDEPENDENT ADVICE

While WSUS seems like the remedy to some of your biggest headaches, it has its limitations. If your budget is an issue, you may need to run more than one of the free patch-management systems that vendors make available. You may also need to look at other creative ways to deploy patches, such as building your own application packages and deploying those packages by being creative with login scripts and other scripting methods.

When we were kids and ripped the knees out of our pants, we would go home and have someone sew a patch over the hole. We did not end up with a new pair of pants; we had the same pants but with a patch. Operating system and application patches are exactly the same. We do not have a new application after applying a patch; we have the same application with an updated piece of code to cover up the hole.

In the past, when applications were single, monolithic executable files, the entire binary executable had to be replaced in order to update an application. Now that applications and operating systems are increasingly modular, patches are used to update or replace executables, Dynamic Link Libraries (DLLs), scripts, and any other application components. Since most attacks spread using un-patched systems, the pressure is on network administrators to quickly supply the patches to the users'. The problem with releasing patches expeditiously is that they must be tested, approved, and deployed to every vulnerable server and workstation in a systematic manner, or else they are installed with a tremendous degree of risk. To minimize the risk and increase the stability and security of your infrastructure, you should introduce patch management.

The definition of patch management from *searchsecurity.com* describes it as "an area of systems management that involves acquiring, testing, and installing multiple patches (code changes) to an administered computer system. Patch-management tasks include: maintaining current knowledge of available patches, deciding what patches are appropriate for particular systems, ensuring that patches are installed properly, testing systems after installation, and documenting all associated procedures, such as specific configurations required."

Shortcuts...

The Truth Is Out There

There is an active patch-management community, specifically regarding WSUS. At *www.patchmanagement.org*, there are links for subscribing to a general patch-management list, and a list specifically for WSUS. On the general patch-management list, most questions come from people building patch and update application packages for deployment using Systems Management Server (SMS) and other vendors' patch-management products. You can sign up for one or both lists and ask questions and receive support from people who are managing systems and using a range of patch-management products. Both lists are very active, and some questions receive responses in minutes. These lists are definitely worth adding to your toolbox.

Microsoft WSUS provides this functionality for the Windows operating systems and applications; however, it is not the only patch-management system available. In fact, it is not the only option available from Microsoft. SMS 2003 has a component entitled "Security Patch Management," which expands the functionality of WSUS to permit the updating of device drivers, and adds other enterprise management features. With the release of SMS 2003, Microsoft expanded the functionality of Security Patch Management (discussed later in this chapter). Furthermore, there are many third-party patch-management products that permit patch management for a range of vendors' products. A major benefit of WSUS for organizations that run Windows and other Microsoft applications is the price; it is available for free.

Why Do We Need It?

If you are reading this book, there is a good chance that you are already aware of the need for patch management; you may have already downloaded and installed WSUS. As discussed earlier, un-patched systems have been subject to and used in Denial of Service (DOS) attacks and a number of de-stabilizing, productivity-stealing events that have had a huge impact. If your colleagues and management are convinced that this will never happen to them, convince them to reconsider their position.

More often than not, updates that are released by Microsoft eliminate bugs in desktop applications and the operating system, which cause incidents that the technician must fix. The technician's time is quantifiable monetarily, as is any lost productivity on the part of the user. Multiply this by the number of users who have not applied a particular patch or any other patches, and the costs start to mount. When the system is a server and all connected users lose access to it, the financial cost of the server's downtime increases exponentially with each passing minute, and also the cost to the organization in terms of loss of reputation or trust. Patch management is important to the security, prosperity, and productivity of everyone (i.e., staff, customers, and clients) who connects to the systems in your environment.

If you are not convinced that patch management is important, it is easy to find evidence to support your arguments. If all else fails, you can fall back on the fact that WSUS cuts down on bandwidth utilization over your Internet connection (see Chapter 5), and WSUS is free.

What System Is Best for You?

As stated earlier, there are a number of patch management options from Microsoft and other vendors. This section discusses the options from Microsoft: SMS, Microsoft Update (formerly known as Windows Update), and WSUS.

Microsoft recommends that its customers use one of its patch management solutions. The most suitable solution depends on the size of the organization, the type of patch management it needs, and what skills are available to administer the system. In general, WSUS addresses most straightforward patch-management requirements, while SMS provides advanced functionality. As shown in Table 1.1, Microsoft recommends the patch-management systems according to the size and complexity of your environment (from www.microsoft.com/windowsserversystem/updateservices/evaluation/faqs.mspx).

Table 1.1 Recommended Microsoft Patch-management Systems

Customer Type:	Scenario:	Customer Choice:
Large or Medium Enterprise	The organization wants a single, flexible patch-management solution with an extended level of control that enables it to update (and distribute) all Windows operating systems and applications, and also includes integrated asset management.	SMS
Large or Medium Enterprise	The organization wants a solution for update management only, which provides simple updating for Microsoft software.	WSUS
Small Business	The business has at least one Windows server and one IT administrator.	WSUS
Small Business	All other scenarios	Microsoft Update
Consumer	All other scenarios	Microsoft Update

SMS is Microsoft's comprehensive system and infrastructure management solution, comprised of Application Deployment, Asset Management, Security Patch Management, Mobility, and Windows Management Services Integration. It is used to return the control over any changes to the management of the infrastructure back into the hands of network administrators. A notable use of SMS is the ability to standardize, deploy, lock down, and manage the configuration of workstations and servers. For the purposes of this book, SMS' Security Patch Management capability takes patch management a step further than WSUS, by delivering the ability to differentiate between stationary and mobile computers, slipstream hardware updates and custom-developed patches in with Microsoft-developed software updates, and enhanced reporting.

Windows Update changed into Microsoft Update, with an expanded selection of Microsoft software now available. Microsoft Update was introduced in tandem with WSUS, and supports Windows Server 2003, Windows XP Service Pack (SP) 2, Windows 2000 SP4, Office 2003, Exchange, and SQL Server. As a rule, Microsoft Update supports the latest versions of these products. Windows Update will continue to be available for older versions of Windows, and should be used for versions starting (or finishing) with Windows 2000 SP 2 and earlier, including Windows 98, 98 Second Edition (SE), and Millennium Edition (Windows ME). An important distinction between Microsoft Update and Windows Update and their internal counterpart, WSUS, is that hardware updates are available through Microsoft and Windows Update. The following sections describe WSUS and its improvements over its predecessor, SUS.

Introducing Microsoft Windows Server Update Services

As discussed earlier, WSUS is one of several Microsoft patch-management offerings. In essence, WSUS enables organizations to take the application and operating system update functionality of Microsoft Update, and move it from outside the firewall to inside, thereby giving the organization the ability to test, approve, schedule, and deploy updates to the latest Microsoft products in a controlled manner. This is something that is often lost when updating workstations and servers are left to the discretion of users and network administrators.

WSUS is more accurately identified as a suite of software, rather than a single application. It consists of the following three components:

1. **Microsoft Update** Rather than have individual workstations and servers connect to Microsoft Update over the Internet, the WSUS server (or servers) downloads updates and stays in synchronization with it. It is the source that WSUS servers use for the updates they deploy.

2. **WSUS Server** WSUS is the component that runs on Windows 2000 and 2003 Servers inside the corporate firewall. Depending on the size, geographic

distribution, management structure, and security requirements of your network, WSUS can run on a single server or be deployed on any number of servers according to the management model that is best suited to your organization. It is available as a free download from Microsoft at http://www.microsoft.com/windowsserversystem/updateservices/downloads/WSUS.mspx.

3. **Automatic Updates** This client software is integrated natively in Windows 2000 with SP3 (or higher), Windows XP, and Windows Server 2003 operating systems. The Automatic Update client is configured on both workstations and servers to download and install updates from a WSUS server.

SOME INDEPENDENT ADVICE

One omission from the list of operating systems supported by Microsoft is Windows NT 4.0. You may be asking, "Why are we talking about Windows NT 4.0 in this day and age?" The answer is simple. There is still a lot of NT 4.0 running legacy software that cannot be updated or does not need to be updated. There is no Microsoft solution for downloading and applying updates. You may want to explore deploying patches, especially if there are a lot of them, using custom-developed scripts and the *qchain.exe* utility. *Qchain.exe* permits the application of hotfixes in a single location to be installed with one reboot instead of having to reboot after every patch.

Shortcuts...

Automate, Automate, Automate

The point of introducing your infrastructure to WSUS is to avoid the practice of visiting every workstation and server when Microsoft releases a patch. As much as possible, use every feature available in WSUS to minimize the time you spend administering it. Use Group Policy Objects (GPOs) to deploy the Automatic Update clients to all supported versions of Windows, and to configure these clients to point to the correct server running WSUS. Enable the automatic scheduled synchronization of updates and enforce the installation of updates, so that all workstations and servers are at the same build level. In the following chapters, these practices and more are described in detail. The goal should be that the only activities you need to perform are the approval and scheduling of updates.

Features

With WSUS, you get much more than you pay for. The current release of WSUS is vastly improved over its predecessor, and the feature set has made it ready for the Enterprise. The following list describes the main features of WSUS:

- **Updates for the Microsoft Family of Products** The most obvious improvement over SUS is that WSUS will upgrade the latest versions of Windows, Office, Exchange, SQL Server, and MSDE.

- **Control Over the Installation (and Removal) of Updates** WSUS permits the approval and scheduling of updates for deployment. In addition, you can enforce the application updates so that they are not ignored by users using the new deadline functionality. Should things go horribly wrong with the installation of an update, WSUS can manage its un-installation on workstations and servers and re-release.

- **Flexible and Scalable Architecture** For small organizations, a single server running WSUS may be all that is required. In larger organizations, WSUS servers can be chained together or replicated, and managed centrally or in a distributed fashion, according to the culture and management style of your organization. There is even accommodation for disconnected networks (see Chapter 10). In addition, you can logically group computers by type, role, location, or any other grouping that makes sense in your organization.

- **Flexible Update Storage Options** Depending on the network and storage constraints of your organization, you have a choice of where you can store updates. If storage is tight, you can keep updates on the Microsoft Update Web site and only download metadata. Alternatively, you can select the most bandwidth-friendly solution and store updates locally on servers inside your firewall.

- **Network Bandwidth Optimization** As mentioned previously, you can decide where clients download the actual updates. If you have a high-capacity, low-cost connection to the Internet, you can opt for keeping updates at Microsoft Update. You still have the ability to approve, schedule, and manage updates without having to manage another file system or partition.

- **Web-based Management Interface** WSUS management is performed exclusively through a robust Web interface, which makes administration flexible and portable wherever you are.

- **Native Integration with Automatic Update Client** Windows 2000 post SP3, XP, and Windows Server 2003, ship with the Automatic Update client installed. Once WSUS is up and running, you can use local settings or GPOs to point the Automatic Update client at the designated server running WSUS, to receive updates without needing additional software installed.

- **Integrated Reporting Capability** One of the key features of WSUS that makes it a truly enterprise-ready management tool, is its ability to deliver a selection of status reports on demand. With the click of a button, you can generate reports on what updates have been approved and what computers have or have not received updates.

Limitations

As robust as it is, there are several limitations that should be considered when selecting and deploying WSUS as your organization's patch-management program. WSUS is limited to updating the latest versions of Microsoft software only, namely Windows 2000 SP4, XP and Server 2003, Office XP and later only, Exchange 2003, SQL Server 2003, and Microsoft SQL Desktop Edition (MSDE). If you are running a variety of operating systems and products from a number of vendors, you may consider running from a number of platform- and application-specific patch-management systems or one from a third-party vendor, to maintain control over the stability of your infrastructure. In addition, the Windows 98 and ME computers that run Microsoft Office 97 still need to use Microsoft Update (or Windows Update and Office Update). Furthermore, you will need to look to another system, such as SMS or a third-party solution, for deploying hardware updates and custom-developed update packages.

Software Update Services vs. Windows Server Update Services

Microsoft's first attempt to bring patch management into its family of operating systems was SUS. WSUS is essentially SUS 2.0, because it builds on SUS functionality by significantly expanding the feature set. In this section, the functionality of SUS is described briefly in relation to the improvements made in WSUS. For those who are running SUS, this may provide you with the comfort to make the switch to WSUS.

Many of the features of WSUS already existed in SUS. Much like WSUS connects with Microsoft Update, SUS connected to the Windows Update site so that network administrators could download all manner of patches (e.g., critical updates, security updates, and service packs) and maintain control over which updates will be applied to workstations and servers. SUS has built-in security using Secure Sockets Layer (SSL), and the ability to select updates for approval and scheduling, the content synchronization between the organizations and Windows Update, and among WSUS servers within the organization.

BEST PRACTICES ACCORDING TO MICROSOFT

- Microsoft will continue to support SUS until December 6, 2006.
- After December 6, 2006, Microsoft will no longer support SUS, and SUS will no longer synchronize or provide new updates. (At the time of writing, SUS has been withdrawn from Microsoft's list of available downloads.)

SOME INDEPENDENT ADVICE

You do not have to do a fast cutover from SUS to WSUS. SUS and WSUS can run in parallel while you transition completely to WSUS (discussed at length in Chapter 4).

Shortcuts...

Start Small and Grow As Required

If there is resistance to implementing enterprise-wide patch management, you may want to consider installing WSUS for servers or workstations over which you are directly responsible. Any software that can make an immediate improvement on a bad situation that can be implemented at little to no cost or effort, can be the "quick win" needed to justify its adoption on a wider scale. WSUS can also be a positive step towards identifying the need for a more robust management product such as SMS.

New Features in WSUS

The following features represent the most significant areas of improvement in WSUS over SUS:

- **Expanded Range of Products that can be Updated** In what is probably the most obvious improvement over SUS, WSUS will upgrade the latest versions of Windows, Office, Exchange, SQL Server, and MSDE.

- **Broader and More Granular Control over the Update Process** WSUS gives network administrators the ability to finely manage updates throughout their lifecycle. From the initial download through approving, targeting, scheduling, installing, and, if necessary, removing updates, you can govern every aspect of the update process.

■ **Ability to Target Updates to Particular Computers** For small organizations, this may not be required; however, in larger, more complex organizations, computer groups can be created based on type, model, role, criticality, and location, among others. This functionality is also useful for creating pilot groups so that you can release an update to a subset of the entire organization before releasing it to all workstations or servers. This can dramatically increase the effectiveness and efficiency of the patch-management process and the stability of your infrastructure.

■ **Consolidated Status Reporting:** Reporting was one of the one of the key features missing from SUS, and gratefully added in WSUS. The ability to generate reports without having to resort to third-party software to define, develop, produce and publish report is deeply appreciated, as is the ability to have a view into the status of updates deployed by WSUS whenever it is required.

Summary

WSUS is an enabling technology solution that supports a patch-management process. This process can be applied as widely or as narrowly as the business culture can tolerate; business processes require it. WSUS is being used successfully in localized or specialized environments, and as an enterprise-wide update infrastructure.

- A patch is designed to address a particular software defect or security flaw. It may not be the best fix, but it is a way to keep the software running until the next full release.

- There are a number of patch-management solutions on the market. Microsoft offers Microsoft Update as a free service, Windows Server Update Services as a free download to bring the service inside the firewall, and SMS as a comprehensive systems management system, which includes Security Patch Management.

- WSUS enables organizations to take the application and operating system update functionality of Microsoft Update and move it from outside the firewall to inside, giving the organization the ability to test, approve, schedule, and deploy updates to the latest Microsoft products consistently across the enterprise in a controlled manner.

- WSUS is essentially "SUS 2.0," and many of its features already existed in SUS. The notable improvements in WSUS are the ability to upgrade desktop and server applications, expanded control over update management, the ability to target computers for upgrade, and consolidated reporting.

The only thing worse than manually deploying patches is not deploying them at all. Leaving control over the downloading and installation of patches to individual users and server administrators will most likely lead to inconsistent patch levels from workstation to workstation and server to server. Patch-management systems have emerged to eliminate, or at least reduce the cost to the organization of not deploying patches or by doing it badly. WSUS is a free solution from Microsoft that can be used to keep Windows-based workstations and servers up-to-date with the latest security patches and bug fixes for both the operating system and for desktop and server applications. The potential for a loss of reputation, and hence, the possible loss of business, may be enough justification for implementing a patch-management process and software solution.

Solutions Fast Track

Patch Management for the Enterprise

- Patch Management is the acquisition, testing, and installation of updates to administered computer systems in a controlled fashion.

- Microsoft has a number of patch-management solutions, including Microsoft Update, WSUS, and SMS.

- Not implementing patch management can be detrimental to the health of your organization's infrastructure. The support effort required for maintaining even a small group of workstations or servers at different patch levels is much higher than a group at the same patch level.

Introducing Microsoft Windows Server Update Services

- WSUS consists of three components: the Microsoft Update Web site, WSUS software running on a server in your enterprise, and the Automatic Update client software running on workstations and servers that will receive updates.

- Updates are limited to the most recent versions of Windows 2000, XP, and Server 2003, Office, Exchange, and SQL Server.

- WSUS is available as a free download from Microsoft.

Software Update Services vs. Windows Server Update Services

- SUS was Microsoft's first foray into a freely available internal patch-management solution and it was introduced to manage and deliver updates to Windows.

- WSUS offers significant advantages over SUS by adding the ability to upgrade desktop and server applications, expanded control over update management, the ability to target computers for upgrade, and consolidated reporting.

- There is a clear upgrade path from SUS to WSUS (covered in Chapter 4).

Frequently Asked Questions

The following Frequently Asked Questions, answered by the authors of this book, are designed to both measure your understanding of the concepts presented in this chapter and to assist you with real-life implementation of these concepts. To have your questions about this chapter answered by the author, browse to **www.syngress.com/solutions** and click on the **"Ask the Author"** form.

Q: With WSUS, do I need to configure all servers and workstations to use it?

A: You can deploy WSUS as narrowly or as widely as you need. If the source of your patch-management pain is a group of Windows servers running SQL Server, you can deploy WSUS for just those servers.

Q: Can I update operating systems other than Windows with WSUS? If not, what can I do?

A: Sadly, the answer is no. WSUS can only be used for updating the Microsoft family of products. As for alternatives, there may be a patch-management system for the other operating systems running in your environment that is freely available from the software vendor. Furthermore, there are third-party patch-management solutions that will update a range of operating systems and software available.

Q: What can I do with PCs running Windows 95 and workstations and servers running Windows NT 4.0?

A: First, WSUS is not an option. Second, if the updates are available, you are left with purchasing a third-party solution that can manage these operating systems, or coming up with your own solution using a combination of scripts and custom-developed update installation packages.

Q: Can I deploy hardware drivers with WSUS just like Windows Update and Microsoft Update?

A: No, WSUS does not give you the ability to deploy drivers. With the Security Patch Management functionality of SMS 2005, you can slipstream drivers in with software updates, which will make it behave much like Microsoft Update.

Chapter 2

Preparing for WSUS

Solutions in this chapter:

- **Assessing Your Current Infrastructure**
- **Selecting a WSUS Management Preference**
- **Designing the WSUS Environment**

☑ **Summary**

☑ **Solutions Fast Track**

☑ **Frequently Asked Questions**

Introduction

This chapter focuses on preparing you to design your Windows Software Update Services (WSUS) implementation. The foundation begins with a thorough assessment of your current infrastructure so that you know exactly how your network is laid out and how it is organized from geographic locations to organizational units (OUs) to security groups and more. Once you have reviewed the infrastructure, you need to look at how you currently manage your infrastructure so that your WSUS environment maps well to your existing structure. At the end of this chapter, you will have all the information you need to effectively design your organization's unique WSUS environment based on both your infrastructure layout and on your current network management practices.

Assessing Your Current Infrastructure

Before you can design your WSUS environment, you must assess your current infrastructure. This assessment includes the current (and near future) geographic distribution of computers, the network architecture in place, the security requirements for your organization, and the types of clients and servers on your network. By having a solid assessment of your infrastructure, you can put together a plan for implementing WSUS across the enterprise. Keep in mind that if your organization is planning major or minor changes to the infrastructure in the next year or so, you should accommodate this in your WSUS planning. In this section, we look at the elements of the infrastructure and discuss how it will shape the choices you make when designing your WSUS implementation.

BEST PRACTICES ACCORDING TO MICROSOFT

- Geographical considerations for WSUS include language, network, and Internet connectivity and local administrative capabilities.
- Each WSUS server should be used to update no more than 15,000 computers. Depending on the locations and types of computers to be updated, you will need to implement one or more WSUS servers to distribute the update load across the enterprise.
- Use a WSUS server to update each operating system. You may choose to organize WSUS servers by operating system type (Windows Server 2003, Windows 2000 Server, Windows XP, and so forth) so that updates for one operating system come from one WSUS server.
- Do not go more than three levels deep when setting up WSUS in a hierarchical model. Exceeding three levels may cause significant lag times between updates and synchronization. When looking at your network layout, keep this limitation in mind.

SOME INDEPENDENT ADVICE

Microsoft stipulates that a single WSUS server with dual 3GHz (or faster) processors and 1GB of random access memory (RAM) can update as many as 15,000 servers; however, when you begin placing a near-maximum load on a server, it can slow down significantly. The WSUS server has essentially two roles. One is to synchronize its internal database with the Microsoft Update site so that available updates are downloaded to the WSUS database, which is primarily an issue of Internet-side bandwidth—how quickly those updates can be downloaded into the local WSUS database. The second function is the distribution of those updates to clients within the organization. This is a function of the number and type of clients as well as the internal network bandwidth available. Other factors such as when the updates occur (high or low network usage time) or whether or not Internet Protocol (IP) traffic is secured (IPSec) will impact server performance. Keep all of this in mind as you assess your infrastructure and later when you plan your WSUS environment. The cost of an additional WSUS server may be a better choice than pushing the capabilities of a single WSUS server with 14,999 clients to update.

Shortcuts...

Asset Database

Most information technology (IT) departments use some type of asset-tracking database to ensure that they know where all of their client, server, and network components are. With the increasing use of mobile devices, knowing who has what becomes even more important. Smaller IT departments can use a spreadsheet or database program to keep track of things; however, as you grow you may need a formal asset tracking application. Assessing your infrastructure is much easier when you have network assets present and accounted for.

Geographic Considerations

The best starting point in assessing your infrastructure is to look at the geographic layout of your network. How you implement WSUS depends greatly on the geography your network has to cover. Clearly, there is a big difference in the implementation approach between a simple, one-location network and a global, distributed network. This section examines how WSUS is implemented in various geographic models, to give you an idea of how assessing your infrastructure ties in with designing your WSUS implementation. When looking at your geographic layout, consider these elements:

- A centralized versus decentralized network management structure
- IT staff at various locations
- A risk to location (natural disasters, and so forth)
- An IT infrastructure at each location, including Internet connectivity, bandwidth, reliability, and so forth

Single Location

If your network assets are all located in one place, the WSUS implementation is fairly straightforward. The most basic WSUS deployment involves setting up a single WSUS server inside the corporate firewall. This single WSUS server can provide update management for up to 15,000 computers across all supported Windows operating systems. Even in a single location, you may choose to use more than one WSUS server. The role of the WSUS server is to *synchronize* and download updates with the Microsoft Update Web site to determine which, if any, updates are needed. These updates are then downloaded to the WSUS server and distributed to the network clients via the internal network.

Multiple Locations

If your network is composed of multiple locations across a wide geographic region (city, state, region, country, world), your WSUS design must address these multiple locations. For each location, you must assess how the locations are currently connected, how they relate to each other, and how they are currently managed.

Mapping your network by geography should also include the number and proximity of offices in a particular location (e.g., your company might have a five-building campus in San Francisco, three manufacturing facilities in Tulsa, OK, and satellite offices in Boston, New York, Miami, Atlanta, and Chicago). Your geographic layout will help you design your WSUS deployment so that you can minimize cost and maximize efficiency.

Creating a location map can help you visualize the relationship between and among locations (see Figure 2.1). Your map will probably have far more detail, but this sample gives you an idea of how to begin mapping your network.

Figure 2.1 Location Map Sample

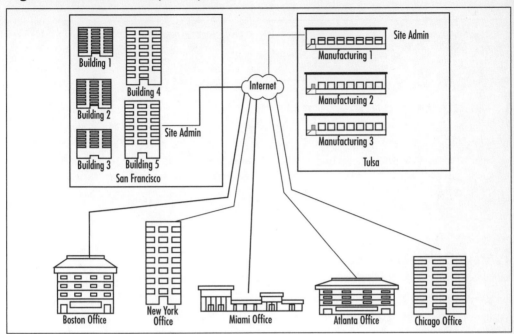

Using this example, you can clearly see your various locations and how they relate to one another and the corporate network. When planning your Active Directory (AD) deployment, you probably created a location map. If one exists, ensure that it is current. If one does not exist, use your AD information and your physical organizational information (actual location of offices) to create a map. Ideally, the map will also list forests, domains, OUs, sites, and IP address ranges, but that level of detail is not specifically required for WSUS implementation. If you do not currently have a site map and are creating one from scratch, you should include the physical locations, number and types of computers, and site link information.

Language Selection

WSUS updates can be targeted to specific language versions of Windows, so understanding where your network locations are and what language they are using is important. It is not a problem if they are all in the U.S. and using English, but if you have locations in other countries and you intend to manage WSUS in a centralized fashion, you should have a complete inventory of the various language versions your company is running.

Shortcuts...

Language Options

By default, WSUS downloads Critical Updates and Security Updates for all Windows products in all languages. Clearly, if you need only English, Spanish, and Japanese, you should limit your language selection in WSUS to just those languages. A complete inventory of the installed version and the language of Windows installed throughout your enterprise is necessary to properly deploy and maintain WSUS.

Network Architecture

Your existing network architecture is another element you should assess prior to implementing WSUS. The purpose of this section is to remind you to look thoroughly at your network architecture with an eye toward WSUS deployment. As you know, you can view your network via connectivity, functional relationship, network topology, and specialized function. Check these elements, at minimum:

- Local area network (LAN), metropolitan area network (MAN), wide area network (WAN)
- Connectivity (T1, T3, CAT 5, and so forth) and bandwidth
- Wired, wireless
- Clients and servers
- AD data
- Topology (bus, star, mesh, and so on)
- Protocols (standard, security, storage, communication, and so on)
- Security components and requirements
- Network components (routers, switches, hubs, firewalls, and so on)

Ideally, you should have a network diagram depicting the locations, architecture, and structure of your entire network infrastructure. If you do, take time to ensure that it is completely up-to-date so that you do not make false assumptions about the status of your network architecture when implementing WSUS. When compiling or reviewing your network architecture, keep the basic design of WSUS in mind to be certain that your review is thorough.

WSUS servers connect via the Internet to the Microsoft Update Web site. The default configuration of the WSUS server is to download all updates in all languages. You can restrict downloads to just those languages and operating systems that your company uses, thereby reducing the amount of Internet traffic between your WSUS server and the Microsoft Update site. Once the updates are on the WSUS server, they are made available to clients based on how the WSUS servers are configured. For instance, you may choose to have a single WSUS server or you may use multiple chained WSUS servers. When reviewing your network architecture, however, you should keep these facts in mind:

- At least one WSUS server must connect to the Microsoft Update Web site. You can choose to have several autonomous WSUS servers at different locations, each of which must connect via the Internet to the Microsoft Update site, or you may choose to have the updates synchronized among chained WSUS servers, where the downstream WSUS server receives its updates from the upstream WSUS server.

- WSUS servers that connect with the Microsoft Update site should be located near the perimeter of your network. Burying it deep in the network configuration uses internal network bandwidth that could be put to better use.

- If you choose to use chained WSUS servers, the connections between those servers should have adequate bandwidth, speed, and reliability to allow the upstream WSUS server to quickly and reliably propagate the changes (*replicate*) across that connection.

- The organization of your network by administrative function, business function, sites, OUs, and more will also come into play as you design your WSUS.

After reviewing these areas, you should also review (and update, if necessary) your AD information, including OUs, group policies, and administrative groups. Your WSUS design and deployment will interact with these elements, and understanding how your network is currently configured is critical for a successful WSUS deployment. Some network administrators already know this information and can simply review it prior to designing their WSUS implementations. Others may have to start from scratch if they are stepping into a new role or if the network architecture has not previously been adequately documented. Starting from scratch may seem like a daunting task to accomplish prior to implementing WSUS, but once complete, it is a valuable resource.

One area to give extra time to is the identification of current network bottlenecks. As you are designing your WSUS deployment, you should make sure that you do not cause further congestion on an already slow connection by using it for WSUS updates. If you are aware of bottlenecks, you should either resolve them before implementing WSUS or make sure that your configuration does not add to the problem. Otherwise, network performance and user productivity will suffer.

Active Directory

Your AD structure should be well documented and should be used in designing your WSUS environment. The following list explains some of the elements that could impact your WSUS environment:

- Number of forests in organization
- Number of domains in organization
- OU design and implementation in your organization
- Site topology

Ideally, you should have a map for your company that lists this detail as well as detailed information about the site topology, which should include computer information, domains relevant to each site, domain controllers at each site, and connectivity between each site. Connectivity information is important because WSUS must connect to the Internet and internally through the private network to clients; therefore, you need a keen appreciation of how sites are connected (the type of links) and the cost associated with each, as well as the current replication schedule and load (AD replication) across those links. If you choose to use the replica model for WSUS, you may be overloading your site links if WSUS replication traffic is large. Understanding the current load will help you design a WSUS environment that works best with your current configuration or allows you to make changes to your infrastructure to accommodate your WSUS design.

Security Requirements and Policies

You must design your WSUS installation according to the security requirements and policies for your organization. For instance, you can (and should) take steps to harden the WSUS server to ensure it remains secure from attack. If you choose to use multiple WSUS servers in a chained fashion, you may also want to consider adding authentication between chained WSUS servers in an AD environment. Finally, you may also want (or need) to use Secure Sockets Layer (SSL) for WSUS server traffic out to Microsoft Updates and back. The WSUS server that connects to the Microsoft Update site should sit behind a corporate firewall and the firewall should be hardened to the greatest practical degree possible.

Understanding how your networks are secured, including physical access, security policies (passwords, authentication, login hours, and so forth), security protocols, and administrative policies (group policy and so forth) is always important, but it is also highly relevant to your WSUS design because you want to maintain (and perhaps improve) security through WSUS implementation. Clearly, one of the compelling reasons to consider using WSUS is the ability to regularly and consistently apply appropriate updates to clients so that security holes are addressed in a timely manner. Many corporate attacks result from hackers learning of a new hole to exploit, and corporations being slow to implement patches. That small gap of time between discovery and repair can make all the difference.

Having a clear understanding of your OUs and how they interact with your Group Policy Objects (GPOs) will also be important when you deploy WSUS.

NOTE

Microsoft does not recommend editing the default domain or default domain controller's GPOs to add WSUS settings.

In a simple environment, the new GPO is linked with the WSUS settings to the domain. In a more distributed network environment, you may have several GPOs linked to OUs, enabling you to apply different WSUS policy settings to different types of computers. The group policies and OUs you have in place will impact how updates are applied to client computers; therefore, a thorough review of these settings is in order.

Your current security needs must be balanced against the additional requirements (administrative, bandwidth, processor) needed for heightened security. You should harden the WSUS server; however, you will have to decide whether implementing authentication between chained WSUS servers or using SSL for WSUS traffic makes sense in your environment. Securing the WSUS server with SSL reduces performance by about 10 percent, because the processor is busy encrypting all of the metadata that has to cross the wire. In addition, if you are using remote Structured Query Language (SQL), the connection between the remote server and the WSUS server will not be encrypted, creating a potential security gap that should be addressed. You have several options if the database connection must be secured. You can place the database on the WSUS server, the default configuration for WSUS, (which eliminates across-the-wire data transfers), you can place the SQL Server and the WSUS Server on a private network (which effectively isolates the across-the-wire data), or you can use the security protocol IPSec to secure the traffic between the two servers, which will reduce performance and throughput.

Servers and Clients

Make sure you have a current listing of all client and server computers. This list should at a minimum contain the following information:

- Computer type (client, mobile client, thin client; domain controllers, print server, application server, Web server, domain name server, proxy, and so on)
- Current operating system and language
- Location
- Use of computer (general categories or descriptions)
- User/owner (user for client, owner, or who manages it for servers)
- Network connectivity type

- Network connectivity speed, bandwidth, and security (if any)
- Special circumstances (if any)

Understanding how your clients and servers are distributed throughout the network will help you design the most efficient WSUS design. For instance, there is a practical limit to how many computers one WSUS server can handle. You need to know in advance how many computers each WSUS server will have to update. Bandwidth issues can come into play as updates are distributed. Busy and slow times should also be noted so that productivity is impacted as little as possible. Understanding the numbers and types of clients and servers that will be serviced by the WSUS servers in your network is critical to a successful deployment.

Additionally, it is important to know the role of each computer on the network. For instance, you may have some custom applications that are critical to the company that must be tested separately. You may discover that some updates are incompatible with these applications; therefore, you may choose not to install those updates. By understanding the nature of each computer on the network, you can create an update plan that allows you to test updates based on computer groups, roles, or other criteria (custom applications, and so on), and apply only the updates that make sense for that computer.

Selecting a WSUS Management Preference

The next step in preparing for WSUS is to decide on the manner in which you are going to manage WSUS. As mentioned earlier, you can manage WSUS centrally or in a more distributed manner. You can also use a combination of the two. For instance, you may choose to centrally administer WSUS in each location comprised of multiple buildings and networks, but you may choose to allow each geographical location to manage WSUS independently. You could also choose to manage all WSUS' through one central location and distribute those changes (via downstream synchronization) to all other WSUS servers in the organization. After reviewing your current infrastructure, you should have a clear idea of your infrastructure components, limitations, and constraints.

BEST PRACTICES ACCORDING TO MICROSOFT

- Use centralized administration if you centrally administer other network functions. You can use both central and distributed management models with WSUS within the same organization, but you should decide how WSUS will be managed before deploying it.
- You must use the distributed management model on disconnected networks. Disconnected networks, especially those that are disconnected from the Internet, require independent management

because you cannot import updates on WSUS servers that are centrally managed.

- Manually synchronize changes to the language options. If you change language options, you should manually synchronize them between the centrally managed WSUS server and its replica servers.

- Ensure that you have adequate storage space on your WSUS servers. You can choose to store updates on the WSUS server or on Microsoft Updates.

- Choose the method of synchronization that best matches your organization's available network bandwidth. Avoid having the Update function slow your network and cause poor network performance during normal business hours.

SOME INDEPENDENT ADVICE

Your choice between centralized and distributed WSUS management is often fairly clear. For instance, if you have locations that have slow WAN links but fast Internet connections, you may choose to use a WSUS configuration where each location is completely autonomous. This allows each WSUS server to connect directly to Microsoft Update and utilize its high-speed Internet connection, rather than forcing it to use a slow-speed WAN connection. If you have locations where you have inexperienced network administrators, you may choose to centrally manage WSUS to ensure that the correct updates are applied to the right computers in the right manner. On the other hand, you might decide to decentralize this function if you have experienced network administrators at other locations, if other locations' update configurations are likely to change frequently, or if you have both fast WAN connections and slow or limited Internet connections.

Available Options

There are several options available to manage WSUS beyond a single server implementation. They are:

- Single WSUS server at single location.

- Multiple WSUS at multiple locations, each autonomous from the other.

- Multiple WSUS at multiple locations, each WSUS replica server subordinate to the WSUS server in the replica server role (centralized management).

- Multiple WSUS at single location, set up in chain or hierarchy. Each downstream WSUS server receives updates from the upstream WSUS server (distributed management).

- Multiple WSUS, one disconnected from the Internet. Updates loaded manually.

Single WSUS

For this section, we will start at the beginning with the most basic WSUS implementation possible, and build from there. First, you can install a single WSUS server behind the corporate firewall, allow it to connect to Microsoft Updates, and have the updates provided to clients from the WSUS server (see Figure 2.2). If you are managing a network for a small or medium-sized business, this is the correct option for you.

Figure 2.2 Single WSUS Configuration

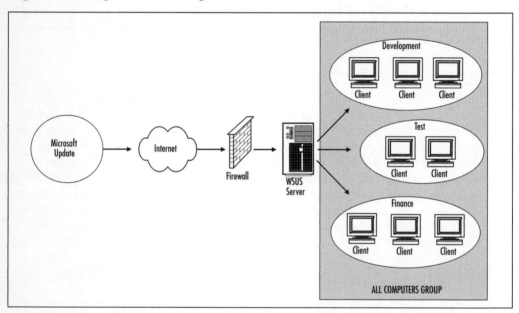

Multiple WSUS Servers

Most organizations' configurations are not as simple as the one discussed previously. If you have multiple locations and thousands of computers to manage, you will probably want to have two or more WSUS servers. A single WSUS server can manage up to 15,000 computers and clients can get updates across the WAN, but you do not want client updates using up that much network bandwidth. This is where your options expand. You can have:

- Multiple autonomous WSUS servers, each configured and managed independently, and each connecting to the Microsoft Update site (see Figure 2.3).

- Multiple WSUS servers with one configured as the master and the others synchronized via replication with the master (much like AD). This is called centralized management (see Figure 2.4).

- Multiple WSUS servers with distributed management, which provides a single source for the updates; however, each WSUS server is configured and managed at the local site (see Figure 2.5).

- Have at least one WSUS connected to the Internet and manually export/import updates to a disconnected WSUS server (typically disconnected for security reasons), as shown in Figure 2.6.

Multiple Autonomous WSUS Servers

With multiple autonomous WSUS servers, each server sits behind a firewall, connects via the Internet to the Microsoft Update site, and synchronizes with the site. During this process, the new updates are downloaded to the WSUS server, effectively synchronizing the WSUS server with the Microsoft Update site. Each server is independently managed, and one does not interact with the others (see Figure 2.3). The WSUS server at Headquarters does not control or influence the WSUS servers at Locations One or Two.

Figure 2.3 Multiple Autonomous WSUS Servers

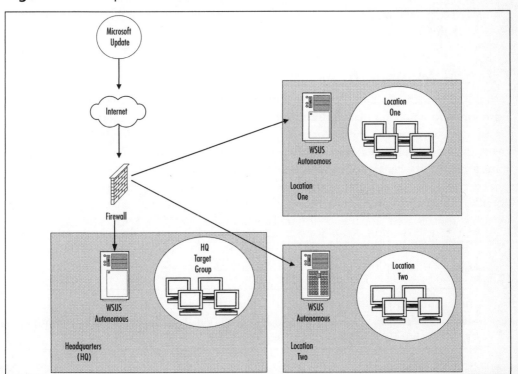

There are several benefits to this type of configuration:

- If one WSUS server goes down, the others are not impacted.

- Each independent location can manage approved updates and computer groups autonomously.

- Updates can be quickly rolled out to client computers, because there is no lag time with replication.

- Each local network administrator can decide how to best implement and manage WSUS for his or her location.

There is also a downside to this type of configuration:

- Each site must have a reasonably fast Internet connection (secured by a firewall) in order to get updates. (Although this is not usually an issue, it is a consideration.)

- If the WSUS server goes down, client computers at that site will not receive updates until the server is repaired.

- WSUS can be managed differently at each location. Mobile users connecting in different locations could potentially create problems.

- If multiple independent WSUS servers are used at one location, they could potentially bog down your Internet connection or your internal network, using network capacity for redundant update traffic.

Central Management

You might initially think that multiple autonomous WSUS servers is the way to go; however, before making that decision, you should review two more multiple WSUS server models: *central* and *distributed management*. This section begins with the central management model, which uses replication to propagate update information across the enterprise. In this scenario, one WSUS server is designated the master and all other servers are subordinate to the master. The master WSUS server connects to the Microsoft Update site and synchronizes with it. WSUS synchronization means that the available updates are compared to the updates stored in the WSUS database. Any new updates not already on the WSUS server are then downloaded to the server.

> **NOTE**
>
> There is an option that can be used where the selected updates are stored on Microsoft Update. Once the master WSUS server is updated, the updates and metadata are replicated to the other WSUS servers (see Figure 2.4).

Figure 2.4 Central WSUS Management (Replica Role)

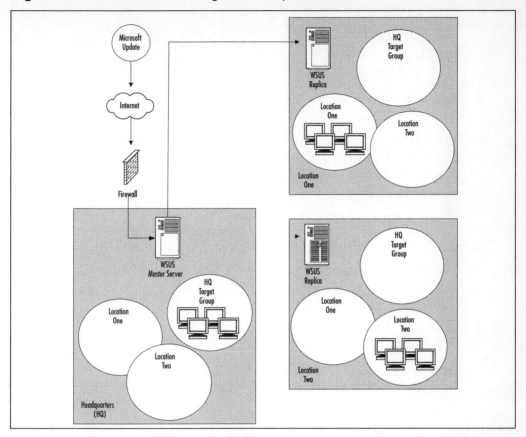

In this scenario, a single master WSUS server is administered. It is configured to use the *replica server role* and other servers are subordinate to this single server (*subordinate replicas*). The update approvals and targeted groups configured on the replica server (or master server), are replicated to the subordinate servers throughout the organization (see Figure 2.4). Not all locations utilize the same computer groups, so you will have to create enough computer groups on the master server to serve the needs of the entire organization. Computers at different sites can be moved into a group appropriate for that site. Computer groups will be empty when not used in that location (see Figure 2.4). Computer group *membership* is not replicated, only the computer groups. This means that you will have to load computers into computer groups.

As with computer groups, all update approvals must be created on the master server. Also, you can only add WSUS servers to the replica group during setup, which is another reason you should thoroughly assess your infrastructure and plan your deployment carefully. Creating the replica group during setup is discussed later in this book, but the essential steps involve pointing the replica WSUS servers to the master WSUS server to inherit (or replicate) from the master. This is called *mirror update settings* and is configured during initial setup.

This type of configuration often makes sense if:

- Remote locations have limited IT staff.

- Remote locations do not have the expertise to manage a WSUS server.

- Remote locations have slow or limited Internet connections but fast WAN connections.

- If a single site's Internet connection goes down, WSUS still updates clients using a WAN connection instead (assuming the WAN connection is separate from the Internet connection).

This type of management model also has its challenges. Among them are:

- If the master WSUS server goes down, the replica servers will not receive updates.

- If errors are made on the master server (update approvals, computer groups, language choices), other locations are impacted and must go through central management to request changes.

- If the WAN link goes down, the specific replica server that is affected will not receive updates.

- If the Internet connection for the WSUS server in the replica server role goes down, clients will not receive updates until the connection is restored.

Distributed Management (Default Mode)

Distributed management means that each WSUS server is *autonomous*. This is the default configuration of WSUS; you do not need to do anything to enable this mode. In this model (see Figure 2.5), each site is separately administered and can manage updates independently. Notice that the empty computer groups required in the centralized management mode are not used in the distributed management model. Downstream servers receive updates from upstream servers, and the last upstream server receives its updates directly from Microsoft Update (see Figure 2.5). In this mode, there are administrators at each site managing the WSUS server. Approval and target groups are not replicated and must be configured at each WSUS server. Servers can then be located throughout a geographically dispersed network to provide optimal connectivity to all client computers, where applicable. Updates and metadata are distributed to other servers. Everything else occurs on the local WSUS server.

Figure 2.5 Distributed WSUS Management

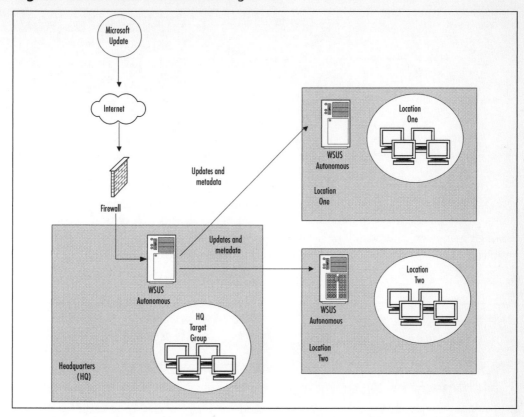

Networks Not Connected to the Internet

One more management option for networks not connected to the Internet is common in companies that require highly secure networks such as those found in the Research and Development (R&D) departments of high-tech or biotech firms. The network security is maintained by physically detaching it from any Internet connection and segmenting the network in a manner that makes it far more secure. The problem, though, is how to implement WSUS when you have a network that cannot be connected to the Internet or to the main corporate network.

In these cases, you can still use WSUS, but you will need at least one WSUS server that can connect to the Internet to synchronize with Microsoft Update (see Figure 2.6). Those updates are then *exported* to portable media, which is then delivered to the unconnected network's WSUS server. The updates are then imported to the unconnected WSUS server via the portable media, and the updates from that server then become available to clients on this network.

Figure 2.6 Using WSUS with Disconnected Networks

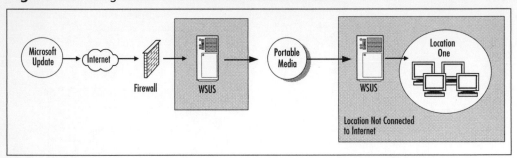

This is the most effective way to manage updates on a network that lacks any external network or Internet connection. Remember, if the network has no external connectivity, all client computers running on that network will lack critical updates. Though many critical updates are security-based, many fix or patch operating system problems that can cause other kinds of problems unrelated to security.

Shortcuts...

Management Options

You can have many WSUS servers connect to the Internet and grab updates. You can also have centralized management where one WSUS server is the master and others replicate with it. You can also distribute management so that the down-stream WSUS servers grab updates from the upstream server, but each WSUS server is autonomously managed in terms of approving updates, creating/managing computer groups, and so forth. There is also the disconnected network management that uses manual exports/imports to synchronize updated data.

Decision Criteria

When we discussed each management model, we discussed the pros and cons of each. The following sections discuss the decision criteria you can use to determine which management model is best suited to your organization.

Single WSUS

The use of a single WSUS server is appropriate in small to medium-sized businesses. The criteria are:

- **Geography** Single location
- **Network architecture** Simple network in single location
- **Security** No different from other management preferences
- **Servers and clients** No more than 15,000 total computers

Multiple Independent WSUS Servers

Each WSUS server independently synchronizes with Microsoft Update. The use of multiple independent WSUS servers might be appropriate for small to medium-sized businesses that meet the following criteria:

- **Geography** Multiple autonomous locations (branch office) or a single location with multiple WSUS servers dedicated to specific operating system updates.

- **Network architecture** One or more networks and subnets at each location, each independently managed. Internet connection is faster (more bandwidth) than WAN connection.

- **Security** Multiple servers connecting to the Internet are slightly less secure. If a fast Internet connection is used with hardened servers behind a firewall, this might be a better solution than a distributed model using a slower WAN link.

- **Servers and clients** Can support more than 15,000 computers across the enterprise. Each location can manage its own computer groups and group membership. The Internet traffic may be reduced slightly because each location can download only approved updates and languages appropriate to that location (rather than global). In cases where multiple independent WSUS servers are in one location, each can be dedicated to a single operating system update, which may be more efficient in some organizations.

Centrally Managed WSUS (Replica Mode)

In this management model, a single WSUS server is assigned the replica server role. All other WSUS servers are subordinate replicas. The WSUS in the replica server role synchronizes with Microsoft Update and then replicates to other servers. This model might be used if the following criteria are met:

- **Geography** Multiple locations and networks. The IT function at branch locations is managed at a central location (e.g., company headquarters) or if the IT staff expertise at branch locations is limited.

- **Network architecture** A LAN/MAN/WAN link is faster than an Internet connection and has adequate bandwidth to accommodate WSUS replication traffic. The network infrastructure is managed from a central location.

- **Security** A single Internet-connected WSUS server is more secure than many connected WSUS servers. Traffic between servers can be secured (will impact performance and bandwidth).

- **Servers and clients** More than 15,000 computers can be handled with this type of scenario. Computer groups for all computers in the organization must be created on the WSUS server in the replica master role. This creates an administrative burden at the central office, but may be desirable if other network administration is also centrally managed.

Distributed Management (Default Mode): Multiple Synchronized WSUS

In this model, a single WSUS server connects to and synchronizes with Microsoft Updates. Additional WSUS servers receive their updates from this single Internet-connected WSUS server. This scenario is considered a *distributed management system* because all of the servers rely on a single WSUS server for updates, but each server is managed independently or autonomously. In other words, computer groups are created on each WSUS server (they are not centrally created or managed); all updates must be approved for each server, and language options are managed at the local WSUS server. This is appropriate when:

- **Geography** Multiple locations and networks where each location/network is semi-autonomous. This might be the case where divisions are located in different regions or countries. This might also be the case where each division manages its own IT function within the corporate framework).

- **Network architecture** Large, complex networks, multiple subnets, distributed network management of other network functions can be used in locations that have LAN/MAN/WAN connections (private network connections) but do not have Internet connections (perhaps due to unreliable or slow Internet availability or for security purposes). Keep in mind that there is a practical limit to the hierarchy. Do not go more than three levels deep with chained WSUS servers.

- **Security** Updates distributed via private network are typically more secure than multiple WSUS servers connecting across the Internet. Updates and metadata are the only data sent from WSUS server to server; other data is not shared (computer groups, approved updates, and so on).

- **Servers and clients** Support more than 15,000 computers. Allows each WSUS server to set local parameters while using the upstream server as the source of updates rather than going out to the Internet for these updates.

Disconnected WSUS Server

This scenario is helpful when you want to use WSUS to manage your updates but do not want to connect your WSUS server (or the network) to the any other network, including the Internet. Using another WSUS server that synchronizes with Microsoft Update, you can use portable media to export updates from the Internet-connected WSUS server and import them to the disconnected WSUS server. This might be used in this situation:

- **Geography** The disconnected WSUS server is within a reasonable distance from the connected WSUS server. The updates needed by the disconnected server are similar to those of the connected server (e.g., language). Updates are transported via physical media, so the transportation of that media must be reliable because updates are released frequently.

- **Network architecture** An isolated network segment or network due to infrastructure limitations or security precautions.

- **Security** Highly secure in the sense that the network is not connected to external computers or networks. However, the portable media itself should be reasonably secure to prevent interception and modification of media while in transport.

- **Servers and clients** You could import updates onto several WSUS servers and chain those servers together so that the disconnected network could conceivably support more than the single WSUS server limitation of 15,000 computers.

SOME INDEPENDENT ADVICE

The management preference for your WSUS deployment should mirror your current network infrastructure management style. If you have several semi-autonomous locations, you may choose to use the distributed model or the multiple independent WSUS server model. The decision should be based on your network administration model, the capabilities of the IT staff at the various locations, and the connectivity of those locations (Internet and LAN/MAN/WAN types of connections). Keeping this implementation consistent with your current network administrative model keeps things simple.

Designing the WSUS Environment

The following section discusses designing the WSUS environment in more detail. The environment includes understanding and organizing computer groups, choosing the database to use with WSUS, reviewing and selecting the location for storing updates, looking at various bandwidth options, determining how you want to filter updates, understanding and deciding on the use of express installation file options, understanding BITS 2.0, and understanding capacity requirements. In this section, we discuss the details of each of these elements so that you can effectively design the WSUS environment that is right for your organization.

BEST PRACTICES ACCORDING TO MICROSOFT

- Choose a management preference before designing your WSUS environment. Your WSUS environment choices are dictated by your management preference decision, so choose the management preference first to avoid reworking your plan later.

- Use computer groups to manage updates. Computer groups are replicated in a centralized management scheme, but computer group membership is not. Computers must be added to the appropriate group.

- Choose the best-fit database solution. You do not have to be a database expert to decide how to handle your WSUS database. Select the database that is right for your organization's unique needs.

- Windows Server 2003 WSUS should use a Windows Microsoft SQL Server 2000 Desktop Engine (WMSDE) or a SQL Server 2000.

- The Windows 2000 Server WSUS should use the MSDE database engine or the SQL Server 2000.

- Filter updates. By default, all updates in all languages are downloaded during synchronization. Filtering updates downloads only the needed updates.

- Determine if you need to conserve Internet or network bandwidth. Various bandwidth configuration options are available, depending on how you want to manage your Internet and network bandwidth.

- Use computer hardware that exceeds minimum capacity standards. If you install the bare minimum, you could run into performance issues very quickly and leave yourself no room for future growth. If you plan on installing additional clients, operating system versions, or languages, make sure your WSUS servers can handle the anticipated load.

Computer Groups

Even in single location scenarios, computer groups are an important part of the WSUS deployment—not only for the implementation phase but also for the ongoing updates. By using computer groups, you can target the appropriate updates to the right computers. Different versions of Windows require different updates; different client configurations may also require different updates. By grouping computers logically, WSUS can be properly configured and updates applied appropriately (see Figure 2.7). Note that there is a computer group named "Test" included in the groups. It is a good idea to create one or more test groups and have computers in those test groups that represent the various configurations in the other groups. This way, you can test updates from the WSUS server prior to deployment. If the update causes problems, it is limited to the Test group or groups. You can troubleshoot the problem or delay rolling out the update until you determine the cause of the problem.

Figure 2.7 Computer Groups in a Single Location

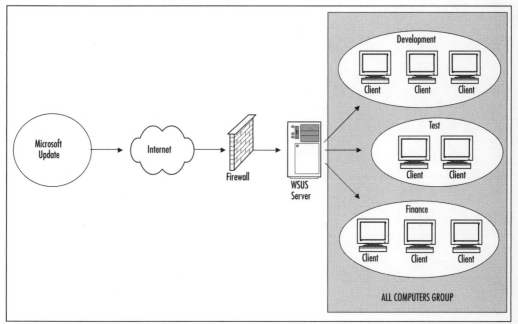

If you have chosen a centrally managed system using the replica model (see Figure 2.8), you must create all computer groups needed by the entire organization on the WSUS server in the replica server role. Notice that the three groups are created on the HQ WSUS server but that only the appropriate groups are populated in the other locations. Location One only has computers from that location in the computer group called Location One. Location Two only contains computers in the computer group called Location Two and so forth. This creates administrative overhead at the centrally managed WSUS server, but reduces or eliminates administrative overhead at the remote locations.

Figure 2.8 Computer Groups in a Multiple Location Scenario

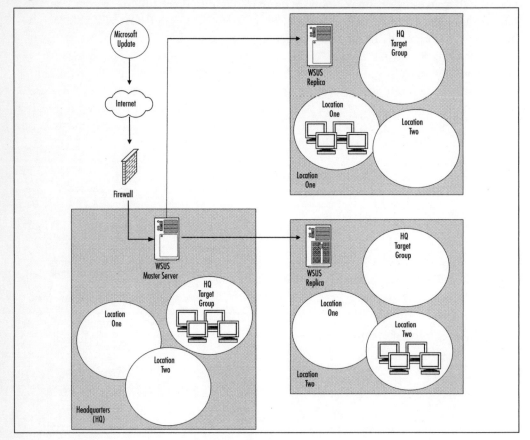

Design your computer groups according to one or more of the following criteria:

- Computers grouped by OUs
- Computers grouped by functional units
- Computers grouped by operating system
- Computers grouped by security needs
- Computers grouped by other criteria

You should create one or more test groups so that you can test the updates before rolling them out globally. This helps you to better manage updates and helps avoid a sce-

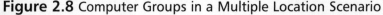

nario where an update is rolled out to 10,000 computers that causes a critical application to fail. The WSUS server must be joined to an AD domain.

Database Selection

In many cases, selecting the database is usually a fairly straightforward decision. WSUS requires the use of a database; however, you do not have to purchase a separate database for this function, because you can obtain one of the three databases listed in this section at no charge (they come with the operating system or can be downloaded for free). The WSUS database is used to store WSUS server configuration information, update metadata (what each update is used for), and information about client computers, updates and client interactions with updates. The WSUS database is not managed directly. Rather, it is managed through the WSUS server console interface or programmatically calling WSUS application programming interfaces (APIs). Each server requires its own database, and if you implement multiple WSUS servers, each must have its own database, even in a chained configuration where only updates and metadata are downloaded.

There are three basic database choices, depending on the operating system used. These options are:

- Microsoft Windows SQL Server 2000 Desktop Engine (WMSDE), which ships with WSUS. This option is available only on a WSUS server running the Windows Server 2003 operating system. It is an improved version of the desktop engine that shipped with Windows 2000. It does not have a user interface nor are there separate database tools available. This engine is intended to be managed through the WSUS console. Use this version if your WSUS server is running Windows Server 2003.

- Microsoft SQL Server 2000 Desktop Engine (MSDE), which is available as a free download. It is based on SQL Server 2000 but has several built-in limitations that restrict the number of connections allowed and restrict the database size to 2 GB. Use this version if your WSUS server is running Windows 2000 Server.

- Microsoft SQL Server 2000, the full version of the database program, which is available from Microsoft. WSUS requires Service Pack 3a to be installed on the SQL Server. If you are running SQL Server 2000 and want to use it as the WSUS server, you may do so but the SQL Server administrator should enable *nested triggers* in SQL Server prior to setting up the WSUS server (which requires specifying the database during setup). WSUS Setup enables *recursive triggers,* which is a database-specific option but it does not enable nested triggers, a global option, that must be set on the SQL Server itself.

NOTE

According to Microsoft documentation, you can use another database application if it is 100 percent compatible with Microsoft SQL Server.

The WSUS database will be named SUSDB during setup, regardless of whether you choose MWSDE or MSDE. Another limitation to be aware of is that WSUS cannot use SQL authentication; it uses Windows authentication only.

WSUS supports running database software on a computer separate from WSUS, but there are some restrictions to be aware of. Remember, if the database is not local to the WSUS server, traffic must travel between the WSUS server and the database server frequently. This could cause security and network traffic issues. If you choose this type of configuration, there are four limitations you should note:

- You cannot use Windows 2000 Server on the front-end computer (the WSUS server).

- You cannot use a server configured as a domain controller for the WSUS server or for the database server.

- You cannot use WMSDE or MSDE for the database on the back end (you must use SQL Server or some other full database program).

- Both computers (WSUS and database server) must be joined to an AD domain.

For more information on setting up the front end and back end of this type of configuration, visit TechNet on the Microsoft Web site and read "Appendix C: Remote SQL" of *Deploying Microsoft Windows Server Update Services Guide.*

SOME **I**NDEPENDENT **A**DVICE

If you are running Windows Server 2003 on the WSUS server, your best choice is to use the MWSDE. It is available, it is ready to go, and unlike the full-blown version of SQL Server, it does not require a SQL administrator to manage. If you are running Windows 2000 Server, you can run the previous version of the Microsoft SQL Server Desktop Engine, but it has more limitations. If you are planning to use the WSUS server to manage near the individual server limit of 15,000, you will probably run into problems with MSDE, because it has connection and storage limitations. In that case, you should consider two or more WSUS servers or use Windows Server 2003 instead.

Update Storage

Before you can decide how to store updates, it is important to understand the update components. Previously, we mentioned updates and metadata; these two elements work together. The updates are the actual updates that are installed on client computers. These can be large files, depending on the nature or extent of the update. Metadata, on the other hand, simply provides information about what the updates are useful for. The metadata also includes End User License Agreements (EULAs). Storing the metadata creates minimal demand for storage, but storing the updates themselves can require large amounts of storage space, depending on your WSUS configuration and the nature of the client computers. As a result, you have two storage options for updates. Remember, the metadata will always be stored on the WSUS server, but the location of the updates can be local or remote.

Local

You can store update information on the local WSUS server. Depending on the nature of the updates, the number of different operating systems, and the number of languages needed, storage demands could be rather large (30GB or more). There is a minimum requirement of 6GB of storage space on the local volume for updates, but 30GB or more is highly recommended. If you choose this storage option during setup, your download settings will be automatically set to *deferred download*.

Pros

The upside to this configuration is that it minimizes bandwidth use over the Internet; clients can receive updates directly from the WSUS server via the private network rather than across the Internet. This is helpful if the Internet bandwidth is limited or if your LAN/WAN link is faster than your Internet connection.

Cons

The downside to this configuration is that the local WSUS server requires more storage space, which means that the WSUS server or the local network could get bogged down while updating thousands of client computers. If your LAN/WAN connection is fast, fine, but if not, you might find performance degraded beyond acceptable limits. If you use the replica model or the distributed system, the updates all originate from a single master WSUS. This should be taken into account when deciding whether or not to store updates locally.

Remote

Another option is to store the updates remotely, to leave them on the Microsoft Update Web site and make them available to clients. This basically creates an Internet-based distribution system. It reduces the amount of local WSUS storage you will need and it can be helpful in certain scenarios. This is the best scenario if your client computers have high-bandwidth Internet connections but slow WAN links, or if you have a relatively few number of client computers. The process of using remote storage is described here and is shown in Figure 2.9:

1. The WSUS server synchronizes with Microsoft Updates. Metadata about the updates is stored on the local WSUS server; no updates are stored.

2. The WSUS administrator reviews and approves the updates.

3. Remote clients connect to the WSUS server (via virtual private network [VPN] connections) and access update approval data.

4. Remote clients connect via the Internet to Microsoft Update and download updates based on WSUS server approvals.

Pros

The upside to this approach is that Internet bandwidth where the WSUS server is located is not used to download all client updates. If clients have a slower WAN connection to the WSUS server, that connection is used only to receive update approval information and not the update itself. The amount of required storage space on your WSUS server is also significantly lower, because you are only storing metadata, not the actual updates.

Cons

The client must have the ability to connect securely to the WSUS server to receive update approval. The client must also have access to a high-speed Internet connection to download approved updates.

Key Differences

You might be asking how this approach differs from or improves upon the current scenario in many companies, where each client can be configured to go out to the Internet and automatically receive (and install) updates. There are several key differences to note. First, you can monitor which clients have updates installed and which do not by using WSUS' *detect* function on the WSUS server. Second, the WSUS administrator can set approval for updates. If you have been managing client computers in the current environment, you no doubt have responded to service requests to restore computers that installed updates that caused system or application problems on that computer. By allowing the WSUS administrator to test configurations (if desired) on various computers and set approvals, you can prevent these kinds of problems. In this way, rather than the client connecting directly to Microsoft Updates and downloading any and all updates available for that particular client operating system, only the approved updates will be downloaded. This provides an additional level of control that the non-WSUS environment does not provide.

Figure 2.9 Remote Storage of Updates

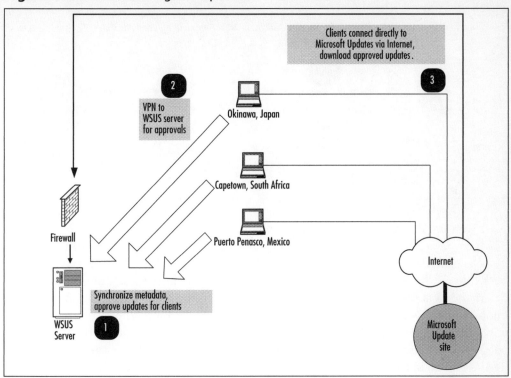

Bandwidth Options

One of the benefits of using WSUS is the ability to manage updates and therefore manage bandwidth usage efficiently. Related to bandwidth, you have four specific options to work with in WSUS. You can defer download, filter updates, use express installation files, and use Background Intelligent Transfer Server (BITS) 2.0.

Deferring Downloads

The out-of-the-box configuration of WSUS downloads all updates in all languages. Aside from being a large download, there is a high likelihood that you do not need all of the updates and you almost certainly do not need all languages. You can synchronize the metadata for the update using deferred downloads. Then you can choose the updates that are relevant to the clients you are managing and download just those (see Figure 2.10). This can significantly reduce the number of updates downloaded and reduce the required bandwidth (and storage) as well.

Figure 2.10 Deferred Downloads

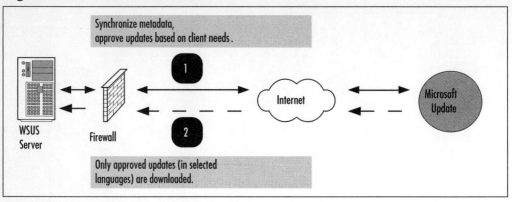

If you use this configuration, make sure you do not go any deeper than three levels down if you are using chained servers (updating from upstream server). All of the servers in a chain must use the same download method; therefore, if the WSUS server connected to the Internet uses deferred downloads, all servers in the chain must use deferred downloads. If the Internet-connected WSUS server downloads metadata and updates during synchronization, all WSUS servers in the chain must also do so. If a downstream server needs an update not downloaded during synchronization, it will trigger a download event on the upstream server to get the needed update. The needed update will be obtained during the next scheduled synchronization. This creates a ripple effect through the WSUS chain, and if it is configured more than three levels deep, there could be significant delays in updates being delivered to clients. This process of detection, update request, and update approval can be automated.

Pros

The upside to this approach is that you can limit bandwidth use for updates across the Internet connection. A WSUS server setting (described later in this book) can *detect* which clients require which updates and only those updates can be downloaded. This is a more efficient method and saves bandwidth.

Cons

The downside to this approach is that if you have a hierarchical setup (chained WSUS servers) and a client needs an update, it can take a while to propagate this through the chain. Exactly how long the delay will be depends on several factors including how many levels deep your WSUS chain is, when synchronization last occurred, and when the update need is detected.

Filtering Updates

WSUS allows you to filter available updates so that you select only the downloads you need based on product, language, and type of update. As with deferred downloads, whatever option is selected on the Internet-connected WSUS server is the option all WSUS servers in the chain must use. This behavior cannot be modified. As mentioned earlier in this chapter, WSUS by default will download Critical and Security updates for all supported Windows versions in all languages. Filtering for just the operating systems and languages needed conserves bandwidth and reduces storage needs.

Express Installation Files

What if your main concern is conserving LAN bandwidth, not Internet bandwidth? The *express installation files* option allows you to better manage network traffic. It is an update distribution management option. This installation method is configured as part of Advanced Configuration options on the WSUS server. By default, WSUS does not use express installation files. To understand how this option works, refer to the following explanation and to Figure 2.11.

The express installation method uses what is referred to as a *delta delivery* model, because only *changes* are downloaded to the client. In this scenario (shown as method 1 in Figure 2.11), all update information is downloaded during synchronization to the WSUS server. The server compares the updated files to the client files and determines the difference (or delta) between the two versions. Only the changes are downloaded to the client and merged into the existing client file. Express installation files are always bigger than the updates they provide, which is why the initial bandwidth requirement during synchronization is larger than the default WSUS method (shown as method 2 in Figure 2.11). The result is higher bandwidth use for synchronization, but lower network use with clients.

Method 2 is the typical bandwidth used for updates when express installation files are *not* used. As a reminder, method 2 is the default method used in WSUS. In this case, the needed updates are downloaded during synchronization and those updates (entire files, not just changes) are passed along to the appropriate target computers (see Figure 2.11).

Figure 2.11 Express Installation Files: Larger Internet Demand, Lower Network Demand

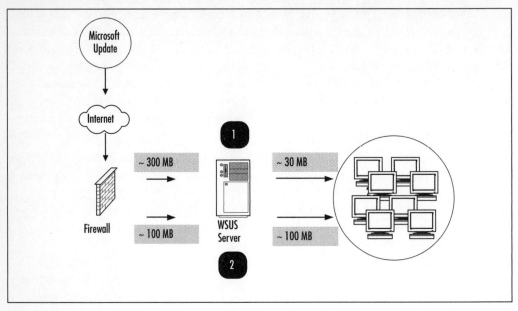

BITS 2.0

WSUS uses BITS 2.0 for all file transfer tasks. The benefit of using BITS is that it maintains file transfers through network disconnects and computer restarts; thus, if an update is interrupted due to a user shutting down the laptop in the middle of an update, BITS will re-start the update from where it left off the next time that computer is back online. BITS is a Microsoft technology that allows programs to download files using very little bandwidth. For additional information on BITS, visit this link on the Microsoft Web site: http://go.microsoft.com/fwlink/?LinkId=15106. Restarting an update where it left off requires less bandwidth than restarting the update from scratch, so using BITS 2.0 helps reduce bandwidth requirements through the WSUS environment.

Capacity Requirements

Some companies will implement WSUS on an existing server; others may purchase one or more additional servers to run WSUS in the enterprise. Ensuring that your servers exceed minimum requirements will avoid problems down the line, especially if your organization is growing and adding computers on a regular basis (see Table 2.1).

Table 2.1 WSUS Server Minimum Server Capacity

Component	Up to 500 Computers	Up to 15,000 Computers
Processor	1GHz or better	3GHz or better (dual processors for 10,000 clients or more)
RAM	1GB	1GB or more
Storage	6GB or more	30GB or more
Database	WMSDE, MSDE	WMSDE/SQL Server 2000 SP 3a

WSUS Server Requirements

The WSUS server is included in the server category; however, it is worth discussing it separately, because there are specific hardware requirements for the server(s) that host WSUS that you should be familiar with as you review your network and design your WSUS deployment. These requirements are baseline (minimum) requirements. As with any server, more is usually better; therefore, do not scrape the bottom of the hardware barrel on WSUS servers. The minimum hardware requirements for a WSUS server serving up to 500 clients are:

- 1GHz processor (> 2GHz recommended)
- 1GB RAM
- System drive must be formatted with New Technology File System (NTFS) (both system partition and partition on which you install WSUS)
- At least 1GB free space on the system partition
- At least 6GB free space for the volume that stores WSUS content (8 GB recommended minimum, 30GB recommended if you want to download all updates)
- At least 2GB free space on the volume where WSUS Setup installs Windows SQL Server 2000 Desktop Engine (WMSDE).

NOTE

A database is required to install WSUS. The default WSUS installation in Windows Server 2003 uses the WMSDE included with Windows Server 2003.

If you are planning to push the envelope and run up to 15,000 clients on the server, you will need to beef up your WSUS server hardware to meet these specs:

- 3GHz dual processors

- 1GB (or more) RAM

- 30GB or more of free disk space on volume storing WSUS content

In addition to hardware requirements for the WSUS installation, your server must also meet the following minimum software requirements:

- Microsoft Internet Information Services (IIS) 6.0

- Microsoft .NET Framework 1.1 Service Pack 1 for Windows Server 2003

- Background Intelligent Transfer Service (BITS) 2.0

Automatic Update Clients

Automatic Updates is the client component of WSUS and has no specific hardware requirements; however, only the following members of the Windows operating system can be updated using WSUS:

- Microsoft Windows Server 2003: Standard Edition, Enterprise Edition, Datacenter Edition, or Web Edition.

- Microsoft Windows XP Professional, with or without Service Pack 1 or Service Pack 2.

- Microsoft Windows 2000 Professional with Service Pack 3 (SP3) or Service Pack 4 (SP4), Windows 2000 Server with SP3 or SP4, or Windows 2000 Advanced Server with SP3 or SP4.

Summary

Preparing to install WSUS involves reviewing the current infrastructure, selecting the manner in which you want to manage WSUS and designing your WSUS environment. Your current infrastructure dictates the manner in which you design and deploy WSUS, and you should have a clear understanding of the following concepts before moving on to the next chapter:

- Your current infrastructure, including geographic locations, network infrastructure, security requirements and policies, and the types of servers and clients WSUS will be updating, should be thoroughly assessed and documented prior to designing your WSUS deployment.

- WSUS can be managed in a centralized or distributed manner. Within each of these options, there are several different types of implementations you can use. The decision about which to use should incorporate your current network administration model as well as IT expertise at remote locations and connectivity issues (both Internet and LAN/MAN/WAN).

- The design of your WSUS environment includes understanding and organizing computer groups, choosing the database to use with WSUS, reviewing and selecting the location for storing updates, looking at various bandwidth options, determining how you want to filter updates, understanding and deciding on the use of express installation file options, understanding BITS 2.0, and understanding capacity requirements.

Solutions Fast Track

Assessing Your Current Infrastructure

- ☑ Geographic locations vary in many ways. IT administration, language differences, and Internet and network connectivity issues all come into play. Understanding the unique needs of each geographic location will help determine the most effective WSUS implementation.

- ☑ The assessment of your network infrastructure should be thorough, because all of it comes into play with WSUS.

- ☑ The network architecture assessment should look at how servers and computers are networked (segmented, subnetted, and connected).

- ☑ Pay special attention to network bandwidth and bottlenecks, and Internet connectivity. Both are important elements in implementing WSUS.

☑ Security requirements and policies should be reviewed prior to designing your WSUS environment. Your objective in designing your WSUS environment should be to support or enhance existing security.

☑ The number and types of servers and clients on your network will drive how you design your WSUS environment.

☑ A single WSUS server cannot manage more than 15,000 computers.

Selecting a WSUS Management Preference

☑ A small network may have a single WSUS server connected to the Internet behind the corporate firewall.

☑ A medium-sized network may have several independent WSUS servers connected to the Internet behind a corporate firewall. Each is independent of the others and all synchronize only with Microsoft Update.

☑ A medium-sized or large network may have several WSUS servers chained together using the replica server model. A single WSUS server synchronizes with Microsoft Update and all other servers replicate with that server.

☑ A medium-sized or large network may also have several WSUS servers autonomously managed through a distributed management model. Servers receive updates and metadata from the master WSUS server, but computer groups? update approval and language preferences are set at the local WSUS server.

☑ A combination of methods can be installed in an organization.

☑ WSUS servers that connect to the Internet should be at the perimeter of the corporate network.

Designing the WSUS Environment

You should consider the following points when designing a WSUS environment:

☑ Computer groups are used to organize computers in WSUS. This allows you to manage updates to client computers more effectively.

☑ WSUS requires the use of a database. You can use the database engine that comes with Windows Server 2003 or Windows 2000 Server. You can also use SQL Server 2000, either on the same server or on a remote (separate) server.

☑ The database engine that comes with Windows Server 2003 is MWSDE.

☑ The database engine that comes with Windows 2000 Server is MSDE.

☑ Updates can be stored locally or remotely. If stored locally, more server storage space and bandwidth is required.

☑ Local storage, by default, uses the deferred download method.

☑ Remote storage of updates is useful when you have a few clients or when clients have a faster Internet connection than network connection.

☑ Approvals for local or remote updates are still managed by the WSUS server.

☑ By default, all updates in all languages are downloaded during WSUS serve synchronization with Microsoft Updates. Applying filters to updates considerably reduces the download size, bandwidth requirements, and storage requirements.

☑ Using Express Installation files allows you to use a delta delivery model by sending only the changes to client files rather than the entire file.

☑ WSUS uses BITS 2.0 to manage file transfers, and provides the capability of managing the file transfer (updates) in the event of client disconnect or network errors.

☑ According to Microsoft specifications, a single WSUS server can handle up to 15,000 clients if it has a 3GHz (or faster) dual processor, 1GB or more of RAM, and 30GB or more of storage capacity.

Frequently Asked Questions

The following Frequently Asked Questions, answered by the authors of this book, are designed to both measure your understanding of the concepts presented in this chapter and to assist you with real-life implementation of these concepts. To have your questions about this chapter answered by the author, browse to **www.syngress.com/solutions** and click on the **"Ask the Author"** form.

Q: We have sites in four different countries and each seems intent on managing their own affairs. However, our recent corporate directive made it clear that we need to take a more integrated approach to security, including patch management. Any suggestions on how we should approach our WSUS environment?

A: The situation you have described sounds like a great candidate for a distributed WSUS management model. As you recall from reading this chapter, the distributed model allows a single WSUS server to connect to the Internet and grab all the updates. From there, each branch or location can synchronize with the master WSUS server and download the applicable updates. Each location can autonomously manage computer groups, set update approvals, and set language preferences. This provides the type of autonomy each location is used to, and also provides a central server that stores information about the update process for all branches.

Q: We have a few locations that have a mix of Windows 95, Windows 2000 Professional, and Windows XP Professional as client machines. Obviously, we cannot update the Windows 95 machines using WSUS, but I know we can update the Win2000 and WinXP machines. The question is, can they all be in the same computer group or do I need to create a computer group for each operating system?

A: The computer groups ideally should contain only computers with the same or similar configuration, so there is no one single answer for you. For instance, do all the Win2000 machines run the same applications? If so, they could go into the same group. On the other hand, if half the Win2000 machines run standard applications and the other half run a customized financial application, you should probably create two groups and separate the machines. The point of WSUS is to ease update and patch management by grouping computers that use the same updates. If you mix and match, you risk installing an update that works for the machines with standard applications but causes serious problems on the computers running the custom financial application.

Q: A portion of our network is highly secure and does not have an Internet connection. It uses IPSec for all network traffic. What is the best way to implement WSUS in this case?

A: There are several ways this can be done and it really depends on how disconnected this secure network is. For instance, if it is not connected to any other part of your corporate network, you must use the manual method of synchronizing updates with Microsoft Update using a WSUS computer connected to the Internet and hand-carrying a portable media device containing the needed updates to the disconnected WSUS server. This is probably the most secure method and enhances security because client computers are kept up-to-date with Critical and Security updates they might not otherwise get (since they would have no way of connecting to the Internet to get those needed updates). A second method is to configure the secure WSUS server to get updates from the WSUS server that is connected to the Internet. This is less secure because there is a physical path from the Internet-connected WSUS server to the "disconnected" WSUS server. However, you can secure the connection both to the Microsoft Update site using SSL, and you can secure the server-to-server traffic with IPSec. This increases processor overhead but provides a more secure environment. The bottom line is that your configuration will depend on how much security you require for this network. Also, no connection is almost always the safest (keeping in mind that a vast majority of network attacks and hacks come from *inside* the organization).

Q: We have a manufacturing facility in rural China. We use our network there for managing inventory and supplies. However, our Internet connectivity is very limited and unreliable. Any suggestions?

A: You actually have several options available to you. If your network is fast but your Internet connection is slow, you can synchronize a single WSUS server to Microsoft Updates. You can choose to download the updates and store them locally (the default option in WSUS). This will require a more robust server but will allow you to store the updates and let clients use the faster network connection to get updates from the WSUS server. If you have widely dispersed clients in this network or location, you can implement additional WSUS servers using one of the models described in this chapter. Remember, WSUS uses BITS 2.0 to manage file transfers, so interruptions to the network will not cause a major disruption to the update process. Your key to designing your WSUS environment is to ensure that you make good use of your fast network connection and minimize the impact of your relatively slow Internet connection.

Chapter 3

Installing WSUS

Solutions in this chapter:

- **System Requirements**

- **Installing Supporting Applications**

- **Installing WSUS on Microsoft Windows Server 2003**

☑ **Summary**

☑ **Solutions Fast Track**

☑ **Frequently Asked Questions**

Introduction

An ounce of prevention is worth a pound of cure. Truer words have never been spoken when referring to the implementation of an enterprise product such as Windows Server Update Services (WSUS). At the end of this chapter, you will have all the information necessary to complete a successful WSUS installation. To accomplish this, a variety of topics are covered, including system requirements, installation of supporting applications and tools, and a step-by-step guide for installing WSUS on Windows Server 2003. We begin with the Microsoft system requirements for installing WSUS.

System Requirements

Microsoft installation requirements for WSUS are very loose, meaning that while they have certain criteria that the server must meet, the requirements are very low and, in theory, can be supported by hardware that isn't necessarily "cutting edge." The software requirements for implementing WSUS are minimal, as opposed to a Systems Management Server (SMS) installation, which has much greater requirements.

Software Requirements

The first thing you need is to obtain a copy of WSUS, which can be downloaded at www.microsoft.com/windowsserversystem/updateservices/downloads/WSUS.mspx. Keep in mind that Microsoft is always changing and moving pages within their Web site, so this link may occasionally change.

Next, you need an operating system (OS) to run your WSUS server. The only two supported server families are Windows 2000 and Windows 2003. Although WSUS runs on Windows 2000, the configuration of WSUS on a Windows 2003 server requires much less interaction. For example, if you plan to run WSUS on Windows 2000, you will want to run the Internet Information Server (IIS) lockdown tool, whereas Windows 2003 is already secured. Likewise, configuring the database for WSUS (either Structured Query Language [SQL] or Microsoft SQL Desktop Edition (MSDE) is easier on a server running Windows 2003.

The remaining software requirements are fairly common, and may already be installed on your server:

- Microsoft IIS 6.0
- Microsoft .NET Framework 1.1 Service Pack 1 for Windows 2003
- Background Intelligent Transfer Service (BITS) 2.0
- SQL Server 2000 or MSDE

IIS will be the front end for Web management once WSUS is installed on the server. By default, WSUS uses the default IIS Web site, so use caution when installing WSUS on a production server that utilizes IIS. The next requirement is Microsoft .NET

Framework 1.1 (Service Pack 1 [SP1]). The Windows Server 2003 distribution CDs come with .NET Framework 1.1; however, Microsoft requires the addition of SP1 to .NET. Although there are multiple updates in the .NET SP1 upgrade, the main focus of the SP revolves around security. The .NET Framework SP can be found at www.microsoft.com/downloads/details.aspx?familyid= AE7EDEF7-2CB7-4864-8623-A1038563DF23&displaylang=en. Because so many people implement SUS to handle functions such as software updates, it is important to keep your WSUS server up-to-date.

BEST PRACTICES ACCORDING TO MICROSOFT

- If you plan to run WSUS on a Windows 2000 server, consider running the IIS lockdown tool.
- If you run the IIS Lockdown tool, you must edit the *Urlscan.ini* file to allow *.exe requests*.
- Windows 2003 does not need the IIS lockdown tool because it has already been secured.

The third software requirement for WSUS is the BITS, which is used for transferring files between a server and a workstation, while providing information about the progress of the transfers. BITS 2.0 is available for download at www.microsoft.com/downloads/details.aspx?FamilyID=b93356b1-ba43-480f-983d-eb19368f9047&DisplayLang=en. For more information on BITS, you can visit http://msdn.microsoft.com/library/default.asp?url=/library/en-us/bits/bits/bits_start_page.asp.

The final software requirement for WSUS is some type of database engine. By default, WSUS uses the MSDE installation that comes with the WSUS distribution (see Figure 3.1). However, Microsoft has provided the ability to use the complete version of SQL Server 2000 in place of MSDE (see Figure 3.2). When planning your WSUS environment, take into consideration the limitations of MSDE as well as the potential added complexity of using a full SQL server installation (either locally or remote). If you have a database administrator (DBA) on staff, consider consulting him or her when planning the WSUS database.

Figure 3.1 WSUS with Default MSDE Installation

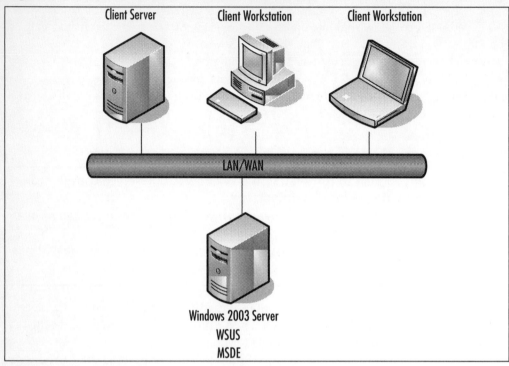

Figure 3.2 WSUS with Remote SQL 2000 Installation

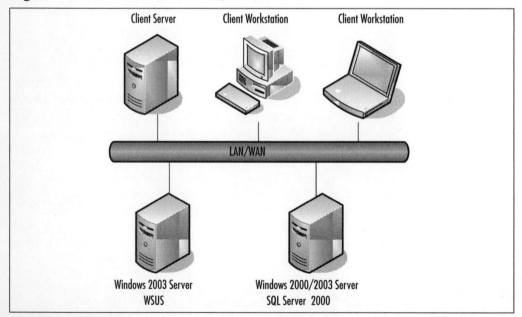

Server Requirements

As mentioned earlier, the server hardware requirements for WSUS are simple. Hardware minimums are listed in Table 3.1.

Table 3.1 WSUS Server Hardware Minimum Requirements

Equipment	500 Clients (or Less)	More than 500 Clients
Processor	750 Mhz Pentium III Processor	1 GHz Pentium III Processor
Memory	512 Megabytes	1GB
Free Disk Space	9GB (1GB free on system partition)	9GBs (1GB free on system partition)

Shortcuts...

Short on Hardware? Virtualize It!

In some environments, justifying hardware for an update server can be difficult. If you have a decent server that meets the minimum specifications and does not have a heavy workload (for instance, a dedicated backup server or SPAM server), consider installing virtual server software, such as VMWare Workstation, VMWare GSX, or Microsoft Virtual Server 2005. In large enterprises, you can make copies of your virtual machine and distribute it to other servers at remote offices, reducing your capital costs and reducing your time to complete your WSUS project. For more information on virtualization with VMWare products, check out Syngress Publishing's *Virtualization with VMWare ESX Server*.

These are the minimums for building an SUS server. However, you need to take the full requirements of the server into consideration when scoping the server. For example, make sure you plan for other applications that will require processing cycles and memory such as anti-virus, zero-day protection (e.g., Cisco's CSA), and so forth. Nine GB of free disk space is an absolute minimum. Although you can try to run with 9GB, Microsoft recommends at least 30GB of space where the WSUS content is stored. Consider separating the store and database partitions for better performance. In other words, don't build a large *C:* drive, which has the system, stores, and database loaded onto it. Table 3.2 shows the recommended server specifications for a WSUS server.

Table 3.2 WSUS Server Recommended Hardware

Equipment	500 Clients (or Less)	More Than 500 Clients
Processor	1GHz Pentium III Processor	3GHz Pentium IV (dual processor for more than 100,000 clients)
Memory	1GB	1GB
Free Disk Space	30GB (1GB free on system partition)	30GB (1GB free on system partition)

SOME INDEPENDENT ADVICE

One thing to keep in mind is network interface card (NIC) speed. For smaller environments (fewer than 500 systems), a 100Mbps network card is probably sufficient. However, in larger environments where several hundreds (or thousands) of systems may be using WSUS for updates, either a gibabit NIC, or at least teamed 100Mbps NICs may be necessary. Always try to plan for more than you need rather than having to fix the problem later. Since the cost of a gigabit NIC (and gigabit switches) has dropped significantly over the past few years, it may make sense to make the investment up front.

Client Requirements

As with the server requirements, there are no extraordinary client requirements to implement WSUS. The most important item to note with WSUS is that it will work with only *current Microsoft supporting operating systems.* Specifically, WSUS will work with the following client operating systems:

- Microsoft Windows 2000 Professional with a minimum of Service Pack 3 (SP3)

- Windows 2000 Server (and Advanced Server) with a minimum of SP3

- Microsoft Windows XP Professional

- Microsoft Windows Server 2003 (Standard, Enterprise Edition, Datacenter Edition, or Web Editions)

Aside from the operating systems, the only other requirement to connect a client machine to WSUS is *automatic updates.* Originally, the intent of automatic updates was to allow Windows clients (both at home and corporate systems) to automatically detect, download, and install Windows patches on a workstation. Automatic updates were a great idea for home users, but in a corporate environment they were notorious for flooding Internet connections as potentially hundreds (or thousands) of clients tried to individually download their updates. Since the concept of automatic updates worked so well, Microsoft used it for the SUS and the WSUS services. Outside of the aforementioned items, no other configuration is necessary from the client perspective.

Shortcuts…

Got Downlevel Clients?
Use GPO to Roll Out Autoupdate

If you have Windows 2000 systems with Service Pack 2 (SP2) (or lower) and want to get the *autoupdate* installed quickly, you can assign a package via a Group Policy Object (GPO). The *autoupdate* client is an MSI file that can be downloaded from Microsoft. If you are using Windows 2003 Active Directory, you can narrow the target of the GPO down even further by using a Windows Management Interface (WMI) filter to determine the OS and SP level.

Installing Supporting Applications

In the previous section we discussed the various applications that are required prior to installing WSUS. This section focuses on how to begin installing the supporting applications for WSUS. Almost all of WSUS management is done via the WSUS Management Web site. Unlike Windows 2000, IIS is not installed by default in Windows 2003.

Assuming this is a greenfield installation, the first thing you should do is install IIS on the server. Before starting, make sure you have the appropriate Windows Server 2003 media or have a copy of the i386 directory copied onto your network.

Microsoft IIS

There are many different ways to install IIS on your server, including Add/Remove Programs, the "Configure Your Server Wizard" wizard page, and from the *autorun* splash screen of the Windows Server 2003 media. Following are the steps needed to begin installing the "Add/Remove Programs" screen of the Control Panel.

1. Click on **Start | Control Panel**.
2. From the Control Panel application list, choose **Add or Remove Programs**.
3. When the "Add or Remove Programs" window opens, select the **Add/Remove Windows Components** button (see Figure 3.3).

Figure 3.3 Add/Remove Windows Components

4. The "Windows Component Wizard" window opens. From the Components lists, select **Application Server** and click the **Details** button. Make sure *not* to check the Application Server checkbox; you only want to *highlight* it.

5. In the "Application Server "window, select the appropriate subcomponents necessary for IIS. For this installation you will only be selecting **Internet Information Services (IIS)**. Note that **Enable network COM+ access** enables itself automatically (see Figure 3.4). Click **OK** to return to the "Windows Components Wizard" window.

Figure 3.4 Selecting Application Server Subcomponents

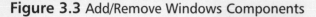

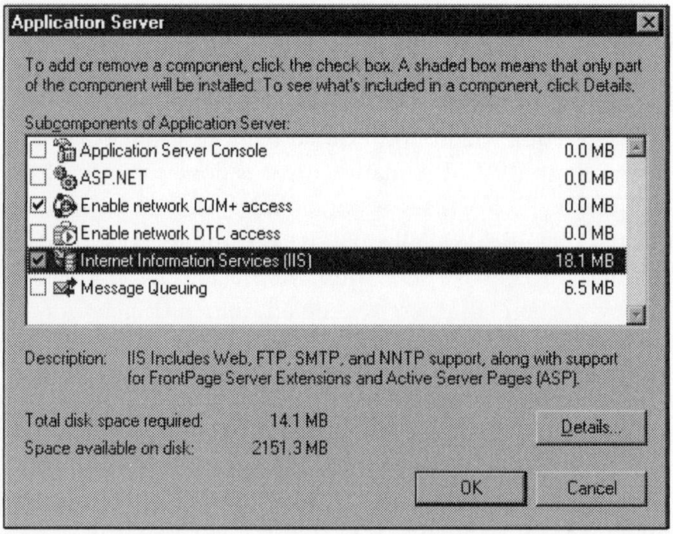

6. Click **Next** to begin installing IIS.

7. Windows begins the installation of IIS on your server. If you are prompted for the Windows media, insert the CD or point the wizard to the directory where i386 lives.

8. Once the installation is complete, you will be notified that IIS was installed successfully (see Figure 3.5). Click **Finish**.

Figure 3.5 Completing the Windows Components Wizard

Databases

The type of database you install depends greatly on the type of organization you work in, as well as several other factors including the number of clients, hardware specifications, and so on. Typically for larger enterprises, there is at least one SQL server already existing, as well as a DBA who takes care of it. You should discuss the situation with your DBA prior to installation. He or she may wish to install the database on an instance of SQL on an existing SQL server (or SQL server cluster) instead of installing MSDE. Many hardcore DBAs frown on MSDE because, not only is it another database server they have to worry about, it has a lot of limitations you must be aware of prior to installation. That said, both SQL Server 2000 and MSDE are valid database solutions.

Since both options give adequate support for a WSUS installation, other criteria need to be examined when determining which database solution to use. In certain environments, cost becomes an issue. Specifically, the cost associated with installing a SQL server versus the free MSDE option. Another area to consider is the necessary skill set needed administer a SQL server. If you're not familiar with SQL and are not sure how difficult it may be, consider that Microsoft actually has a certification based around database administration—the Microsoft Certified Database Administrator (MCDBA) certification. In an environment where SQL servers and DBAs exist, neither of these issues should be of concern.

Microsoft SQL Server

Microsoft SQL server is a very robust, scalable relational database server. SQL was originally developed by IBM, but has taken on many different flavors including Oracle, MS SQL, and MySQL. As mentioned, in some situations it may be more sensible to use a SQL back-end server for your database. WSUS allows for this type of front-end/back-end solution, but it is more complicated to install compared to an MSDE installation.

This section focuses on only the back-end configuration; the front-end configuration will be addressed later in this chapter. Before you begin, make sure your SQL server meets certain requirements:

- The SQL server must be set up to use Windows Authentication. SQL Authentication will not work with WSUS.

- SQL server must be SQL SP3a or higher.

- SQL must have the *Nested Trigger* feature turned on.

- The Microsoft .NET framework with SP1 must be loaded on the SQL server.

BEST PRACTICES ACCORDING TO MICROSOFT

- Do not use Windows 2000 server as the front-end computer in a remote SQL installation.
- Both the front-end and back-end computers must participate in an Active Directory domain.
- Neither the front-end nor the back-end can be a domain controller.
- You must run SQL on the back-end; MSDE and Windows Microsoft SQL Server 2000 Desktop Engine (WMSDE) are unsupported.

If all of these prerequisites have been met, you can move forward with your WSUS back-end configuration:

1. Open a Web browser and go to www.microsoft.com/wsus. On the WSUS homepage, you will see an option for downloading "Windows Server Update Services." Download the file and place it in a directory on your SQL server.

2. Open a command prompt (**Start| Run | cmd.exe)** and go to the directory (*cd <drive>\directory*) where you have placed the *WSUSSetup.exe* file that was downloaded in step 1.

3. At the command prompt, type **WSUSSetup /b** and press **Enter** (see Figure 3.6).

Figure 3.6 WSUSSetup Command Line for Back-End Server Configuration

4. When the "Welcome" window opens, click **Next**.

5. Read the license agreement, select "I accept the terms of the License Agreement," and click **Next**.

6. The next window to open will be the "Database Options" window (see Figure 3.7). Choose **Use an existing database server on this computer**, and select the SQL instance name from the drop-down box, and then click **Next**. WSUS will attempt to connect to the SQL server database specified.

Figure 3.7 Database Options Window

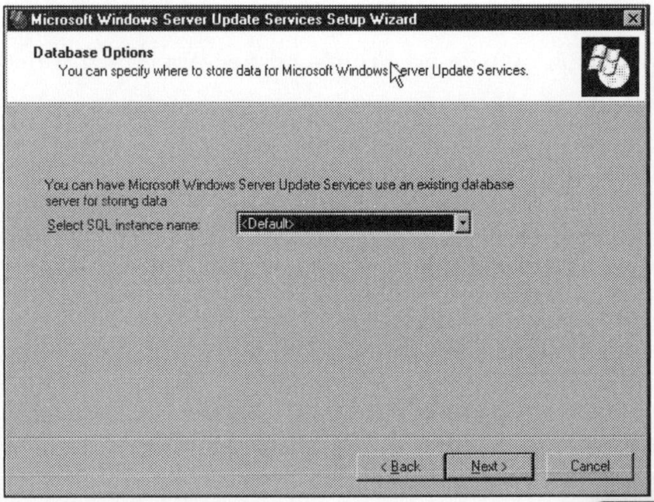

7. When WSUS successfully connects (see Figure 3.8), click **Next**.

Figure 3.8 WSUS Successfully Connects to SQL

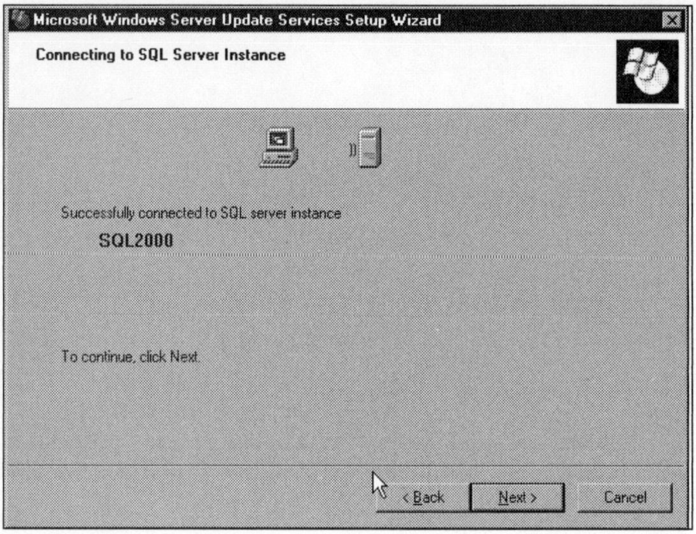

8. When the "Mirror Update Settings" window appears, click **Next**.

9. Verify the settings are correct, and click **Next** to begin the installation.

10. Click **Finish** to complete the installation.

There are also some permission issues to take care of on your servers.

1. On a domain controller or a system running the Windows Admin Pack, open **Active Directory Users and Computers**.

2. Right-click on the "Users" folder or an Organizational Unit (OU). From the menu, click **New | Group**.

3. Enter a name for the group; **Front-end Servers** is used as the group name in this example.

4. Change the Group Scope to **Global**.

5. Change the Group Type to **Security**.

6. Click **OK** to save the group.

7. Find the group you created, and double-click to open it.

8. Click on the **Members** tab.

9. Click **Add**.

10. From the "Select Users, Contacts, or Computers" window, click the **Object Types** button (see Figure 3.9).

Figure 3.9 The Select Users, Contacts, or Computers Window

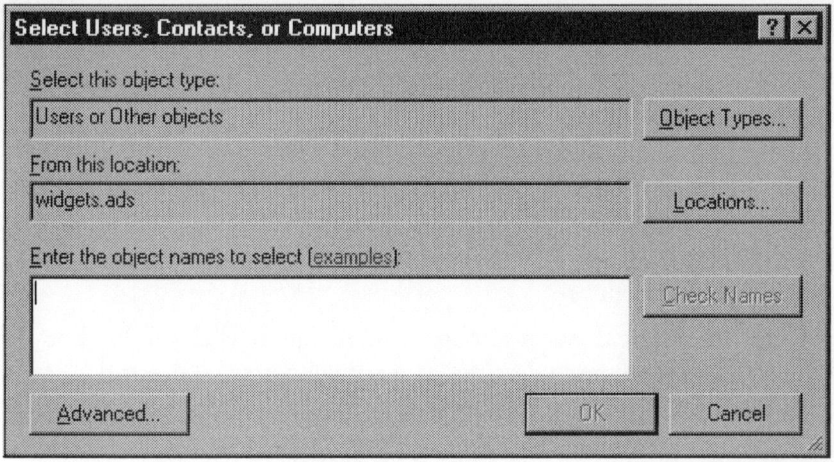

11. Remove the "Other" objects and "Users" objects, and select **Computers** so that it is the only object type selected.

12. When you return to the "Select Users, Contacts, or Computers" window, type the name of the front-end server in the Enter the object names to select (*examples*): window (see Figure 3.10). In this example, the front-end server name is WSUS.

Figure 3.10 Enter the Name of the Front-End Server

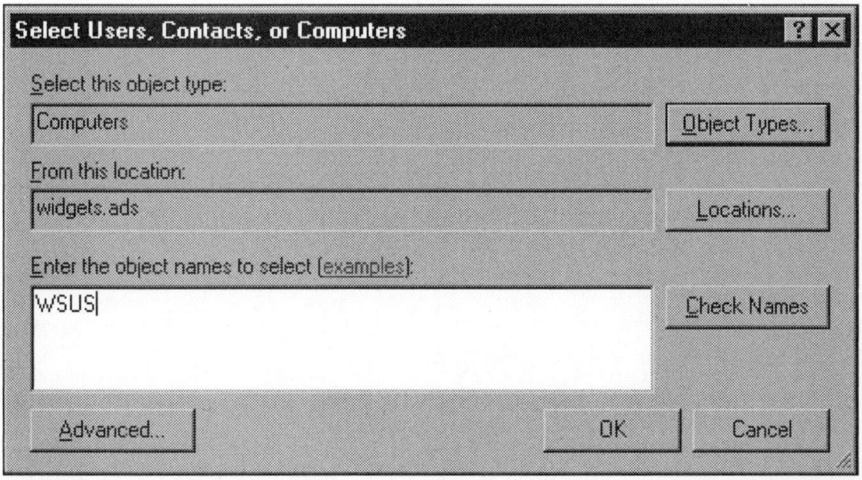

13. Click the **Check Names** button to verify that the name is correct and is registered in Active Directory, and then click **OK.**

14. Click **OK** again to close the Group Properties window.

Now you need to take the group you just created, and apply it to the SQL server:

1. On the SQL server, click **Start | Programs | Administrative Tools | Computer Management**.

2. Click on **Local Users and Groups**.

3. Double-click on the **Groups** folder to open it.

4. Double-click on the **WSUS Administrators** group.

5. Click the **Add** button.

6. When the Select Users or Groups window opens, click on the drop-down box next to **Look in:** and select the name of your Active Directory domain.

7. Click on the Global group you created earlier, and then click the **Add** button.

8. Click **OK** twice to close the group properties.

Although you are not quite done with the back-end configuration, you have to complete the front-end installation before you can move forward with the remaining pieces. Therefore, this will be put on hold while we discuss MSDE installations. If you do not plan to use MSDE, you can jump ahead to the next section, "Microsoft SQL Server Desktop Engine (MSDE)."

If you're installing WSUS on a Windows Server 2003 platform and plan to use MSDE, skip this section and go directly to ***Installing WSUS on Microsoft Windows Server 2003***. Do not pass go, do not collect $200.

Installing MSDE on Windows 2000

To install WSUS on a Windows 2000 server, the first thing you will need to do is download a copy of *Microsoft SQL Server 2000 Desktop Engine* from either the Microsoft Download Center, or directly from http://go.microsoft.com/fwlink/?LinkId=47366. While you're there, you should also pick up a required security patch for MSDE 2000. Again, you can find it at the Download Center or go directly to http://go.microsoft.com/fwlink/?LinkId=37271. Now you will install MSDE on your server:

1. Go to the directory where you downloaded the MSDE 2000 self-extracting executable.

2. Double-click on **MSDE2000a.exe**.

3. Read through the license agreement, and then click **I agree.**

4. When the **Installation Folder** window opens, type the path where you want to decompress the MSDE installation (see Figure 3.11) and click **Finish.**

Figure 3.11 Decompressing the MSDE files

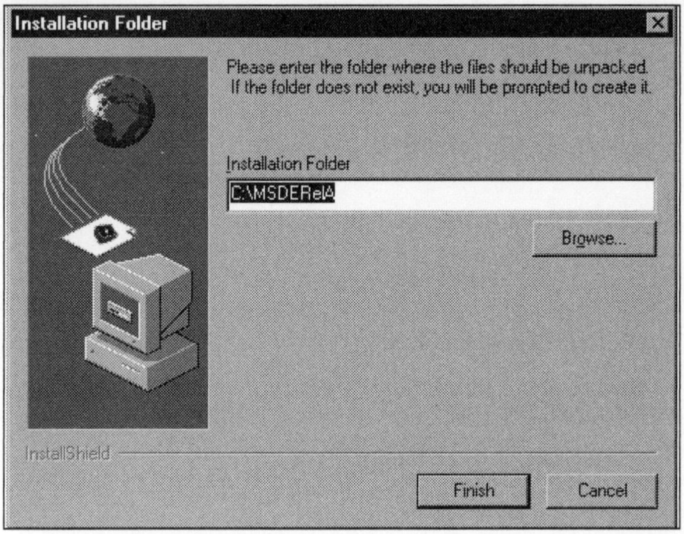

5. Next, open a command prompt (**Start | Run | cmd.exe**), go to the directory specified in step 4 (*cd <drive>\directory*), and type **setup sapwd="WSUSServer" instancename="WSUS"**. This gives MSDE one instance named WSUS, and a Systems Administrator (SA) account with the password "WSUSServer" (see Figure 3.12). The password can be changed to anything you choose.

Figure 3.12 Command Prompt Syntax for MSDE Installation

```
C:\WINDOWS\system32\cmd.exe

C:\MSDERe1A>setup sapwd="WSUSServer" instancename="WSUS"
```

Next, patch the MSDE installation using the security patch that you downloaded earlier:

1. Using Windows Explorer, navigate to the directory where you downloaded the patch.

2. Double click on **SQL2000-KB815495-8.00.0818-ENU.exe**.

3. When the "Welcome" window opens, click **Next**.

4. You will be presented with another *End User License Agreement*, which you must read.

5. When you are done reading the license agreement, click **I accept the license terms and conditions** and click **Next**.

6. In the Instance to Update window (see Figure 3.13), use the **Instance** box to select the WSUS instance you just created and then click **Next**.

Figure 3.13 Selecting an Instance

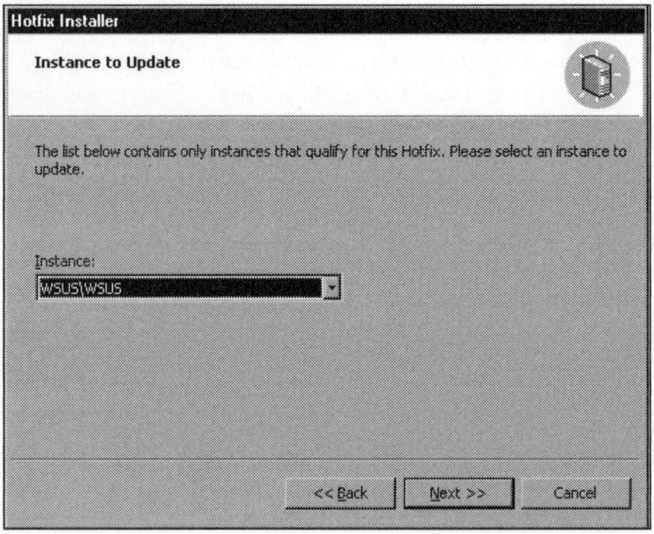

5. In the Authentication Mode window, choose **Windows Authentication** and click **Next**.

6. In the Hotfix Installer window, click **Install** and the security patch installation will begin. When the installation is complete, click **Finish**.

Installing WSUS on Microsoft Windows Server 2003

You are now ready to install WSUS on your server. However, ironically, the first thing you need to do is patch your patching server. As mentioned in the system requirements, you will need a .NET Framework SP (www.microsoft.com/downloads/details.aspx?familyid= AE7EDEF7-2CB7-4864-8623-A1038563DF23&displaylang=en) as well as the BITS 2.0 update (www.microsoft.com/downloads/details.aspx?FamilyID=b93356b1-ba43-480f-983d-eb19368f9047&DisplayLang=en).

Patches

Let's start with the .NET Patch:

1. Assuming you have downloaded the patch, go to the directory where you saved the patch and double-click on it (**KB867460**).

2. When the "Windows Server 2003 KB867460 Setup Wizard" window opens (see Figure 3.14), click **Next**.

Figure 3.14 Windows Server 2003 .NET Patch Welcome Screen

3. Read through the *License Agreement*, click on the **I Agree** radio button, and then click **Next**. The patch will begin applying the updates.

4. If you are prompted to start and re-start the World Wide Web (WWW) Publishing Service (see Figure 3.15), click **Continue**; otherwise, abort the update. If you choose to continue, Windows will stop the WWW Publishing Service, apply the changes, and restart the service when complete.

Figure 3.15 Prompt to Stop and Restart the WWW Service

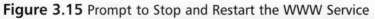

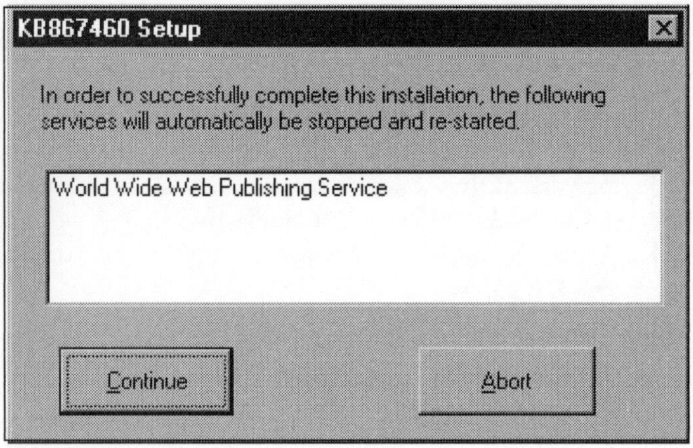

5. When the patch is complete (see Figure 3.16), click **Finish**. If prompted, restart your computer before applying the second patch. Even if you are not prompted, it's always good to restart after completing a new update.

Figure 3.16 Completing the Update Wizard

Next, you need to complete the update for BITS 2.0. The process for this upgrade is pretty much the same as the .NET patch:

1. Assuming you have downloaded the patch, go to the directory where you saved the patch and double-click on it (**KB842773**).

2. When the Windows Server 2003 KB842773 Setup Wizard window opens (see Figure 3.17), click **Next**.

Figure 3.17 Windows Server 2003 BITS Patch Welcome Screen

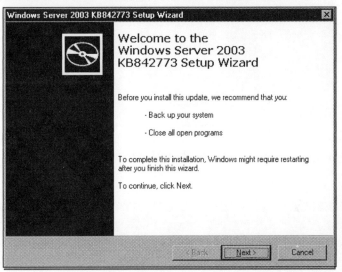

3. Read through the *License Agreement*, click on the **I Agree** radio button, and then click **Next**. The patch will begin applying the updates.

4. When the patch is complete (see Figure 3.18), click **Finish**. If prompted, restart your computer before applying the second patch. Even if you are not prompted, it's always good to restart after completing a new update.

Figure 3.18 Completing the Update Wizard

When the server reboots, you are ready to begin installing the WSUS software.

Shortcuts...

Save Time and Pack Your Server!

If you have already installed SP1 on your WSUS server, or plan to SP it prior to installing WSUS, you can skip the steps listed in the previous section. SP1 has all of the patches included. You can still attempt to install the patches if you choose, but you will be informed that the patch has already been installed. Note that the individual patch numbers will not appear in Add/Remove Programs on a server that has SP1 installed.

Typical Server Installation

Now it is time to install WSUS. You have patched your servers, and hopefully you have verified that your server meets the minimum requirements, and all decisions have been made about the database location. Now, find the WSUS installation media or the directory where you saved the *WSUSSetup.exe* download. The following steps assume you are using the downloaded version (since it is typically the most up-to-date):

1. Launch the WSUS setup file. The setup file will begin extracting the components to a temporary directory.

2. The "Microsoft Windows Server Update Services Setup Wizard" screen will open (see Figure 3.19). Read through the brief description of the installation. When you are finished, click **Next**.

Figure 3.19 Microsoft Windows Server Update Services Setup Wizard

3. Read through the *License Agreement*, and select the radio button next to **I accept the terms of the License agreement**. Click **Next** to continue.

4. Now you need to specify where you to store the updates that clients will be acquiring via WSUS (see Figure 3.20). By default, WSUS will try to store the updates on *C:\WSUS*. Since this is typically the system partition, it's probably not a good idea to store them here. Choose another drive, or you can optionally decide to use WSUS in a "proxy" mode and redirect clients to download the updates directly from Microsoft. When you have selected a location, click **Next**.

Figure 3.20 Selecting an Update Source

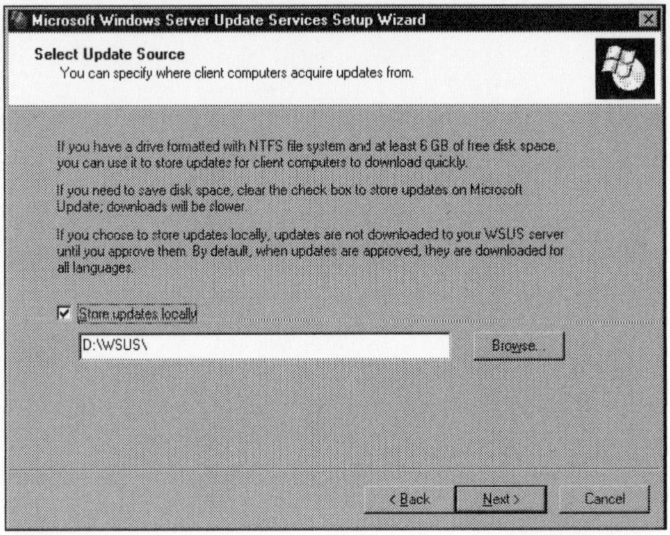

5. Now you have come to the database options. For Windows Server 2003 users, you need to decide where to install MSDE on this server. By default, WSUS will attempt to use the same drive and folder used in the previous step (see Figure 3.21). You can either select another directory (or drive) on this server, or use an existing database server running on this computer.

Figure 3.21 Selecting a Database Option

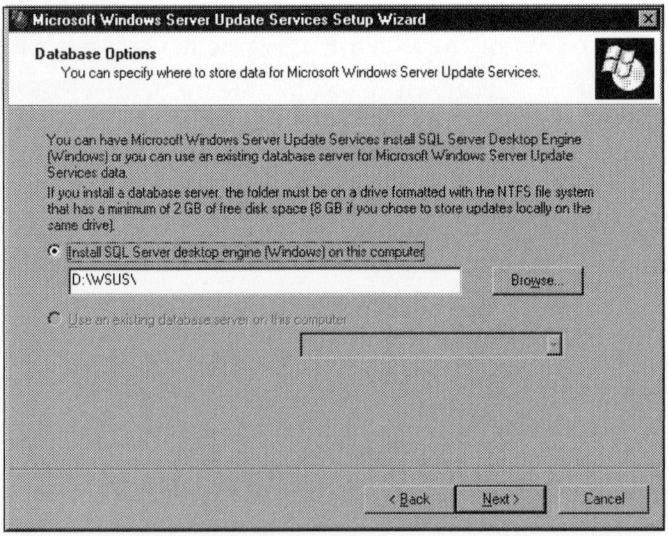

6. Now select the Web site where the WSUS administrative tools and Web services will be accessed. By default (and Microsoft recommendation), the WSUS console will use the IIS Default Web site (see Figure 3.22). If this server does not host any other WSUS sites, this is not an issue. If it is a multi-purpose server, consider creating a WSUS site. Make note of the site and ports specified on this page, and click **Next**. For this example, we will use the default Web site.

Figure 3.22 Selecting a Web Site for WSUS

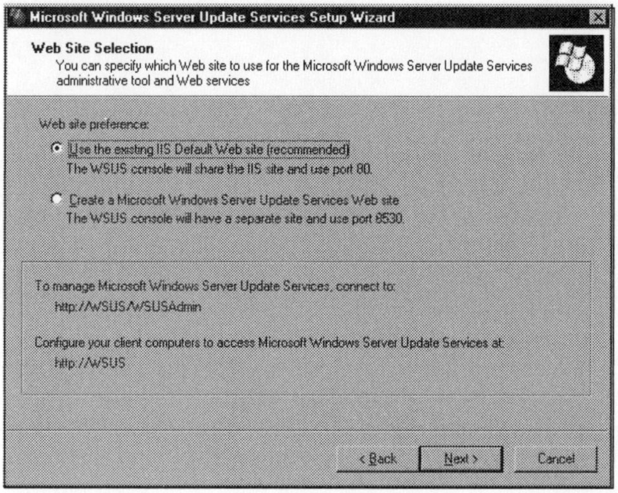

7. The next window is the "Mirror Update Settings" window (see Figure 3.23). In larger enterprises, you may have multiple WSUS servers for updating remote offices. Since this will be the first server in the enterprise, you can simply click **Next**.

Figure 3.23 Selecting Mirror Update Settings

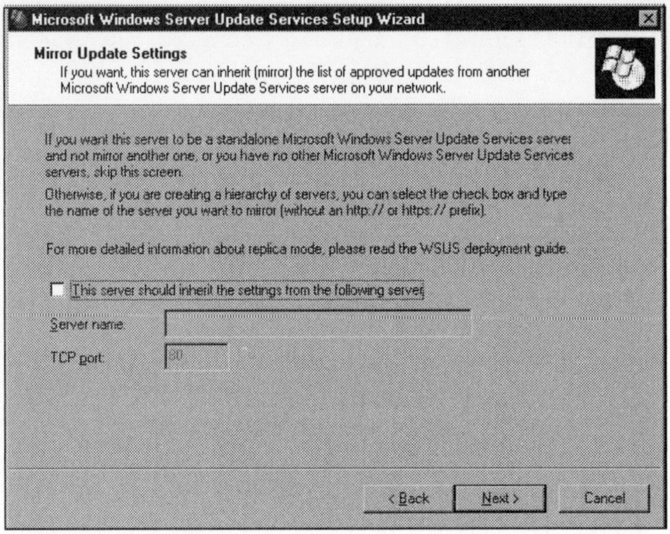

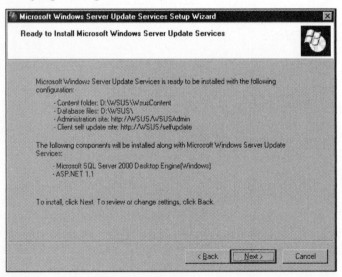

8. All of the pre-installation configuration options are complete. Now you need to review and verify the settings that you just made (see Figure 3.24). Verify that all of the information is correct, and click **Next**. Windows Server 2003 users should note that "Microsoft SQL Server 2000 desktop engine (Windows)" installs automatically (see Figure 3.21).

Figure 3.24 Verifying Configuration Options

9. When the installation is complete (see Figure 3.25), click **Finish.**

Figure 3.25 Completing the WSUS Installation

Your WSUS server installation is complete. Unless you unchecked the box, WSUS will launch automatically after completing the installation. The first screen you will see is the *Windows Server Update Services* homepage (see Figure 3.26). Here, you will find a summary of all of the information pertaining to this WSUS server and the clients that it services.

Figure 3.26 The WSUS Homepage

![The WSUS Homepage showing Windows Server Update Services welcome page]

Windows Server Update Services

Home Updates Reports Computers Options

Home   Help

Welcome to Windows Server Update Services

You can use Windows Server Update Services to quickly and reliably deploy the latest updates to your machines. Get the latest WSUS news from Microsoft

Status as of Saturday, August 20, 2005 9:29 PM

Updates		Synchronization Status	
Total:	0	Last synchronization:	Never run
Approved updates:	0	Last synchronization result:	N/A
Updates not approved:	0	Next synchronization:	Manual
Declined updates:	0	Current status:	Idle
Updates with computer errors:	0	Synchronize now	
Updates needed by computers:	0		
		Status of Downloads	
Computers		Updates needing files:	0
Total:	0		
Computers with update errors:	0		
Computers needing updates:	0		

To Do List

Get started by synchronizing your server
To be able to view available updates you first need to synchronize your server. By default Critical and Security updates for Windows will be synchronized in all languages. Or before synchronizing you can select the products and languages you want on the Synchronization Options page.

Unattended Server Installation

In certain situations where either physical access or access via Remote Desktop is either not possible or is unreasonable (such as across slow network links), using an unattended installation of WSUS may be necessary.

Microsoft has made unattended installations of WSUS very easy for even the novice command line user. As simple as it is, don't be fooled—it still has all the functionality and flexibility as the graphical user interface (GUI) installation. Before performing an unattended installation, you should collect as much configuration information as possible (e.g., what partitions have enough free space to hold the updates and the database, and so on).

Let's walk through a simple unattended installation. This example explains how to configure several options:

- The directory where the content will be stored
- The directory where the WSUS database will be stored
- The name of the SQL server instance to be used

These are just some of the many properties and parameters that can be specified in a WSUS unattended installation. Table 3.3 shows a complete list of the properties that can be set, and Table 3.4 lists the different parameters available.

Table 3.3 WSUS Unattended Properties

Property	Description
CONTENT_DIR	The directory where WSUS will store its content.
CONTENT_LOCAL	The location of the .cab files. This determines if a client will download updates locally or from Microsoft.
INSTANCE_NAME	The name of the SQL server instance. WSUS by default
WMSDE_DIR	The directory where the WMSDE directory will be stored.
RETAIN DATA	During uninstallation, this is used to determine what (if any) data will be retained.

Table 3.4 WSUS Unattended Parameters

Parameters	Description
/b	Used for remote SQL database installations, sets up the back-end database.
/d	Use the existing SQL database server
/f	Also used for remote SQL installations, but performs all the front-end functions.

Continued

Table 3.4 continued WSUS Unattended Parameters

Parameters	Description
/l	This parameter can be used to run setup in a different language than the default system language.
/o	Overwrite the existing database
/q	Perform a silent installation.
/u	Uninstall WSUS
/v	Used in conjunction with the properties in Table 3.3.
/?	Display the help file.

So, now that you've covered some of the basic background information, it's time to do the installation.

1. Click the **Start** button.

2. Click **Run**.

3. Type **cmd** and either press **Enter** or click on **OK**.

4. Change directories to the location where the *WSUSSetup.exe* file resides.

5. To begin, type **WSUSSetup /?** to display the full list of parameters, switches, and languages available (see Figure 3.27). Note that the *.exe* file temporarily extracts its contents to a directory on the server.

Figure 3.27 WSUSSetup Command Line Parameter and Properties

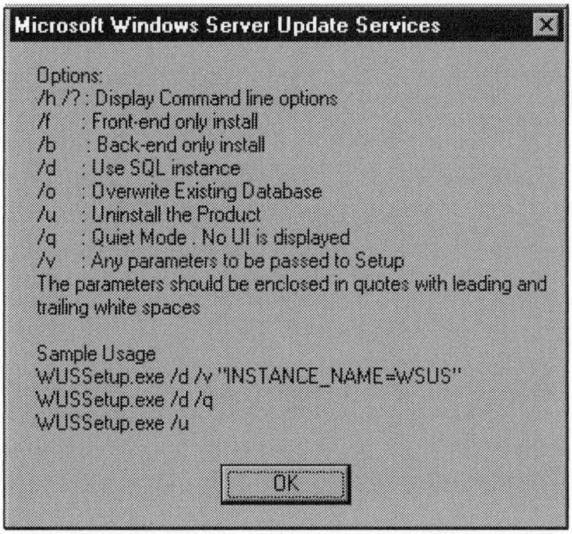

```
Microsoft Windows Server Update Services          [X]

Options:
/h /? : Display Command line options
/f    : Front-end only install
/b    : Back-end only install
/d    : Use SQL instance
/o    : Overwrite Existing Database
/u    : Uninstall the Product
/q    : Quiet Mode . No UI is displayed
/v    : Any parameters to be passed to Setup
The parameters should be enclosed in quotes with leading and
trailing white spaces

Sample Usage
WUSSetup.exe /d /v "INSTANCE_NAME=WSUS"
WUSSetup.exe /d /q
WUSSetup.exe /u

                    [   OK   ]
```

6. Click **OK** to close the window. As mentioned earlier, you will configure three parameters in your installation. The first parameter is the directory where the WSUS content will be stored (see Figure 3.28). Remember to *not* press **Enter** after completing the syntax, as you will be adding to it.

Figure 3.28 Specifying the WSUS Content Directory

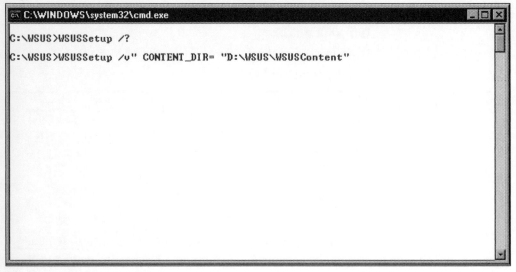

```
C:\WINDOWS\system32\cmd.exe

C:\WSUS>WSUSSetup /?

C:\WSUS>WSUSSetup /v" CONTENT_DIR= "D:\WSUS\WSUSContent"
```

7. Next, you must specify the directory where the WSUS database will be stored (see Figure 3.29). Again, make sure *not* to press **Enter**.

Figure 3.29 Specifying the WSUS Database Directory

```
C:\WINDOWS\system32\cmd.exe

C:\WSUS>WSUSSetup /?

C:\WSUS>WSUSSetup /v" CONTENT_DIR= "D:\WSUS\WSUSContent" WMSDE_DIR = "D:\WSUS"_
```

8. Specify the SQL instance name to be used by WSUS. Figure 3.30 shows the complete command line to be used for your unattended installation. Make sure to add the second quotation at the end of the command, otherwise the installation may fail. Also, make sure to use the **/q** switch to perform the installation in the background, otherwise the installation will continue as expected, using the parameters you set.

Figure 3.30 Specifying the WSUS Instance Name

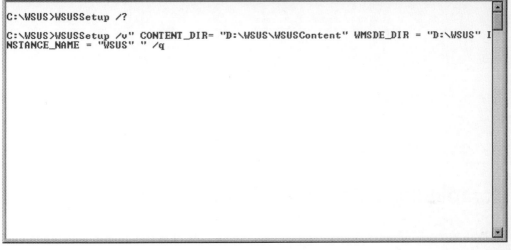

9. After verifying the command line, press **Enter.** The WSUS executable will once again extract to a temporary directory.

10. To verify that the installation is running, open the Task Manager by right clicking on the Taskbar, and selecting **Task Manager**. Click on the **Processes** tab, and sort by CPU usage by clicking on the **CPU** column header (see Figure 3.31). Notice the running processes. You will see *msiexec.exe*, *WusSetup.exe*, *WSUSSetup.exe*, as well as *WUSInstaller.exe*. When the installation is complete, these processes will disappear, and you will be able to browse to the WSUSAdmin Web page on the server.

Figure 3.31 Task Manager Showing Processes Sorted by CPU Usage

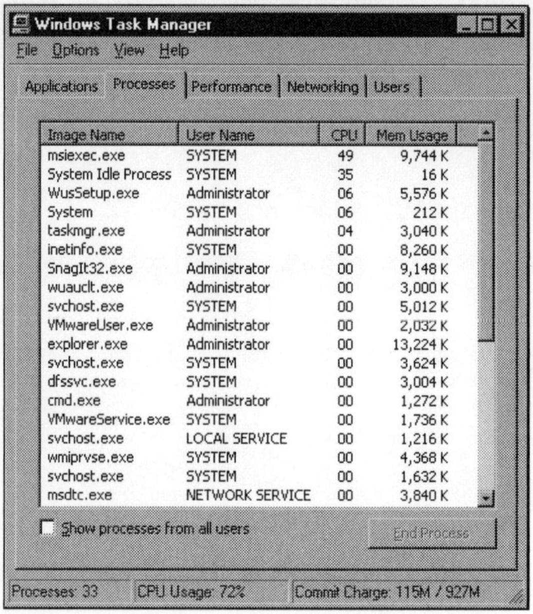

Completing a Remote SQL Installation

In "Installing Supporting Applications," we left the SQL server installation in limbo. Now that you have an understanding of how a typical WSUS installation is completed, you can finish the front-end/back-end configuration.

Configuring the Front-end Server

In a typical installation, you would normally complete this piece *before* configuring the back-end server; however, switching the order will not affect the installation. With the front-end installation, you still need to determine where the updates will be stored, how the server will be accessed (Web site and port), and tell the front-end server where the database actually lives. For now, you should focus on the first two items.

1. Open a Web browser and go to *www.microsoft.com/wsus*. On the WSUS home-page, you will see an option for downloading **Windows Server Update Services**. Download the file and place it in a directory on your SQL server.

2. Open a command prompt (**Start| Run | *cmd.exe***) and go to the directory (*cd <drive>\directory*) where you have placed the *WSUSSetup.exe* file that was downloaded in step 1.

3. At the command prompt, type **WSUSSetup /f** and press **Enter** (see Figure 3.32).

Figure 3.32 Configuring the WSUS Front-End Server

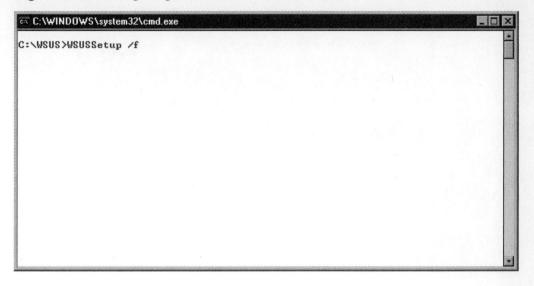

4. When the "Welcome" window opens, click **Next**.

5. Read the *License Agreement*, select **I accept the terms of the License Agreement**, and click **Next**.

6. Now you need to specify where you to store the updates that clients will be acquiring via WSUS (see Figure 3.33). By default, WSUS will try to store the updates on *C:\WSUS* Since this is typically the system partition, it's probably not a good idea to store them here. Choose another drive, or you can optionally decide to use WSUS in a "proxy" mode and redirect clients to download the updates directly from Microsoft. When you have selected a location, click **Next**.

Figure 3.33 Selecting a Location for the Updates

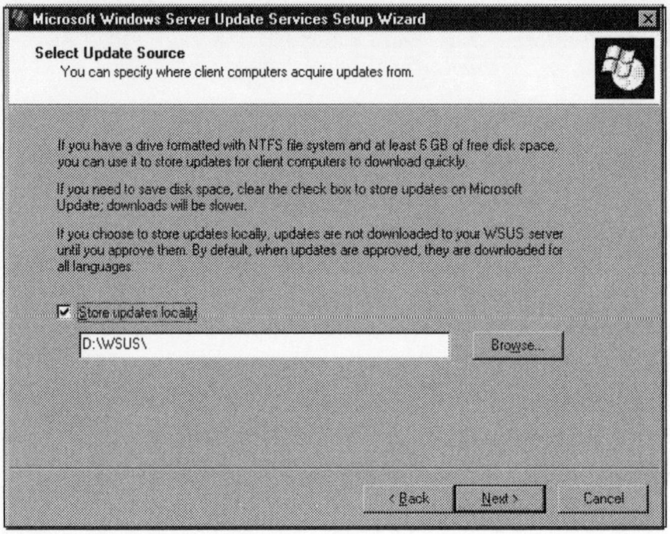

7. Now you will select the Web site where the WSUS administrative tools and Web services will be accessed. By default (and Microsoft recommendation), the WSUS console will use the IIS Default Web site. If this server does not host any other WSUS sites, this is not an issue. If it is a multi-purpose server, consider creating a WSUS site. Make note of the site and ports specified on this page, and click **Next**. For this example, we use the default Web site.

8. All of the pre-installation configuration options are complete. Now you need to review and verify the settings you have just made. Verify that all of the information is correct, and click **Next**.

9. When the installation is complete, click **Finish**.

Finishing the Back-End Configuration

The SQL server was left in limbo waiting for us to complete the back-end configuration. However, we had to complete the front-end configuration before we were able to configure. Specifically, we had to already determine where the WSUS updates would be stored so that we could make SQL aware of it. This can be a little tricky, so be careful of typos and directory locations:

1. From the SQL back-end server, open a command prompt (**Start | Run | cmd.exe**) and go to the — *<drive>:\Program Files\Update Services\tools\osql* Directory.

2. Type the following string: **osql.exe –S <sqlservername> –E –b –n –Q "USE SUSDB UPDATE dbo.tbConfigurationA SET HostOnMu = '0' UPDATE dbo.tbConfigurationB SET LocalContentCacheLocation = N'<WSUSdirectory>'"** where **<sqlservername>** is the name of the SQL back-end server, and **<WSUSdirectory>** is the path on the front-end server where the updates are stored (see Figure 3.34). If the script executes properly, it will return a message that one row was affected.

Figure 3.34 Configuring SQL Server at the Command Line

Connecting the Front-End Server to the Back-End Server

The front-end/back-end configuration is nearly complete. The last thing you need to do is tell the front-end server how to contact the back-end server, and then start the WSUS service. To configure the front-end server, you will need to open the Registry Editor (*regedit.exe*):

1. From the WSUS front-end server, open the registry editor (**Start| Run | *regedit.exe*)** and go to *HKEY_LOCAL_MACHINE\SOFT-WARE\Microsoft\Update Services\Server\Setup*.

2. Double-click on the **SQLServerName** key.

3. In the Value data: field, type the name of the SQL server.

The last thing you need to do is turn on the WSUS service:

1. Click on **Start | Administrative Tools | Services**
2. Right-click on **Update Services** and click **Start**.

If you configured the back-end and the front-end servers correctly, you should now have a functioning WSUS server with Remote SQL. If it doesn't work on the first attempt, try rebooting.

Some Independent Advice

If this configuration does not work the first time, don't get frustrated and give up. The first thing you should do is reboot the WSUS server, since you made changes to the system registry. If that does not work, it is very easy to uninstall WSUS and delete the SQL database and start over. There is a good chance it was a simple typo.

Summary

As you have seen, Microsoft has made the installation of WSUS as simple as possible, while still leaving you with a variety of options for configuration. Let's recap some of the key points of installing WSUS:

- The most important thing to remember when building WSUS is to scope it properly. Make sure that your WSUS server meets the minimum requirements, and make sure you decide on the location and type of database prior to installation.

- Save some time and download all of the necessary patches at once, which will prevent multiple visits to the Microsoft Web site.

- If you are planning to implement a front-end/back-end solution, be mindful of your typing. A simple typo can have you troubleshooting for hours.

Solutions Fast Track

System Requirements

- ☑ Very loose hardware requirements, with the main focus being storage space.
- ☑ MSDE or SQL must be used for WSUS database.
- ☑ Additional patches and updates are required on the WSUS server prior to installation.

Installing Supporting Applications

- ☑ Make sure IIS is installed and secure it as needed.
- ☑ Plan your database type and location prior to WSUS installation.
- ☑ Be careful when using the front-end/back-end database configuration.

Installing WSUS on Microsoft Windows Server 2003

- ☑ Make sure you have sufficient drive space before attempting the installation.
- ☑ An unattended installation is a good option for systems with limited console access.
- ☑ WSUS servers in a front-end configuration are not started by default. You have to make the appropriate registry change and start the service.

Frequently Asked Questions

The following Frequently Asked Questions, answered by the authors of this book, are designed to both measure your understanding of the concepts presented in this chapter and to assist you with real-life implementation of these concepts. To have your questions about this chapter answered by the author, browse to **www.syngress.com/solutions** and click on the **"Ask the Author"** form.

Q: How difficult is it to build a front-end/back-end solution?

A: It is not difficult; however, you must make sure that it is done properly. A good idea is to make a checklist of the various items that must be completed. You should also think about writing your command line strings on a notepad prior to attempting to type the command line.

Q: Do I need to store the updates on a local drive? Can I use a drive mapping?

A: Yes, you can use a mapped drive. However, make sure that this is a persistent mapping; you don't want to be in a situation where the updates cannot be accessed because of a broken mapping.

Q: I have a PII-400MHz server I want to use for WSUS. Will this work?

A: It may; however, it does not meet the minimum requirements for Windows 2003 or WSUS.

Q: My company uses WSUS for Windows updates but we run on a Novell network. Do I really need Active Directory to complete a front-end/back-end configuration?

A: Yes. You need Active Directory because of the security permissions and the requirement for integrated Windows authentication.

Q: I want to perform an unattended installation, but I want to watch while it is running for testing purposes. If I do not use the **/q** switch, what will happen?

A: All of your variable will still be applied; however, you will be prompted to click **Next**, accept License Agreements, and so forth.

Q: Does WSUS work with SQL Server 2005?

A: There is no official word on this yet, but it is very likely that they will be compatible.

Chapter 4

Upgrading from SUS to WSUS

Solutions in this chapter:

- **In-Place Upgrade**
- **Across-the-Wire Upgrade**

☑ **Summary**

☑ **Solutions Fast Track**

☑ **Frequently Asked Questions**

Introduction

A Software Update Services server (SUS) cannot be upgraded to a Windows Server Update Services (WSUS) server; however, you can migrate updates and approvals from a SUS server to a WSUS server. Doing so prevents you from having to download and approve all of your updates again. This is done in one of two ways. You can install WSUS onto the server already running SUS and perform a local migration known as an *in-place upgrade*, or you can install WSUS onto another server and migrate everything across the network, which is known as an *across-the-wire upgrade*.

In-Place Upgrade

An in-place-upgrade is the easiest way to migrate from SUS to WSUS. It involves installing WSUS onto the existing SUS server. Both will run successfully at the same time, which allows you to become familiar with WSUS before switching over all of your clients. Once WSUS is working as expected, you can switch over all of your clients and decommission SUS. The in-place upgrade is a one-way process; you can migrate from SUS to WSUS, but not from WSUS back to SUS.

Even though SUS and WSUS will run on the same machine at the same time, they will never synchronize with each other. This means that if you want to run both of them at the same time for an extended period of time, you must administer them separately.

> **NOTE**
>
> Microsoft is ending support for SUS updates on June 6, 2006. To continue updating your clients, you will have to move to WSUS at that time.

There are a few things to look out for when doing an in-place upgrade. If you have been running a beta version of WSUS on your SUS server, you should remove it before installing WSUS. If you plan to promote your server to a domain controller, you should do it before you install WSUS. Also, if you want to demote your server to a member server instead of it being a domain controller, you should do so first.

Steps to Success

Performing an in-place upgrade from SUS to WSUS contains many phases:

1. You must first make sure that the server meets the minimum hardware and software requirements for WSUS.

2. You must install and configure WSUS.

3. Once WSUS is working, you must migrate the approval status of your SUS updates and the content of those updates to WSUS.

4. You must configure all of your clients to start using WSUS instead of WSUS.

5. Lastly, you can decommission the SUS service all together.

Meeting the Prerequisites

Before installing WSUS on the SUS server, you must make sure that the server meets the minimum hardware and software recommendations for WSUS. If you have been keeping your existing SUS server up-to-date, it is probably already prepared for WSUS. If you do not meet the prerequisites for WSUS, you will be given a window when you start the installation (see Figure 4.1).

Figure 4.1 Resolving Issues During Setup

The hardware requirements are the same for Windows 2000 Server and Windows Server 2003. Microsoft recommends using at least a 1-gigahertz (GHz) processor with a minimum of 1 gigabyte (GB) of random access memory (RAM), even though it is supported on a 750-megahertz (MHz) processor with 512 megabytes (MB) of RAM. (See Table 4.1 for a list of recommendations based on the number of clients.)

Your WSUS server should have a minimum of 9GB of free disk space, which should allow sufficient space to hold the operating system (OS), the page file, the Microsoft SQL Desktop Edition (MSDE)/Windows Microsoft SQL Server 2000 Desktop Engine (WMSDE), and all of the WSUS files and updates. The disk space is allocated as follows:

- At least 1GB for the system partition (must be formatted as New Technology File System [NTFS])

- At least 2GB for the partition containing WMSDE or MSDE

- At least 6GB (30GB recommended) for the partition containing the WSUS content (must be formatted as NTFS)

Table 4.1 Choosing Hardware for WSUS

Number of Clients	Recommended RAM	Recommended CPU	Recommended Database
500 or less	1GB or more	1 GHz or faster	WMSDE (2003) or MSDE (2000)
500–10,000	1GB or more	3 GHz or faster	SQL server
10,000 or more	1GB or more	Dual 3 GHz or faster	SQL server

BEST PRACTICES ACCORDING TO MICROSOFT

Use a larger drive than required to allow room for growth. Installing WSUS on a drive with at least 9GB of free disk space will meet the minimum require-ments. However, Microsoft recommends using a drive with at least 40GB of free disk space. They recommend having 30GB just for the drive that contains the WSUS updates.

The software requirements are different depending on whether you are running Windows 2000 Server or Windows Server 2003. WSUS can be installed on all versions of Windows 2000 Server and Windows Server 2003, except Windows Server 2003 Web Edition and 64-bit editions of Windows. If installing on Windows 2000, you must take extra steps to install and secure WSUS (see Table 4.2 and Table 4.3 for a list of software download locations).

SOME INDEPENDENT ADVICE

Do not worry if you do not have 40GB of free space on your drive. You can use the *WSUSUtil.exe* command (explained later in this chapter) to move the loca-tion of where WSUS looks for. Thus, if the drive you start with becomes full, you can easily move the updates to a new larger drive.

Windows 2000 Server has the following software requirements:

- Microsoft Internet Information Services (IIS) 5.0
- Background Intelligent Transfer Service (BITS) 2.0 (installation requires rebooting)
- Microsoft Internet Explorer 6.0 Service Pack 1
- Microsoft .NET Framework Version 1.1 Redistributable Package
- Microsoft .NET Framework 1.1 Service Pack 1

- A database compatible with Microsoft Structured Query Language (SQL)
- Windows 2000 Server Service Pack 4

Windows Server 2003 has the following software requirements:

- Microsoft IIS 6.0
- BITS 2.0 (installation requires a reboot)
- Microsoft .NET Framework 1.1 Service Pack 1

Table 4.2 Downloading Software for Windows 2000

Software	Download Location
BITS 2.0;	*http://go.microsoft.com/fwlink/?LinkId=46794*
MSDE	*http://go.microsoft.com/fwlink/?LinkId=47366*
MSDE patch described in Security Bulletin MS03-031	*http://go.microsoft.com/fwlink/?LinkId=37271*
Microsoft Internet Explorer 6.0 Service Pack 1	*http://go.microsoft.com/fwlink/?LinkId=47359*
Microsoft .NET Framework Version 1.1 Redistributable Package	*http://go.microsoft.com/fwlink/?LinkId=47369*
Microsoft .NET Framework 1.1 Service Pack 1	*http://go.microsoft.com/fwlink/?LinkId=47368*
Windows 2000 Service Pack 4	*http://go.microsoft.com/fwlink/?LinkId=13228*
WSUS	*http://go.microsoft.com/fwlink/?LinkId=47374*

Table 4.3 Downloading Software for Windows 2003

Software	Download Location
BITS 2.0	*http://go.microsoft.com/fwlink/?LinkId=47251*
Microsoft .NET Framework 1.1 Service Pack 1	*http://go.microsoft.com/fwlink/?LinkId=35326*
WSUS	*http://go.microsoft.com/fwlink/?LinkId=47374*

Shortcuts...

Getting All Your Software Together

Use the links on Table 4.2 and Table 4.3 to download all of the required software before you begin installing WSUS. Create a support folder on your hard drive and save all of the software there. This way, as you are working through this chapter, you will have everything you need to follow all of the exercises.

Installing MSDE

If you are running WSUS on Windows 2000 Server and do not have a Microsoft SQL Server, you must install the MSDE manually. If you are installing WSUS on Windows Server 2003, the WSUS installer will install and configure the WMSDE automatically. Even if you do have access to a SQL server, you may choose to use MSDE or WMSDE instead. If you implement WSUS with SQL Server, you need to purchase a SQL Client Access License (CAL) for each computer serviced by WSUS, or use per-processor licensing for SQL Server.

MSDE can be downloaded from Microsoft's Web site (see Table 4.2). After downloading, you must expand the files to a folder on the SUS server. Next, from the command prompt set the SQL instance name and Systems Administrator (SA) password. After the install finishes and you make sure that the service is running, you must patch MSDE to make it secure.

To install MSDE on Windows 2000 Server, follow these steps:

1. Download MSDE from *http://go.microsoft.com/fwlink/?LinkId=47366*.

2. Expand the MSDE archive by double-clicking on **MSDE2000a.exe**.

3. This gives you the "License Agreement" screen shown in Figure 4.2. Click on **I Agree** to accept the license agreement and continue with setup.

4. You will now be prompted for a location to hold the unpacked MSDE files (see Figure 4.3). You can click **Browse** and choose an alternate location. For this exercise we are using default location *C:\MSDERelA*. Click **Finish** to continue.

5. Because this folder does not yet exist, you will be prompted to have setup create it (see Figure 4.4). Click **Yes** to create the folder and continue with the setup.

Figure 4.2 Accepting the License Agreement

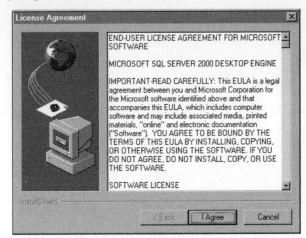

Figure 4.3 Selecting a Location for the MSDE Files

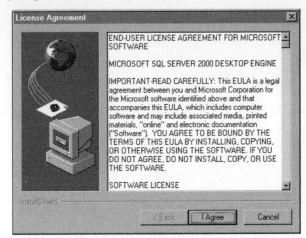

Figure 4.4 Confirming Folder Creation

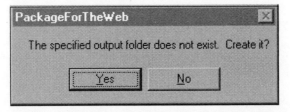

6. As the files unpack, you will see the progress window shown in Figure 4.5.
    Once the unpacking is complete, you will be notified with the window shown
    in Figure 4.6. Click **OK** to accept confirmation.

Figure 4.5 Unpacking the MSDE Files

Figure 4.6 Confirming That the Files Have Been Extracted

7. MSDE installation must be initiated from the command line. If you try to run setup by double-clicking on *setup.exe*, you will get the error shown in Figure 4.7. To start setup, open command prompt **Start | Run | CMD | Enter** and navigate to the installation folder listed in Step 4. Execute the following command (where "password" is the password used for the SA account in MSDE):

```
setup sapwd="password" instancename=WSUS
```

8. You will now see setup progressing, as shown in Figure 4.8. After setup is complete, you will see the window shown in Figure 4.9. Click **Yes** to reboot you server and finish the install of MSDE.

9. After your server reboots, go to **Services | Start | Run | Services.msc | Enter** and make sure MSDE is installed and running. You should have a service list named MSSQL$WSUS, as shown in Figure 4.10. This service should be started and set to run automatically.

Figure 4.7 Running Setup Incorrectly

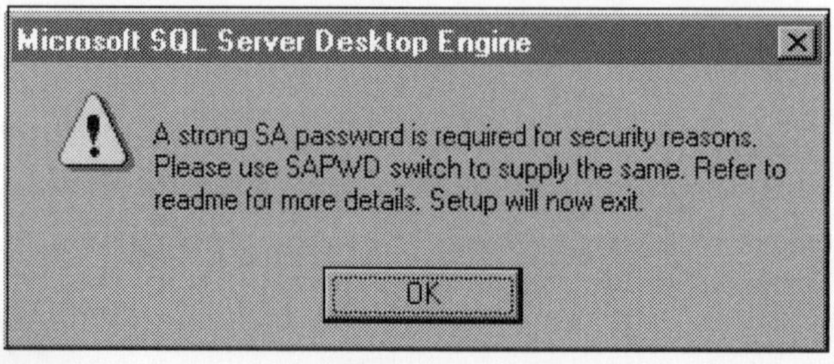

Figure 4.8 Running Setup Correctly

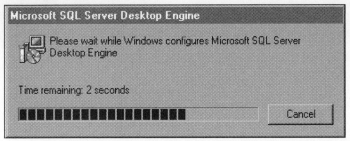

Figure 4.9 Rebooting Your Server

Figure 4.10 Verifying the Installation of MSDE

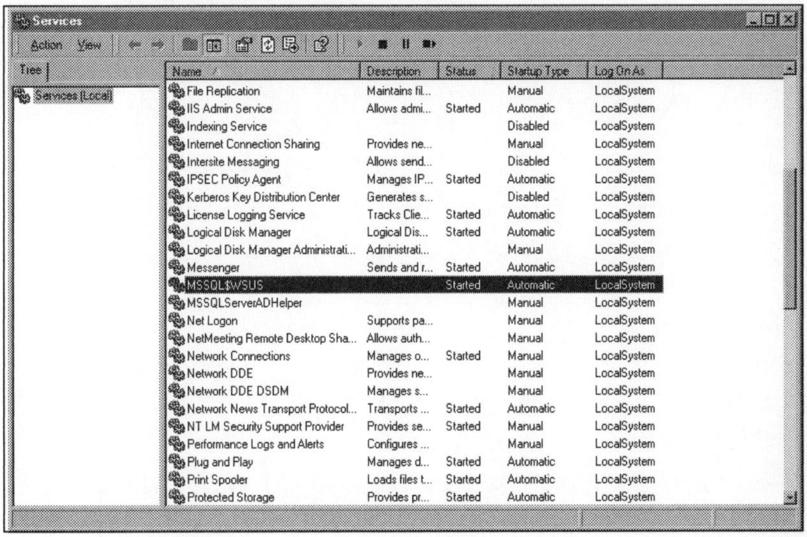

After installing MSDE, you must install the security patch discussed in Security Bulletin MS03-031. There are vulnerabilities in MSDE that will potentially let a hacker run their code of choice. This patch helps prevent named pipe hijacking, named pipe denial of service (DOS), and SQL Server buffer overruns. To install this patch, follow these steps:

1. Download the patch from http://go.microsoft.com/fwlink/?LinkId=37271.

2. Double-click on **SQL2000-KB815495.exe**. This will extract the patch, as shown in Figure 4.11.

Figure 4.11 Reading the Package

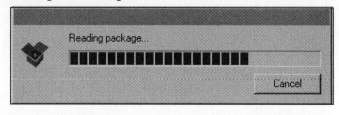

3. You will now see the Welcome window shown in Figure 4.12. Click **Next** to continue.

Figure 4.12 Starting Setup

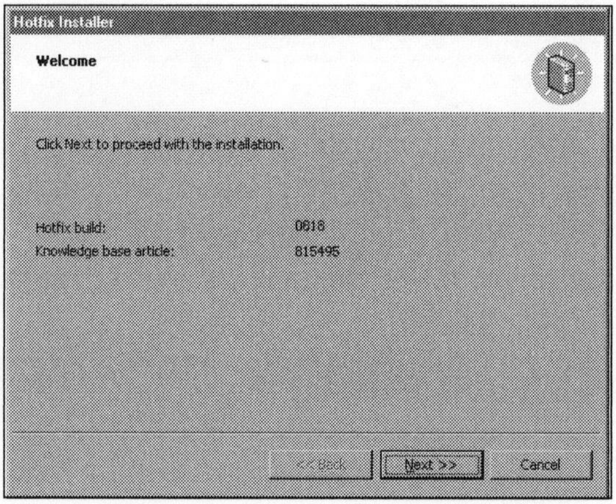

4. You must now agree to the License Agreement shown in Figure 4.13. Check the box next to "I accept the licensing terms and conditions" and then click **Next** to proceed.

5. Select **SERVERNAME\WSUS**, as shown in Figure 4.14. Click **Next** to continue.

Figure 4.13 Accepting the License Agreement

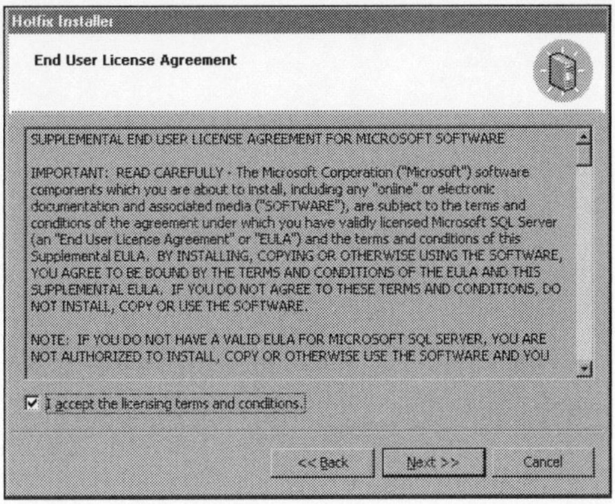

Figure 4.14 Choosing an Instance to Update

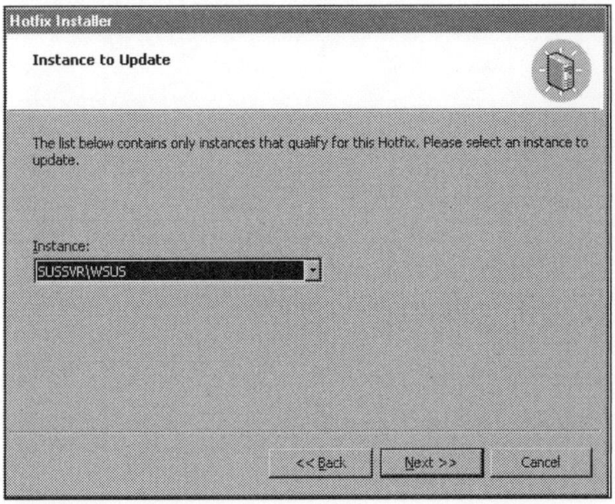

6. Choose **Windows Authentication**, as shown in Figure 4.15, and click **Next** to proceed.

7. Click **Install** on the "Ready to Install" window shown in Figure 4.16. You will now see the "Progress" window shown in Figure 4.17.

8. Once the setup is complete, you will see the "Hotfix Complete" window shown in Figure 4.18. Click **Finish** to end the setup.

Figure 4.15 Selecting an Authentication Mode

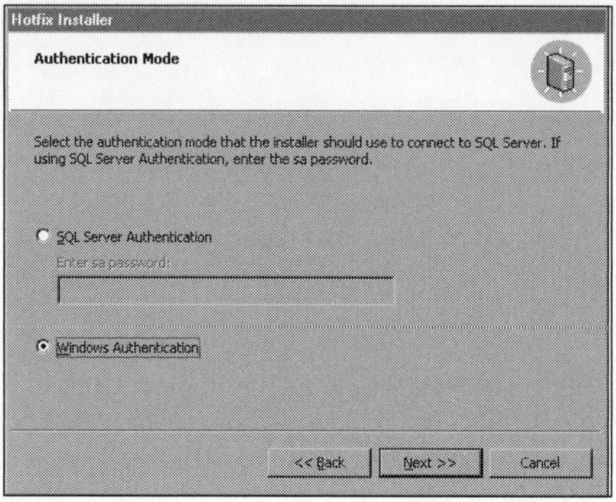

Figure 4.16 Applying the Patch

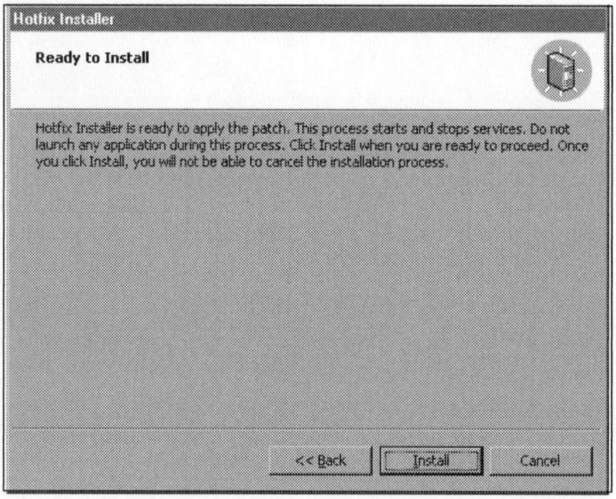

Figure 4.17 Watching the Install

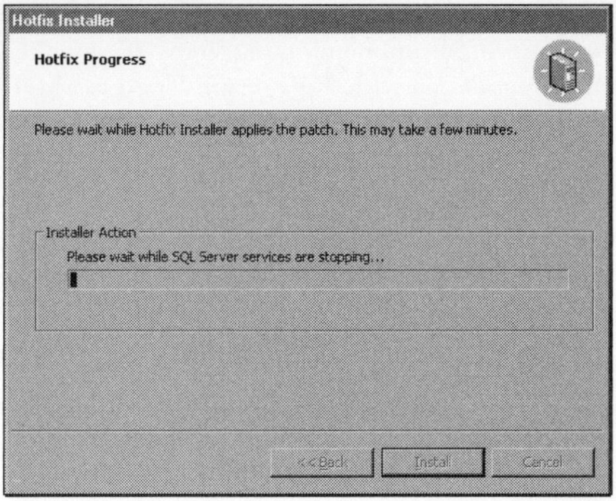

Figure 4.18 Completing the Install

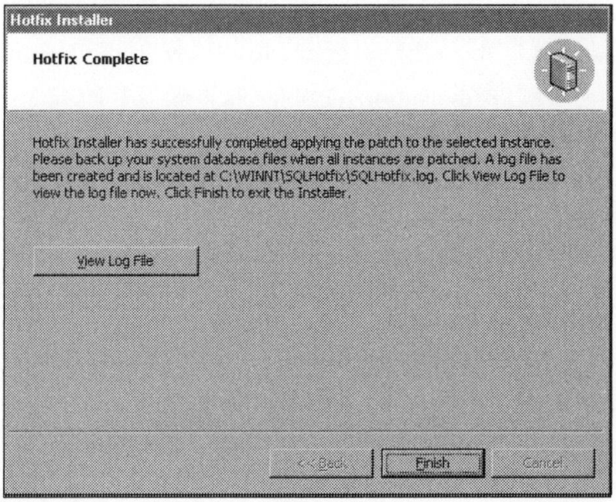

Installing WSUS onto the SUS Server

Since SUS is already using port 80, you must install WSUS using a custom port number. The default custom port is 8530, although you can choose any number not currently in use. To install WSUS, you must be logged on with administrative rights to the local machine. Installing WSUS does not require a reboot, although it will temporarily stop the IIS services. If the only application running in IIS is SUS, you can perform the install during production time without interfering with your users, as IIS will only be stopped for a few minutes.

During installation, you must indicate which database to use. You can use a local MSDE, WMSDE, SQL Server database, or a remote SQL Server database. If you have fewer than 500 users, Microsoft recommends using WSMDE or MSDE. If you have more than 500 users, you should go with SQL Server. If you use SQL Server for your database, you should use SQL 2000 with Service Pack 3a. Also, you must use Windows authentication instead of SQL authentication. If running SQL Server on a remote server, the server must be joined to the domain.

You must choose where to store updates, which can be stored locally or left on Microsoft's servers. It is preferred to store them locally so that all clients do not have to go out to the Internet to install their updates. To install WSUS, follow the steps outlined in the next section.

Installing WSUS on a Server with SUS Already Installed

In this exercise, we will install WSUS onto a server that already has SUS installed. We will use a local database and install everything to the *E:* drive. We will not mirror another WSUS server, because this will be the first WSUS server in our environment.

1. Download WSUS from http://go.microsoft.com/fwlink/?LinkId=47374.

2. To start the WSUS installation, double-click on the ***WSUSSetup.exe*** file. This will start the extraction process shown in Figure 4.19.

Figure 4.19 Extracting Files

3. Once extraction is complete, you will see the "Preparing Installation Windows" screen shown in Figure 4.20. During this phase, the prerequisites for WSUS are being verified.

Figure 4.20 Preparing to Install WSUS

4. After verification is complete, you will get the "Welcome to WSUS Setup Wizard" screen shown in Figure 4.21. Click **Next** to continue with the setup.

Figure 4.21 Starting the WSUS Setup Wizard

5. You will see the "License Agreement" window shown in Figure 4.22. Choose the button next to "I accept the terms of the License agreement" and click **Next** to continue. You can optionally click the **Print** button to print a copy of the license agreement.

Figure 4.22 Agreeing to the End User License Agreement

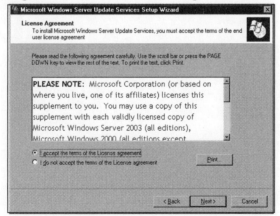

6. You will now be asked where you want to store your updates, as shown in Figure 4.23. This can be any drive in your system as long as there is at least 6GB of free disk space and the drive is formatted as NTFS. The option to store

them locally is checked by default. Use the **Browse** button to navigate to the location where you want to store the updates or type in the path manually. Once the path is set, click **Next** to continue.

Figure 4.23 Selecting the Update Source

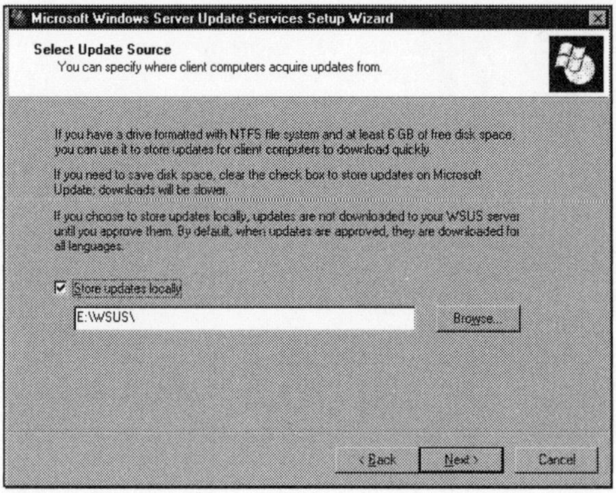

7. You must now choose where to store the data for WSUS (see Figure 4.24). You can install WMSDE locally or connect to an existing database. For this exercise, we are installing WMSDE. Use the **Browse** button to select the database installation path and click **Next** to continue.

Figure 4.24 Choosing the Database

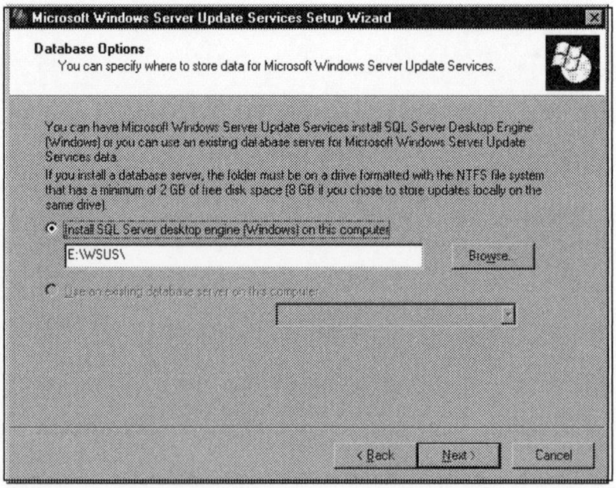

8. Since you are running SUS on the same server on which you are installing WSUS, you will be given the "Web Site Selection" window shown in Figure 4.25. Click **Next** to continue.

Figure 4.25 Acknowledging Web Site Selection

9. Since this is the first WSUS server in our environment, we will not use mirroring. Take the defaults shown in Figure 4.26 and leave "This server should inherit setting from the following server" unchecked. Click **Next** to continue.

Figure 4.26 Mirroring Updates from Another Server

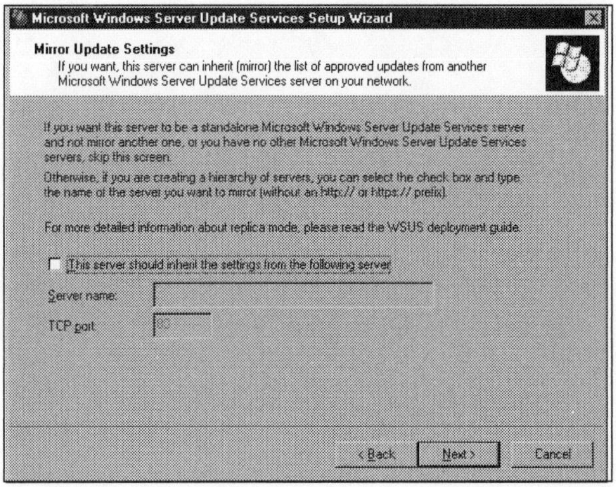

10. You will now see the confirmation window that is shown in Figure 4.27. Verify that the settings are correct and click **Next** to continue. While the installation is being completed, you will see the screen shown in Figure 4.28.

Figure 4.27 Confirming Installation Settings

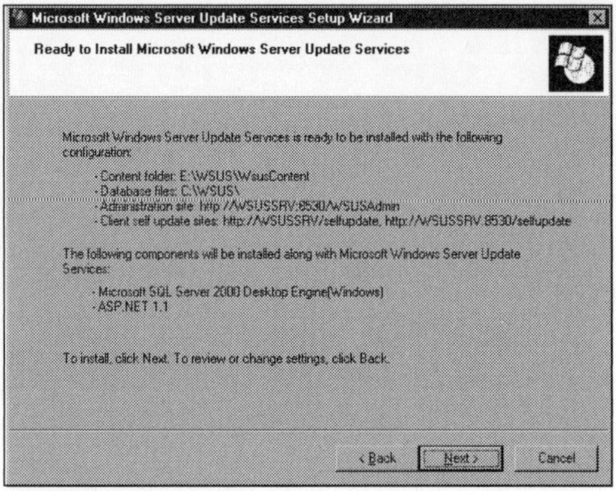

Figure 4.28 Installing WSUS

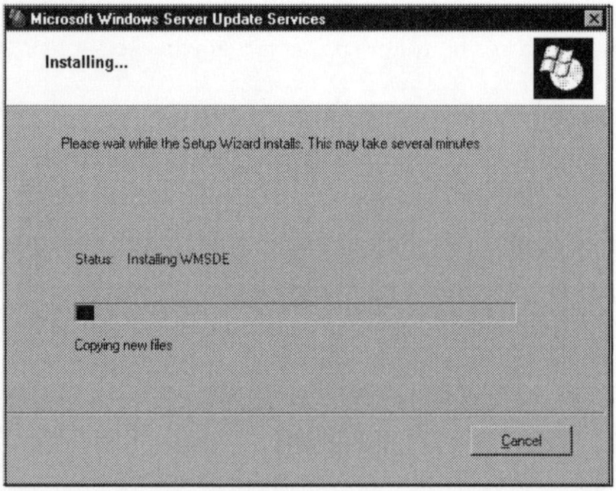

11. Once setup has finished, you will see the "Completing the Microsoft WSUS Setup Wizard" shown in Figure 4.29. Click **Finish** to end the wizard and launch the administration tool.

Figure 4.29 Completing the Setup

Configuring WSUS

After installing WSUS, you should connect to the console and configure it. You can access the administration console by going to **Start** | **All Programs** | **Administrative Tools** | **Microsoft Windows Server Update Services** on the WSUS server or by using Internet Explorer on any machine and going to *http://WSUSServer:portnumber/ WSUSAdmin* (where *WSUSServer* is the name of your WSUS Server and *portnumber* is the port number used by WSUS). For example, you could get to WSUS on the server DC1 by going to *http://dc1:8530/wsusadmin*. If you are using port 80 for WSUS, you do not have to append the port number to the Uniform Resource Locator (URL). In our example, you can type in *http://dc1/wsusadmin*. To access the administration console, you must be logged in with administrative rights.

Configuring the various options of WSUS is covered in great detail in the other chapters of this book. This chapter focuses on the things that must be configured immediately after installing WSUS to successfully migrate from SUS. To get WSUS up and running, you must configure your server to access the Internet, choose the languages supported, and configure the synchronization settings.

Setting Proxy Settings

If you are using a proxy server on your network, you must configure WSUS with the proxy server's name and port number. WSUS uses port 80 (Hypertext Transfer Protocol [HTTP]) and port 443 (Hypertext Transfer Protocol Secure sockets [HTTPS]) to communicate with Microsoft's servers. These ports must be open on your firewall to allow WSUS to synchronize updates. If you do not want your server to have unrestricted access to the Internet over these ports, you can only allow the sites needed for WSUS. These sites are listed in Table 4.4.

Table 4.4 Allowing Internet Access to the Site Required for WSUS

Sites Needed for WSUS
http://windowsupdate.microsoft.com
http://*.windowsupdate.microsoft.com
https://*.windowsupdate.microsoft.com
http://*.update.microsoft.com
https://*.update.microsoft.com
http://*.windowsupdate.com
http://download.windowsupdate.com
http://download.microsoft.com
http://*.download.windowsupdate.com
http://wustat.windows.com
http://ntservicepack.microsoft.com

Configuring Proxy Settings for WSUS

In this section, you will configure your WSUS server with the correct proxy settings to get out to the Internet. To continue, you must know the name or Internet Protocol (IP) address of your proxy server and what port it is listening over. If you are not using a proxy server or do not require authentication to access the Internet, you may skip this step.

1. Launch the WSUS Web Administration Console by typing http://server-name:8530/WSUSAdmin into the address bar of your Internet browser (where servername is the name of your WSUS server).

2. Click on the **Options** link on the upper right-hand corner of the console, as shown in Figure 4.30. This will take you to the "Options" window shown in Figure 4.31.

3. Click on the **Synchronization Options** link at the top of the page, as shown in Figure 4.31. This will take you to the "Synchronization Options" page shown in Figure 4.32.

Figure 4.30 Using the WSUS Administration Console

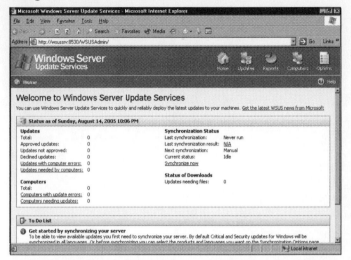

Figure 4.31 Selecting Options for WSUS

4. Scroll down to the section labeled "Proxy Server." Check the box next to **Use a proxy server when synchronizing**. Next, type in the proxy server name or the IP address, and the port number. If your proxy server requires authentication to access the Internet, key in the user name, password, and domain information for a valid user account. After keying in the correct information, click the **Save settings** link under the **Tasks** pane; this will make your new settings take effect.

Figure 4.32 Configuring Proxy Settings

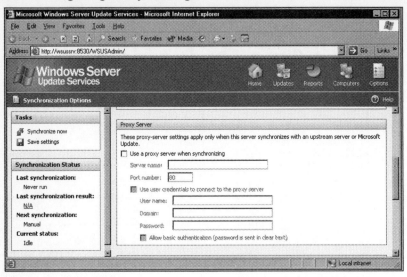

Configuring Languages and Download Options

By default, WSUS is configured to download updates for all languages. You should change this to match the languages being downloaded by SUS. If you do not have machines using different languages, do not waste the disk space on the WSUS server to download updates that will never be installed.

You must also determine how you want WSUS to handle downloads. You can choose to install updates locally on the WSUS server, or to have clients install them from the Internet. If you do not have much disk space on your WSUS server, have all of your clients download their updates from Microsoft. This will cause a lot more Internet traffic, because the clients will be downloading their own copies instead of just downloading one copy to the WSUS server.

You can configure WSUS to use deferred downloads. This way, updates will not be downloaded until they are approved for installation. If you have the disk space, it is preferred to download the updates ahead of time so that they can be deployed immediately, once approved. WSUS has an option called "Express Installation Files." These are larger than the standard updates, but they deploy faster to your clients. If you have the disk space, you should choose this option to reduce the bandwidth and time required to update clients.

Choosing the Languages Supported by WSUS

In this section, we will choose the language supported by WSUS and configure the download options. By default, all languages are supported. You can choose to have WSUS use the same language locale of the local server or you can choose the language from a list. This step should be done immediately after installing WSUS, as it will reset the download state for all updates. For this example, we are using the English language. We are configuring WSUS to store updates locally and to use express installation files.

1. Navigate to the "Synchronization Options" window, as explained previously.

2. Scroll down to the section called "Update Files and Languages."

3. Click the **Advanced** button to access the files and the "Languages" window, as shown in Figure 4.33. Clicking **Advanced** will cause WSUS to display the warning shown in Figure 4.34.

Figure 4.33 Updating Languages

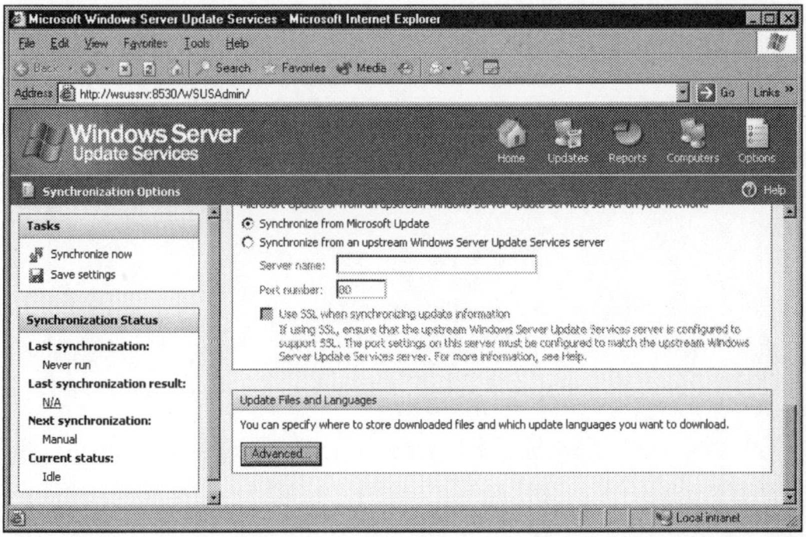

4. Click **OK** to acknowledge the warning about changing advanced settings.

Figure 4.34 Warning about Changing Advanced Settings

5. In the "Advanced Synchronization Options" window shown in Figure 4.35, under the "Update Files" section choose the button to **Store update files locally on this server** and check the box next to **Download express installation files**.

6. Under the "Languages" section, select **Download updates only in the selected languages**, and select **English**. Selecting a language will launch the warning window shown in Figure 4.36. Click **OK** to the warning.

Figure 4.35 Selecting Languages

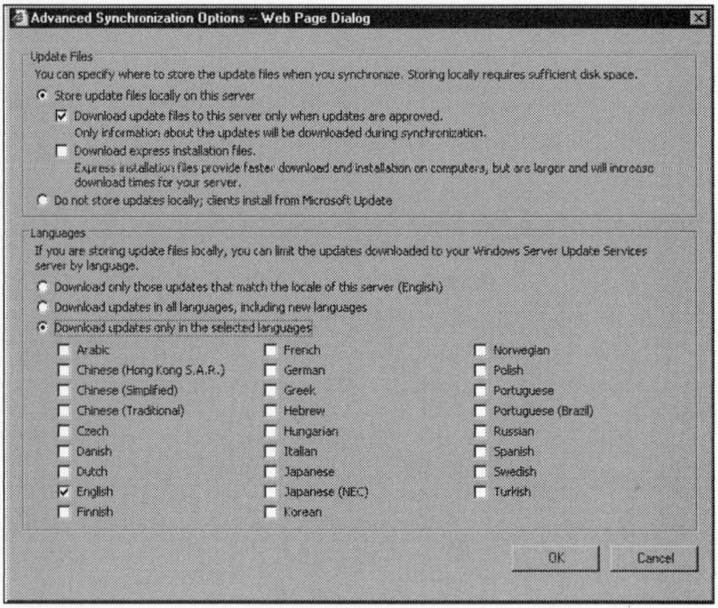

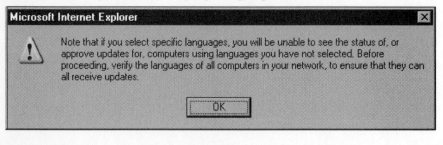

7. Click **OK** in the "Advanced Synchronization Options" window, as shown in Figure 4.35.

8. To save your settings, click the **Save settings** link under the Tasks pane, as shown in Figure 4.33.

Figure 4.36 Warning about Specifying Languages

Configuring Synchronization

WSUS must be synchronized at least once before you can migrate approvals and content. Synchronizing does not download all updates. By default, it only downloads information about the updates. You can choose to manually synchronize or you can schedule a synchronization to occur daily at a set time. You should schedule WSUS to synchronize daily during a time of low activity. If you choose to schedule synchronization, WSUS will start synchronizing within 30 minutes of the configured time. The following walks you through configuring WSUS to synchronize everyday at 3:00 A.M.

1. Navigate to the "Synchronization Options" window, as explained in Exercise 4.4.

2. Scroll down to the section labeled "Schedule," as shown in Figure 4.37.

3. Click the **radio** button next to "Synchronize daily at."

4. Select **3:00 A.M.** from the drop-down arrow.

5. Click the **Save settings** button under the "Tasks" pane.

Figure 4.37 Setting the Synchronization Schedule

Migrating SUS Approvals and Content

After configuring WSUS, you are ready to migrate SUS approvals and content. Migrating content is the process of copying over all of the physical update files that WSUS will push to the clients. This way, you do not have to download all of the updates again, which will save a lot of time and bandwidth. Approvals refer to the status of what to do with your updates, meaning do you want them to be installed, not installed, removed, and so forth. The benefit of migrating approvals is that you do not have to tell

WSUS what to do with each update. If you already configured the update in SUS, WSUS will use those settings.

Approval and content migrations are accomplished with *WSUSutil.exe*. This tool is located in the *program files\update services\tools* folder on the drive where WSUS is installed. *WSUSutil.exe* allows you to migrate approvals or content. You can do both if you choose, but it is not required.

You must be logged in with administrative rights to use *WSUSutil.exe*. This tool must be run locally on the WSUS server; it cannot be used across the network. SUS does not have to be running to perform the migration. However, if SUS is running, it must not be synchronizing its updates or the migration will fail. Table 4.5 explains the syntax for *WSUSUtil.exe*.

To use *WSUSUtil.exe* to migrate approvals and local content from SUS, go to command line **Start | Run | CMD | Enter** and type in the following command (be sure to type the command as one string):

```
wsusutil.exe migratesus /content PathToLocalSUSContent /approvals SUSServer
/log filename
```

where *PathToLocalSUSContent* is the location of the SUS updates folder and *SUSServer* is the name of the SUS server. For example, to migrate update data from *c:\sus\content\cabs* (the default location for SUS updates) use the following command on the server dc1:

```
wsusutil.exe migratesus /content c:\sus\content\cabs /approvals cd1 /log
migration.log
```

Table 4.5 Understanding the Syntax for *WSUSUtil.exe*

Switch	Purpose
Export	Exports update information in the database to a package file. Does not export update approvals, update files, or server settings.
Import	Imports update information from a package file into the database.
migratesus	Migrates update approvals from SUS to WSUS.

Continued

Table 4.5 continued Understanding the Syntax for *WSUSUtil.exe*

Switch	Purpose
movecontent	Changes the location WSUS uses for update files. Copies update files from old location to new.
Reset	Checks that every update entry in the database has a matching update file stored on the WSUS server. If files are missing, WSUS will download them again.
deleteunneeded revisions	Deletes the update information in the database for unneeded updates.
listinactiveapprovals	Shows inactive approvals due to a change in language support on WSUS.
removeinactive approvals	Removes inactive approvals due to a change in language support on WSUS.

Decommissioning SUS

Do not rush this step. It does not hurt to leave SUS in place for a while to make sure that WSUS is working as expected. You can use SUS for your production machines and use WSUS for your test environment. After successfully testing WSUS, you can decommission SUS. This involves stopping the Web site in the IIS Management Console and changing the WSUS port to 80. You do not have to use port 80 for WSUS to work, but it is recommended so that machines installed with the SUS client will automatically update themselves to the WSUS client. Here are the steps involved in decommissioning SUS:

1. Open IIS Manager **Start | Administrative Tools | Internet Information Services**, as shown in Figure 4.38.

2. Navigate to the Web site containing SUS (in this example it is the default Web site). Right-click on the Web site and choose **Stop** from the context menu. This will stop SUS from servicing clients.

3. Next, change WSUS to use port 80 instead of the custom port used by default (8530). Right-click on the **WSUS Administration** Web site and choose **Properties** from the Context menu, which gives you the window shown in Figure 4.39.

Figure 4.38 Stopping SUS

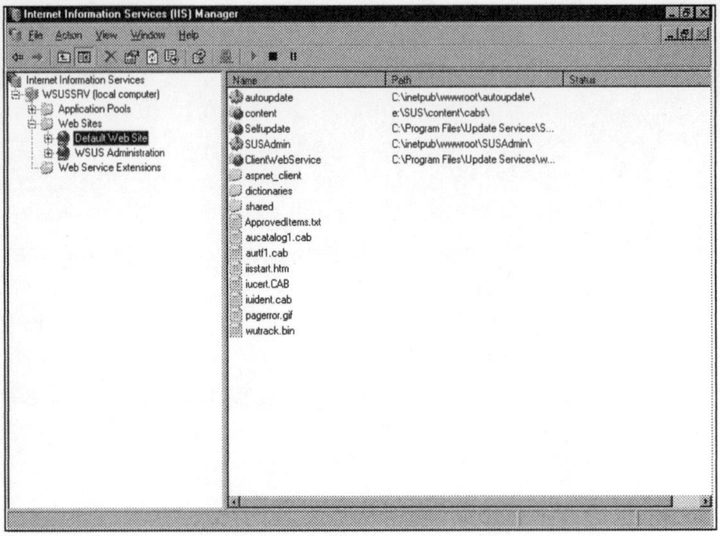

Figure 4.39 Changing the Port for WSUS

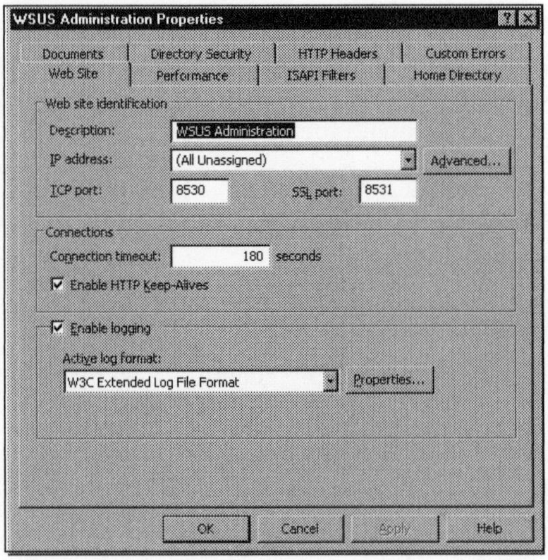

4. Change the number in Transmission Control Protocol (TCP) port from 8530 to **80**.

5. Click **OK** to save your changes.

Changing the Shortcut to WSUS

If you change the port number used by WSUS to 80 from 8530, your shortcut on the Start menu will no longer work. You must create a new shortcut with the correct port number. You can easily create a new shortcut by right clicking on your desktop and choosing **New Shortcut** from the Context menu. Type the URL into the WSUS server Administration Console (*http://WSUSServer/WSUSAdmin*) along with a name for the shortcut.

Across-the-Wire Upgrade

An across-the-wire upgrade involves installing WSUS onto a different server than the one holding SUS, and migrating over the approvals and update data. If for any reason you are not pleased with the performance or reliability of your SUS server, now is a good time to replace it. One problem with an in-place-upgrade is that any problems with your server will still be there once you install WSUS. An across-the-wire upgrade gives you the opportunity to start fresh with your WSUS server.

You may want to use a new server for a variety of reasons. Maybe you are putting WSUS onto more powerful hardware (i.e., more RAM, faster central processing unit (CPU), and so on). Perhaps SUS is running on Windows 2000 Server, but you want to install WSUS onto Windows Server 2003. It would be easier to use a new server than to upgrade the old one. The most common reason to use an across-the-wire migration is to consolidate SUS servers.

Steps to Success

There are a lot of similarities between an in-place upgrade and an across-the-wire upgrade. Both methods involve installing WSUS and configuring it to synchronize updates. They both also require using *WSUSUtil.exe* to migrate approvals and update content. The last step for each method is to decommission the SUS server. This section focuses on the steps that are unique to an across-the-wire upgrade. These steps include creating WSUS target groups for consolidating SUS servers, sharing remote content on the SUS server, migrating remote update content and approvals, and pointing the clients to the new WSUS server. Before you start this section, you must complete the following (all of these steps are covered earlier in this chapter):

1. Meet the hardware requirements for WSUS.

2. Install all prerequisite software.

3. Install WSUS.

4. Configure WSUS for Internet access.

5. Select the languages to be supported by WSUS.

6. Tell WSUS how to handle update downloads.

Using WSUS Target Groups

One limitation of SUS is the inability to approve updates separately for different groups of computers. In SUS, you either approve an update or you do not. Once an update is approved, it is applied to all machines supported by that SUS server. This method of patching is flawed. Most companies will roll updates out to their clients sooner than they roll them out to their servers. Also, depending on the type of server, you may or may not want to roll out the updates right away. It may be okay to update your file servers and domain controllers on the fly, but you may want to do more testing before updating your application servers (Exchange, SQL, Internet Security and Acceleration [ISA], and so forth).

The need for different update approvals leads a lot of companies to implement multiple SUS servers (one SUS server for each group of machines). For example, you may have one SUS server for workstations and another for servers. Some companies have one SUS server for production and another for testing. In larger environments it is not uncommon to have a separate SUS server for each location or department.

In WSUS, you can create computer groups; updates can then be approved separately for each group. This allows you to have one WSUS server handle all of your patching needs. You may still need multiple WSUS servers to keep up with the load or if your machines are all geographically dispersed.

As part of an across-the-wire upgrade, you must create computer groups to mimic your SUS structure. For example, say you have two SUS servers, one for patching workstations and another for patching servers. You would need to create two computer groups, one called "workstations" and one called "servers." You would then migrate your SUS approvals to the corresponding group.

Creating a Computer Group

1. Open the "WSUS Administration Console" shown in Figure 4.40.

2. Click the **Computers** link in the upper right-hand corner. This will take you to the "Computers" page shown in Figure 4.41.

3. Click on **Create a computer group** under "Tasks." This will give you the "Create a Computer Group" screen shown in Figure 4.42.

Figure 4.40 Accessing the WSUS Administration Console

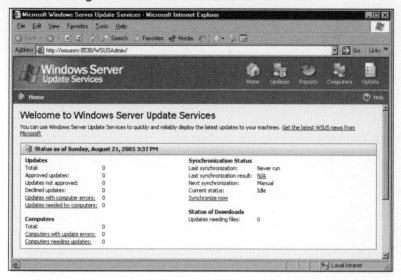

Figure 4.41 Creating Computer Groups

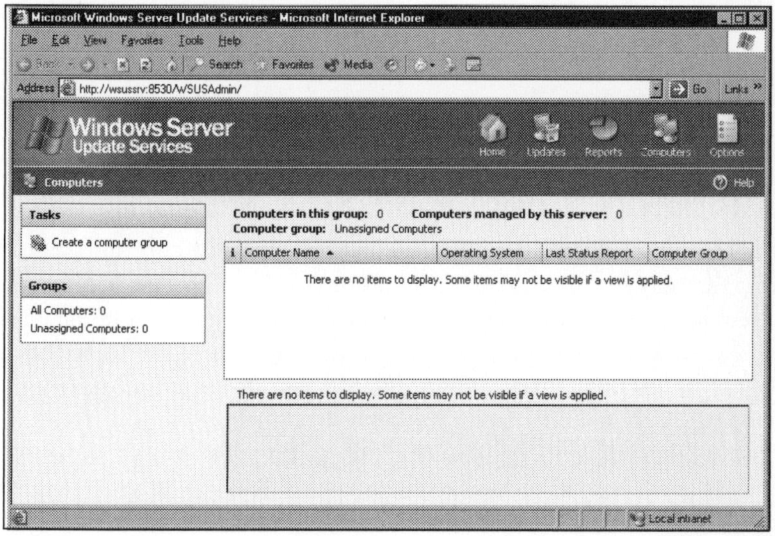

4. Type in the name of your group (for this exercise we are creating a Servers group) and click **OK** to continue. Your group will now be listed under "Groups," as shown in Figure 4.43.

Figure 4.42 Naming Computer Groups

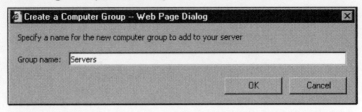

Figure 4.43 Verifying New Computer Groups

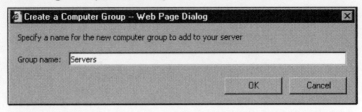

Sharing Remote Content on SUS Server

One drawback of an across-the-wire upgrade is that you must copy all of the SUS updates across the network to your WSUS server. This is still better than having to download them all from the Internet, but it is not as quick as when doing an in-place upgrade. Before you can copy over the updates, you must share the folder on the SUS server containing the updates. The following walks you through this process.

Sharing the Content Folder on the SUS Server

1. Double-click on **My Computer** from the desktop. This will open a window similar to the one shown in Figure 4.44.

2. Double-click on the drive containing the SUS updates and navigate to the content folder, as shown in Figure 4.45. The default location is *c:\SUS\Content*.

3. Right-click on the "Content" folder and choose **Sharing and Security** from the "Context" menu. This will take you to the "Content Properties" window shown in Figure 4.46.

Figure 4.44 Navigating to the Content Folder

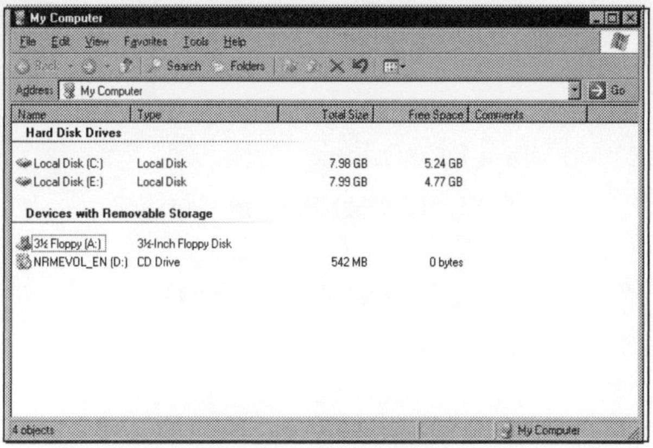

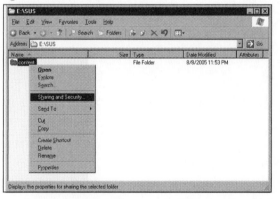

Figure 4.45 Sharing the SUS Content Folder

Figure 4.46 Naming the Share

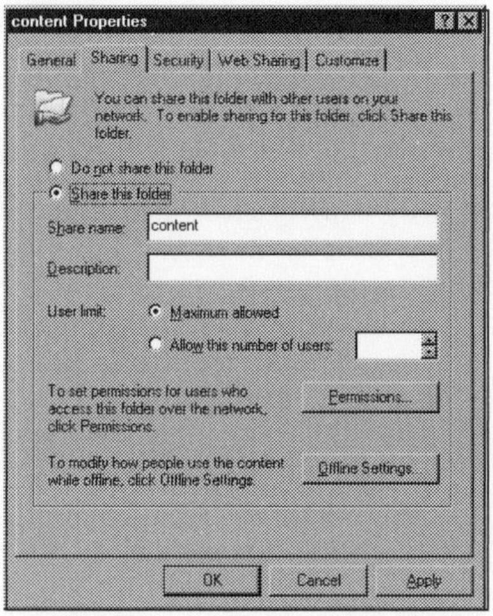

4. You can type in whatever name you want for the share. In this exercise we use the default name "Content." After typing in the share name, click on the **Permissions** button. This will take you to the "Share Permissions" window shown in Figure 4.47.

Figure 4.47 Assigning Share Permissions

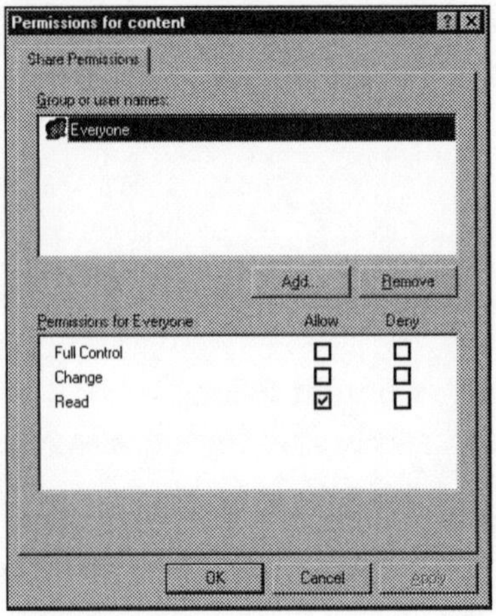

5. Verify that the "Everyone" group has the Read share permission. Click **OK** to continue.

6. On the "Content Properties" window (Figure 4.46) click on the **Permissions** tab (Figure 4.48).

7. Verify that the "Everyone" group has the Read NTFS permission. Click **OK** to save your choices and create the share.

Figure 4.48 Assigning NTFS Permissions

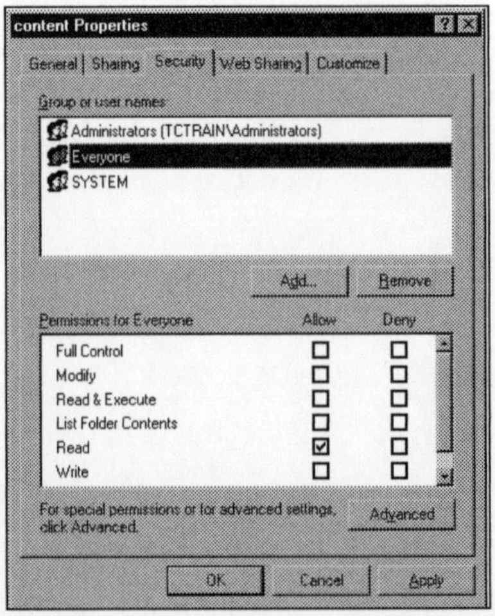

Migrate Remote Content and Approvals

The *WSUSUtil.exe* tool is used to migrate approvals and update data for in-place upgrades and for across-the-wire upgrades (its syntax was shown earlier in Table 4.5). For this tool to work, you must have HTTP access and Server Message Block (SMB) access to the SUS servers from the WSUS server. HTTP is used to migrate the approvals and SMB is used to migrate the updates. HTTP uses port 80 and SMB uses port 445. To migrate update data and approvals, use the following command (be sure to enter the command as one continuous line at the command prompt):

```
wsusutil.exe migratesus /content PathToRemoteSUSContent /approvals
SUSServer "WSUSGroupName" /log filename
```

PathToRemoteSUSContent is the location of the remote SUS updates folder, *SUSServer* is the name of the SUS server, and *WSUSGroupName* is the name of the target WSUS computer group. For example, to migrate update data and approvals from the server dc1 (with the SUS content folder shared as content) to the servers computer group, use the following command:

```
wsusutil.exe migratesus /content \\dc1\content\cabs /approvals dc1
"servers" /log migration.log
```

Pointing Clients to the New WSUS Server

After installing and configuring a new WSUS server, you must configure all of your clients to stop using SUS and start using WSUS. This step is not needed in an in-place upgrade, because the server name is the same. This setting is configured through group policy. Microsoft recommends disabling your old Group Policy Object (GPO) and replacing it with a new one for WSUS. This way, if there is a problem, you can easily revert back to your SUS server. (Exercise 4.9 walks you through creating a new GPO to reflect the new WSUS server.)

Creating a New GPO for WSUS

We will now use "Active Directory Users and Computers" to create a GPO at the domain level to push down the new WSUS settings. This could also be accomplished using the Group Policy Management Console, but the steps would look a bit different. There are ten total settings that can be configured for WSUS. For this example, we are configuring every machine to automatically download updates and install them at 3:00 A.M. without forcing a reboot.

BEST PRACTICES ACCORDING TO MICROSOFT

Microsoft recommends against editing the Default Domain Policy or the Default Domain Controllers Policy.

1. Open "Active Directory Users and Computers" be going to **Start | All Programs | Administrative Tools | Active Directory Users and Computers**.

2. Right-click on the **domain object** and select **Properties** from the Context menu, as shown in Figure 4.49. This will give you the domain "Properties" window shown in Figure 4.50.

Figure 4.49 Viewing Properties of the Domain

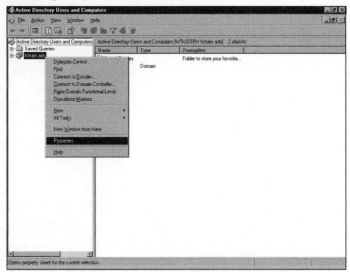

Figure 4.50 Creating a New Group Policy Object for WSUS

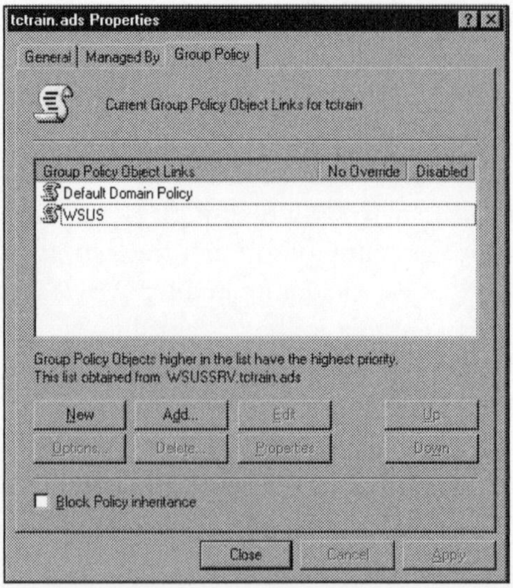

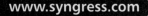

3. Click **New** to create a new GPO, and give it a descriptive name. For this exercise, it is named **WSUS**.

4. Select the new GPO and click the **Edit** button. This will open the GPO Editor shown in Figure 4.51.

5. Navigate to **Computer Configuration | Administrative Templates | Windows Components** and select **Windows Update**, as shown in Figure 4.51.

Figure 4.51 Configuring Windows Update Options

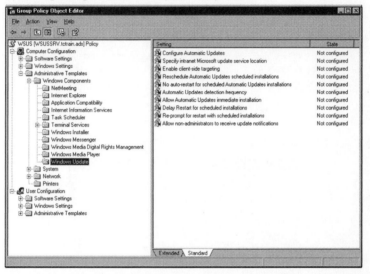

6. Double-click on the setting labeled **Configure Automatic Updates**. This will open the window shown in Figure 4.52.

7. This setting specifies whether this computer will receive updates through the Windows automatic updating service. Select option **4 – Auto download and schedule the install** from the drop-down lists.

8. Choose the **0 – Every day** option from the drop-down box next to "Scheduled install day."

9. Choose **03:00** from the drop-down box next to "Scheduled install time."

10. Click **OK** to save your settings. This will take you back to the "GPO Editor" window shown in Figure 4.51.

11. Double-click on the **Specify intranet Microsoft update service location** setting. This will open the window shown in Figure 4.53.

Figure 4.52 Configuring Automatic Update Properties

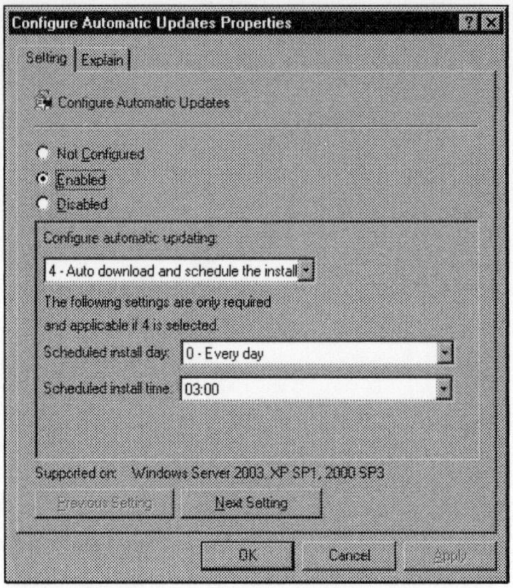

Figure 4.53 Specifying the Location of the WSUS Server

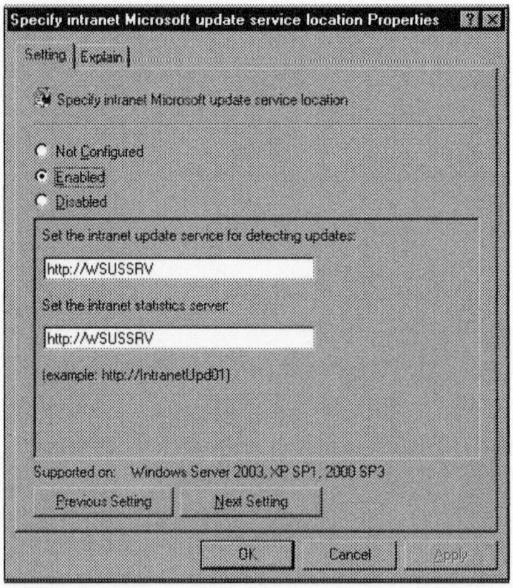

12.   Type ***http://WSUSServer*** (where *WSUSServer* is the name of your WSUS server) into both boxes. This will tell the client which server to use for updates and statistics.

13.   Click **OK** to save your settings. This will take you back to the "GPO Editor" window shown in Figure 4.51.

14. Double-click on the setting called **No auto-restart for scheduled Automatic Updates installations**. This will give you the window shown in Figure 4.54.

Figure 4.54 Configuring Clients Not to Automatically Restart

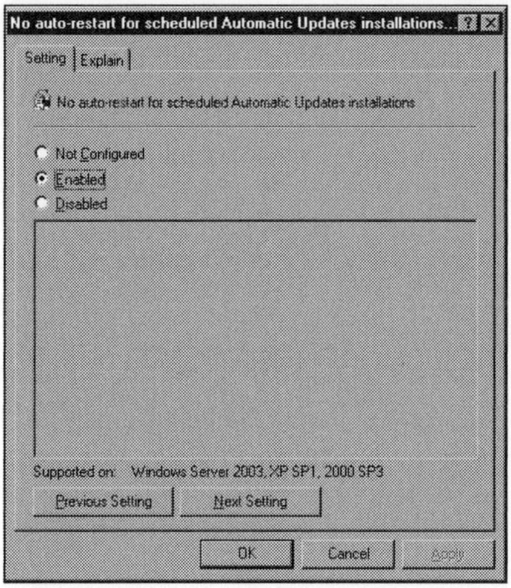

15. This step is not a requirement for WSUS to work, but if you do not configure it all of your machines (servers and workstations) will automatically reboot after they install their updates. Select the button next to **Enabled**.

16. Click **OK** to save your settings.

17. Close the GPO Editor.

18. "Close Active Directory Users and Computers."

Remember that GPO changes do not take effect immediately. These settings will take place about 20 minutes after your Group Policy refreshes. Workstations and member servers (by default) refresh their policy every 90 minutes. They vary their updates by up to 30 minutes to ensure that all machines are not updating at the same time. This means that Group Policy may not begin for up to 120 minutes. Add the 20 minutes for this setting to take effect and it will take up to 140 minutes before you notice the change.

SOME INDEPENDENT ADVICE

If you do not want to wait 120 minutes for Group Policy to refresh, you can force it to refresh immediately by using command-line tools. On Windows XP and Windows 2003 Server, type in the following command:

gpupdate /force

On Windows 2000 machines type in the following command:

secedit /refreshpolicy machine_policy /enforce

Summary

You have two choices available when migrating from SUS to WSUS. You can perform an in-place upgrade or an across-the-wire upgrade. The main deciding factor is how your SUS environment is currently set up. Are you using one server for everything? If so, an in-place upgrade would be the way to go. Do you have a reason to move to a new server? Perhaps you have outgrown your existing SUS server and an across-the-wire upgrade would be better. Maybe you will be performing a combination of the two methods; upgrading one server in-place and then consolidating the other SUS servers across-the-wire.

If you choose an in-place upgrade, you must complete the following tasks:

- Install prerequisite software
- Install WSUS
- Configure WSUS for languages supported
- Configure WSUS to access the Internet
- Locally migrate SUS approvals and update data
- Decommission the SUS server

If you choose an in-place upgrade, you must complete the following tasks:

- Install prerequisite software
- Install WSUS
- Configure WSUS for languages supported
- Configure WSUS to access the Internet
- Create WSUS target computer groups
- Share update data on the SUS servers
- Remotely migrate SUS approvals and update data

- Point clients to the new WSUS server
- Decommission the SUS server.

Solutions Fast Track

In-Place Upgrade

☑ An in-place upgrade involves installing WSUS onto your existing SUS server and locally migrating over the SUS approvals and updates.

☑ Microsoft recommends a server with at least a 1 GHz CPU and 1GB of RAM.

☑ WSUS will run on Windows 2000 or Windows 2003.

☑ WSUS can use MSDE, WMSDE, or SQL Server for its database.

☑ When running WSUS on Windows 2000, you must manually install MSDE and patch it with the Hotfix discussed in Security Bulletin MS03-031.

☑ When installing WSUS onto a machine with SUS already installed, you must use a custom port for WSUS. The default port is 8530.

☑ You must synchronize WSUS with Microsoft at least one time before you can migrate over SUS approvals and updates.

☑ If you are running a proxy server in your organization, you must configure WSUS with the proxy name and port number before it will be able to synchronize with Microsoft.

☑ Before allowing WSUS to synchronize the first time, you should select the languages that will be supported by WSUS.

☑ You must have administrative rights to install WSUS or to use the WSUS Administration Console.

☑ SUS approvals and updates are migrated with the *WSUSUtil.exe* command.

☑ *WSUSUtil.exe* is located in the program *files\update services\tools* folder on the drive where WSUS is installed

☑ *WSUSUtil.exe* must be run locally on the WSUS server.

☑ After completing the migration, you should decommission SUS and configure WSUS to use port 80.

Across-the-Wire Upgrade

☑ An across-the-wire upgrade involves installing WSUS onto a different server than the ones currently running SUS. Updates and approvals are then migrated over the network to the new WSUS server.

☑ Across-the-wire upgrades have the same hardware and software requirements as in-place upgrades.

☑ If you are using multiple SUS servers to handle different patching needs, you can map each SUS server to a computer group in WSUS. You can then configure each group's updates separately.

☑ If you want to migrate SUS updates across the network, you must first share out the Content folder on the SUS server.

☑ You must have HTTP and SMB access to the SUS server from the WSUS server to migrate approvals and update data.

☑ After installing the new WSUS server, you must point all of your clients to the new server. The easiest way to accomplish this is by using Group Policy.

Frequently Asked Questions

The following Frequently Asked Questions, answered by the authors of this book, are designed to both measure your understanding of the concepts presented in this chapter and to assist you with real-life implementation of these concepts. To have your questions about this chapter answered by the author, browse to **www.syngress.com/solutions** and click on the **"Ask the Author"** form.

Q: When will Microsoft stop supporting SUS?

A: Microsoft will support SUS until July 6, 2006. At this time, they will no longer offer technical assistance and will stop providing updates.

Q: Why should I upgrade from SUS to WSUS?

A: If you want to continue to update your clients, you will have to upgrade to WSUS by June 6, 2006, because Microsoft will no longer be offering updates for SUS. The main benefits for upgrading are the ability to target which clients get updates, detailed reporting, and being able to update Office, Exchange, and SQL.

Q: Do I have to deploy a new WSUS client to my machines?

A: All deployments of the SUS client will be automatically updated to the new client for WSUS.

Q: Is it better to deploy WSUS on Windows 2000 or Windows 2003?

A: Windows 2003 is recommended as it is more secure out of the box. Also, you can get WSUS installed and running quicker on Windows 2003. Windows 2000 requires you to manually install and patch MSDE. Also, you have to run the IIS Lockdown tool to secure WSUS. All of these steps happen automatically on Windows 2003.

Q: What will WSUS update that SUS will not?

A: Microsoft plans for WSUS to eventually update all Microsoft corporate software. Out of the box it will update Windows 2000, Windows XP, Windows 2003, Office XP, Office 2003, SQL Server 2000, MSDE, and Exchange 2003.

Q: SUS was free. Are there any costs associated with WSUS?

A: Yes. Even though Microsoft does not charge for the WSUS software, you must have a CAL for all clients being updated by WSUS. This is because WSUS runs on a Windows server and uses Windows authentication. For clients to connect to the Windows server, they must have the appropriate license.

Q: Does WSUS run on Windows Small Business Server 2003?

A: Yes. WSUS is supported on SBS 2003.

Q: Do you recommend an in-place upgrade or across-the-wire upgrade?

A: That depends on the state of your current SUS server. If your SUS server is on a healthy and functional server, go with an in-place upgrade. If you are not happy with your existing SUS server, do an across-the-wire migration.

Chapter 5

Deploying WSUS in the Enterprise

Solutions in this chapter:

- Installing Multiple Servers
- Deploying WSUS Client Software
- Managing Bandwidth Concerns
- Using Computer Groups
- Creating Group Policies

☑ Summary

☑ Solutions Fast Track

☑ Frequently Asked Questions

Introduction

Deploying Windows Server Update Services (WSUS) on anything but a one-server net-work introduces a layer of complexity that requires further research and reading. This chapter walks through the many features, enhancements, and "gotchas" that you will confront and take advantage of as you create an enterprise patch management infrastruc-ture based on WSUS.

Installing Multiple Servers

You may find that the size of your network and the number of clients you have requires that you install and deploy more than one WSUS server to support your network. Fortunately, Microsoft built into WSUS the ability to synchronize one WSUS server with another, instead of having to grab the same downloads from Microsoft Update every time. By chaining these servers together, you create a hierarchy in which one machine, known as an *upstream Software Update Services (SUS) server*, host updates and metadata for all subordinate servers known as *downstream servers*. It's important to note that when you configure such a chain of servers, the upstream server shares only updates and metadata with its downstream servers during synchronization, so that other configu-ration information such as computer group information or update approval remain machine-specific. If you want to set up WSUS to distribute information about which updates are approved, research it using *replica* mode.

To chain a group of servers together, use the following procedure (see Figure 5.1):

1. On the WSUS console toolbar, click **Options**, and then click **Synchronization Options**.

2. In the Update Source box, click **Synchronize from an upstream Windows Server Update Services** server.

3. Enter the server name and port number in the corresponding boxes.

4. Under Tasks, click **Save**.

5. Click **OK** when the confirmation box appears.

Figure 5.1 Synchronization Options

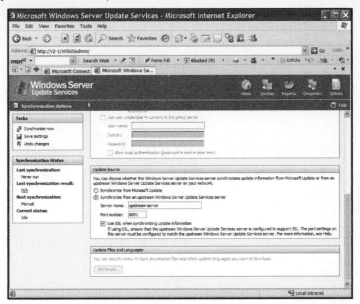

BEST PRACTICES ACCORDING TO MICROSOFT

- Use chain mode to download updates from the Internet, and then distribute those updates to branch offices with downstream servers.
- Chain mode is appropriate to scale patch management services to the size of your network.
- You can also use chain mode to move updates closer to the point where they will be deployed, making network traffic more efficient.
- Use only three levels of hierarchy when establishing a chain.

Distributed vs. Central Management

You may want to go further than just chaining servers together. For example, what if you want to synchronize not only updates and meta-information but also the actual configuration information and management data? WSUS can be deployed in two different management models. These models allow you to manage how the actual patch management process operates within your network, without forcing you to deploy the solution in a way that doesn't make sense for you. You can also choose more than one management model throughout your organization, so that one department can use one model while another uses a different model. In short, it's all about flexibility.

The first model is the *central management* model. Centrally managed WSUS servers use a replica server paradigm, in which an administrator configures a single server directly, exactly how he wants it, and then one or more subordinate machines make an exact replica of that configuration (i.e., a mirror) and operate using that set of options and specifications. The update approval information and computer groups you create on the master server are duplicated throughout the subordinate replica servers on your networks. All update approvals, such as computer groups, must be created on the master server (see Figure 5.2).

Figure 5.2 Central Management of WSUS Servers

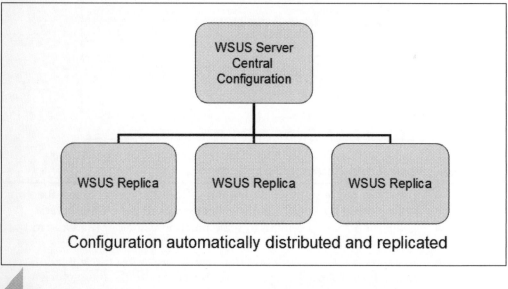

NOTE

You can add WSUS servers to replica groups only during setup.

To set up a replica group:

1. Install WSUS on a computer at a site where an administrator can manage it.

2. Install WSUS on a computer at a remote site.

3. When you get to the Mirror Update Settings page during WSUS setup, enter the name of the WSUS server from step 1.

4. Repeat steps 2 and 3, as necessary, to add additional machines to your new replica group.

You can also choose to deploy WSUS in the *distributed management* scheme. Using distributed management offers you full control over approvals and computer groups for the WSUS server that you yourself control. With the distributed management model, this may mean that you need an administrator at each site with WSUS deployed. Distributed management is the default installation option for all WSUS installations; therefore, you do not need to take any further action to enable this model (see Figure 5.3).

Figure 5.3 Distributed Management of WSUS Servers

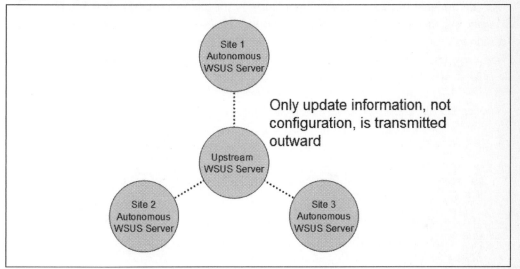

SOME INDEPENDENT ADVICE

If you have a network that is primarily contained within one site, you will find management much easier by configuring your WSUS deployment to use the centralized management scheme. The distributed management model is mainly meant for networks that cross geographical or structural boundaries, and for networks where very distinct, segregated groups have different update manage-ment needs (e.g., college/university networks and subsidiary businesses that are run separately).

If you are the only administrator on your network, choose central manage-ment so that you spend less time deploying each server.

Deploying WSUS Client Software

When your client computers first contact the WSUS server, the latest Automatic Updates (AU) software installed on your client computers self-update to the latest version. The one exception to this is the version of AU included with the initial release of Windows XP (the so-called gold RTM version without any service packs), which cannot update itself automatically. This must be manually pushed out via Group Policy, a login script, or the tried and true *sneakernet* method.

The updated AU client can be installed on your clients using the MSI install package, self-updating from the old Critical Update Notification (CUN) tool, installing Windows 2000 Service Pack 3 or 4, installing Windows XP Service Pack 1, or installing Windows Server 2003. You can download the AU client from the Microsoft Web site located at *http://www.microsoft.com/WSUS*. On a stand-alone machine, the AU client can be added by running the MSI file on the machine.

Manually installing a file, however, can quickly become a pain when you have more than just a few machines to handle. Fortunately, because the client installation program is in the form of an MSI, you can easily push the program to clients by using Group Policy if your clients are joined to a Windows-based domain.

To create a new Group Policy object (GPO), assign it to your computers and have it installed automatically:

1. Open the Active Directory Users and Computers MMC snap-in.

2. Right-click the **domain** or **organizational unit** that you are interested in deploying to the client, and select **Properties**.

3. Click the **Group Policy** tab.

4. Click **New** to create a new Group Policy object (GPO), and type in a name for the GPO.

5. Select the **new GPO** from the list, and click **Edit** to open the Group Policy Object Editor.

6. Expand **Computer Configuration**, and select **Software Settings**.

7. Right-click **Software Installation** in the left pane, select **New**, and then click **Package**.

8. Enter the path to the AU MSI file you downloaded from the Web. Make sure you use a network path (not a local path) to ensure that your clients can find the file at boot time.

9. Choose **Assigned** to assign the package to the computers in the domain or organizational unit, and then click **OK**.

10. Allow time for polices to replicate through the domain (usually accomplished within 15 minutes).

11. Restart the client computers. The client software should be installed before the Logon dialog box is displayed.

NOTE

The application will be installed in the context of the local computer; therefore, make sure that authenticated users have rights on the source folders.

If you are not currently using a domain, you can still deploy the client MSI through a logon script by calling **MSIEXEC** followed by the client software file name as an argument. The software will be installed as requested.

Shortcuts…

Quick Ways to Push Out the AU Software to Clients

If you are like me, you will try to avoid sneakernet if possible; however, deploying GPOs can be more trouble than it's worth. Or perhaps you are not authorized to edit GPOs on a domain-wide basis. Following are some options to get the latest AU software out to clients:

- Deploy Windows XP Service Pack 2.

- E-mail the MSI to your users and ask that they install the file immediately. There are holes in this method, however, because you will need to make sure your users follow through, and you will need to ensure that your users can execute the file.

- To get the file to your users, ask them to download the MSI file from a Web page. You can then write a script to execute the file within an administrative context.

Managing Bandwidth Concerns

No matter the amount of network bandwidth available, WSUS offers features that allow you to shape the deployment to best fit your organization's needs. The decisions you make about how to synchronize with Microsoft Update have a dramatic effect on the efficient use of available bandwidth.

Deferring Some Downloads

WSUS supports deferring the download of update metadata, separating that information transfer from the downloading of the update itself during synchronization. When you use this deferral method by approving an update, WSUS downloads all of the files used to install that particular update, thus, saving bandwidth and WSUS server disk space since only approved updates are downloaded in full to the WSUS server.

Deferral works with WSUS server chaining in some interesting ways. In a chain of machines, WSUS automatically configures downstream servers to use the deferred download option that is selected on the upstream server (i.e., the computer that connects to Microsoft Update). You cannot change this configuration, meaning the entire chain of WSUS servers must either defer the download of updates or download both metadata and updates during synchronization. If you enable deferred downloads and a downstream server tries to request a file not yet approved on the upstream server, the upstream server downloads the file. The downstream server then gets that content on a later synchronization. If you have a deep hierarchy of WSUS servers using deferred downloads, there is greater potential for delay as content is requested, downloaded, and then passed down the chain during successive synchronization cycles.

The option to defer downloads is particularly useful when used in conjunction with a special approval setting that only detects whether a client needs a specific update. The WSUS server does not download any unprompted update and clients do not install any unprompted update; rather, the client machines figure out whether or not they require a specific update. If they do, they send an event to the WSUS server, which is recorded in a server report. When you review the report and notice that your clients need updates that were approved for detection, you can then approve them for installation; only then does download take place.

If you chose to store updates locally during the WSUS setup process, deferred downloads are enabled by default. You can change this option manually using the following procedure:

1. On the WSUS console toolbar, click **Options** and then click **Synchronization Options**.

2. Under Update Files and Languages, click **Advanced**.

3. Acknowledge the warning that appears by clicking **OK**.

4. In the Advanced Synchronization Options box (see Figure 5.4), under Update Files, select **Download updates to this server only when updates are approved** to enable deferred downloading. If you want to disable it, clear the same checkbox.

Figure 5.4 Advanced WSUS Synchronization Options

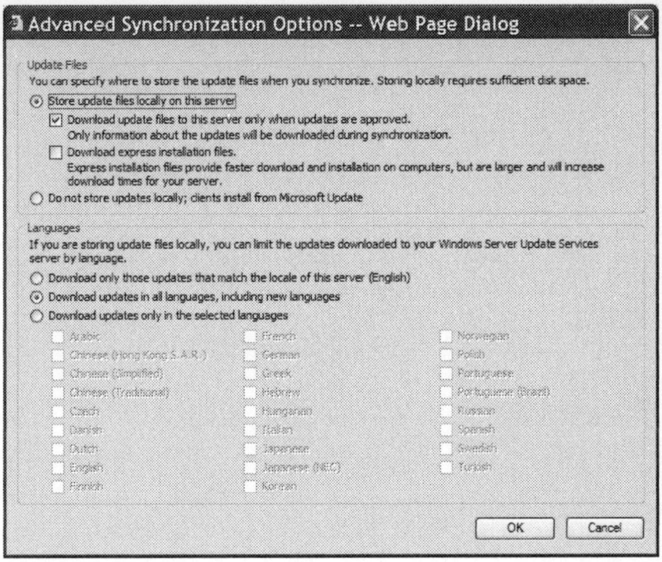

Limiting Superfluous Downloads

WSUS offers the ability to choose only the updates your organization requires during synchronization. The most common way to filter downloads is by language, product, and type of update.

In the chain, all downstream servers use the update filtering options that are selected on the upstream server; therefore, you can only set a filter for updates on the upstream server. However, you can defer the download of updates to get a subset of language, product, or types of updates on a downstream server (described in the previous section).

By default, WSUS downloads critical and security updates for all Windows products in every language. You should configure WSUS to limit languages to only those you need, to conserve bandwidth and disk space.

To specify these language options:

1. On the WSUS console toolbar, click **Options** and then click **Synchronization Options**.

2. Under Update Files and Languages, click **Advanced**.

3. Acknowledge the warning that appears by clicking **OK**.

4. In the Advanced Synchronization Options box, under Languages, select either **Download only those updates that match the locale of this server**, **Download updates in all languages, including new languages**, or **Download updates only in the selected languages** (see Figure 5.5).

Figure 5.5 Specifying WSUS Language Options

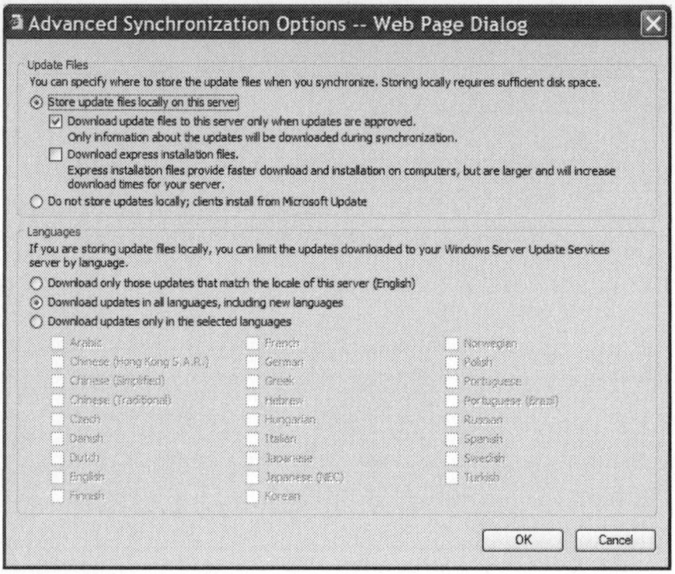

If you change language options after downloading updates, you should manually synchronize such updates between a master server and its subordinate
replica members.

Express Installation

The *express installation files* feature distributes updates that are geared toward limiting the
bandwidth consumed on your local area network (LAN), which it does by increasing
the bandwidth consumption over your Internet connection.

Updates typically consist of new versions of files that already exist on the target computer. On a binary comparison level, the existing files are similar to the new versions. The
express installation feature is a way of identifying only the changed sections within the old
updated versions of the files, creating and distributing updates that include just these differences and not the entire file package, and then merging the original file with the
update on the client computer. This method is called *delta delivery* because it downloads
only the differing sections, or the delta, between two versions of a file.

Distributing updates using express installation requires more than the usual amount
of bandwidth over your Internet connection, because files designed to be used with this
method are larger than the updates they send out. The express installation file must contain all of the possible variations of each file it is meant to update, rather than just a

complete, unaltered version of the target file. You will generally incur an initial download expense that is approximately triple the size of a normal update. In most cases, however, this cost is mitigated by the reduced amount of corporate network bandwidth required to update client computers. Conversely, if you do not use this feature, your initial download of updates is smaller. Whatever you download must then be distributed to each of the clients on your corporate network.

Not all updates are good candidates for distribution using express installation files. If you select this option, you obtain express installation files for any updates being distributed this way, and by default, WSUS does not use express installation files.

To enable this option, use the following procedure:

1. On the WSUS console toolbar, click **Options** and then click **Synchronization Options**.

2. Under Update Files and Languages, click **Advanced**.

3. Acknowledge the warning that appears by clicking OK.

4. In the Advanced Synchronization Options box, under Update Files, check the **Download express installation files** box. To disable express installation, clear the check box (see Figure 5.6).

Figure 5.6 Disabling Express Installation

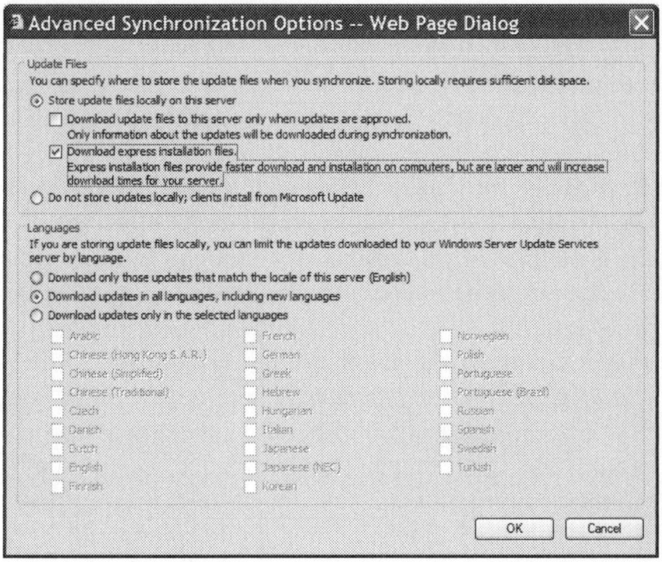

BEST PRACTICES ACCORDING TO MICROSOFT

- Use the deferred downloading feature to save network bandwidth and to make downloading updates and accompanying meta-information more efficient.
- Limit downloading updates localized for languages that do not exist on your network. There is no need to waste network throughput and disk storage space for a foreign version of a security update, when all of your users are native English speakers.
- If you change language options after downloading the updates, you should manually synchronize these updates between a master server and its subordinate replica members.
- Use express download on busy internal networks only if you can afford significantly larger initial downloads over the Internet from Microsoft Update.

Using Computer Groups

Computer groups are an important part of the most basic WSUS systems. Computer groups enable you to target updates to specific sets of computers that share some common criteria. WSUS ships with two default groups, called *All Computers* and *Unassigned Computers*. When each client computer initially contacts the WSUS server, the server adds it to both these groups. Of course, it is very likely that you will want to create your own computer groups, since you can control the deployment of updates much more granularly with them. For example, you can create a group named *Test* that contains some lab machines. You can initially deploy a new patch to the test group, and then, once you have verified the patch works on those machines, roll it out to other groups. Since there is no limit to the number of custom groups you can create, you can also block off machines into departments, function, roles, or any other denominator you wish to use.

Remember that computer group membership is not distributed throughout a replica group that you create. In other words, you always have to load client computers into computer groups. It is possible that not all the sites in your organization require the same computer groups, in which case you should have a sufficient number of computer groups on the administered server to satisfy the needs of the rest of the organization. Computers at different sites can be moved into a group appropriate for the site. Meanwhile, computer groups inappropriate for a particular site remain empty.

Setting up computer groups takes three steps. First, specify whether you intend to use server-side targeting, which involves manually adding each computer to its group by using WSUS, or client-side targeting, which involves automatically adding the clients by using either Group Policy or registry keys. Next, create the computer group on WSUS. Finally, move the computers into groups using whichever method you chose in the first step.

This section talks about server-side targeting, since it's the most likely method you will use.

To specify that you will use server-side targeting to select members of computer groups:

1. In the console toolbar, click **Options**, and then click **Computer Options**.

2. Click **Use the Move computers** task in Windows SUS in the Computer Options box. This is shown in Figure 5.7.

3. Within Tasks, click **Save** settings and then click **OK** to confirm your selection.

Figure 5.7 Server-Side Targeting

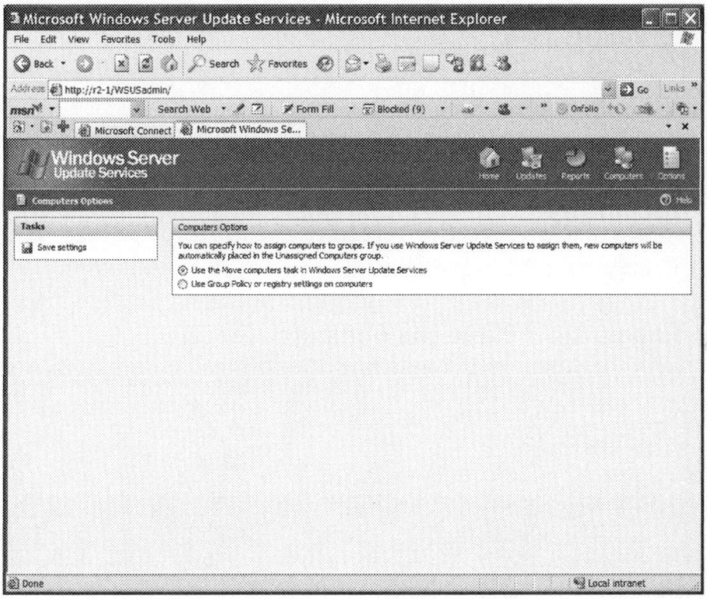

Next, create a computer group. In this example, we will create the Test group mentioned earlier in this chapter:

4. In the console toolbar, click **Computers**.

5. Within Tasks, click **Create** a computer group.

6. Enter **test** into the Group name box (see Figure 5.8) and then click **OK**.

Figure 5.8 Creating a Computer Group

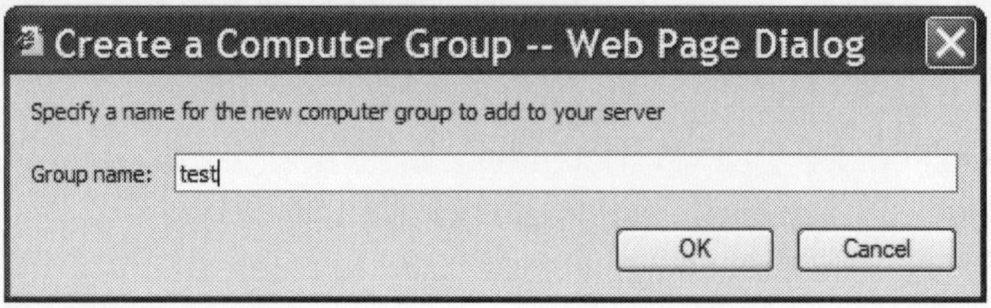

Finally, add a machine to that group. You will need to follow the instructions within the client-side portion of this chapter to get the AU software deployed, which will populate the WSUS console with a list of available computers. Once that's done, follow these steps to add a machine to a group:

1. In the console toolbar, click **Computers**.

2. In the Groups box, click the **All Computers group** and then click the computer you want to move into the Test group.

3. Under Tasks, click **Move the selected computer**, and then select the **Test group** and click **OK** to perform the move (see Figure 5.9).

Figure 5.9 Adding a Machine to the Computer Group

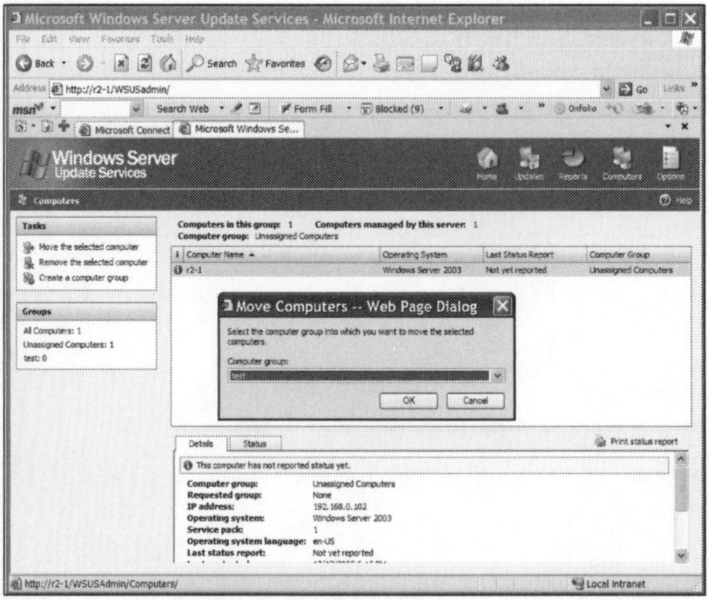

Repeat until you have a group structure appropriate to your network and deployment methodology.

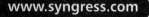

> ### Shortcuts...
>
> ## Using Client-Side Targeting
>
> By using client-side targeting, WSUS can figure out how to assign computers to different groups by looking at Group Policy or Registry keys on each machine to automatically collect computers into a group. Client-side targeting saves you the trouble of manually adding computers, moving them around in groups, and generally resorting to tedious administrative methods.
>
> To enable this, use Group Policy to configure the AU software on each computer. Enable the **client-side targeting** option by clicking the **Enabled** option, type the name of the group to which this computer should belong on the WSUS, and then click **OK**.
>
> Keep in mind that you need to create the group on the WSUS server for this to take effect.

Creating Group Policies

The AU client does not have any user-interface options for determining the origin of updates to install. Set this using a Registry change on each of the client computers or through Group Policy, either locally or based through a domain. Once the changes take effect, you will be able to see the machines within the Computers page of the WSUS console.

Group Policies in Active Directory

Through a domain-based Group Policy, direct clients to the WSUS server should use the following procedure:

1. Open the Default Domain Policy GPO in Active Directory Users and Computers and click the **Edit** button.

2. Expand **Computer Configuration | Administrative Templates | Windows Components**.

3. Select **Windows Update**. The right pane will contain several options that pertain to the AU client (see Figure 5.10).

Figure 5.10 Group Policy Settings

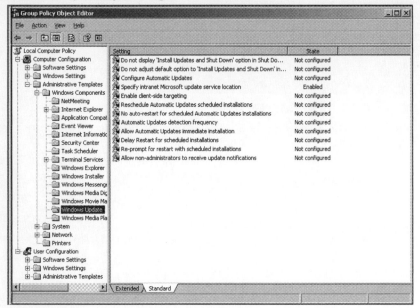

These options are described here in more detail:

- **Configure AU** This option specifies whether a computer will receive security updates and critical bug fixes. The first option ensures that the currently logged-on user is notified before downloading updates. The user is notified again before installing the downloaded updates. The second option ensures that updates will automatically be downloaded but not installed until a logged-on user acknowledges the updates' presence and authorizes the installation. The third option makes sure that updates are automatically downloaded and installed on a schedule that can be set in the appropriate boxes on the sheet. The fourth option, which appears if the AU software has updated itself to the version compatible with WSUS, allows local administrators to use AU in Control Panel to select their own configuration. To use this setting, click **Enabled**, and then select one of the options.

- **Specify Intranet Microsoft Update Service Location** This option designates a WSUS server from which to download updates. To use this setting, you must set two values for the server names: the server from which the AU client detects and downloads updates, and the server to which updated workstations upload statistics. Both values can be set to be the same server.

- **Enable Client-Side Targeting** This option enables client computers to automatically populate groups on the SUS server. To use this option, click the

Enabled option and then type the name of the group to which this computer should belong on the WSUS. Click **OK**. Keep in mind that you need to actually create the group on the WSUS server for this to take effect.

- **Reschedule Automatic Update's Scheduled Installations** This option specifies the amount of time to wait after booting before continuing with a scheduled installation that was missed previously (e.g., power outage, system powered off, network connection lost, and so on). If the status is set to Enabled, a missed scheduled installation will occur a specified number of minutes after the computer is next started. If the status is set to Disabled or Not Configured, a missed scheduled installation will roll over to the next scheduled installation.

- **No Auto-restart for Scheduled Automatic Updates Installations** This option designates whether a client computer should automatically reboot when an update that is just installed requires a system restart. If the status is set to Enabled, AU will not restart a computer automatically during a scheduled installation if a user is logged in to the computer. Instead, it will notify the user to restart the computer to complete the installation. If the status is set to Disabled or Not Configured, AU will notify the user that the computer will automatically restart in 5 minutes to complete the installation.

- **Automatic Update Detection Frequency** This option details the hours that Windows will use to figure out how long to wait before pinging the WSUS server to see if new updates are available. This time is actually determined by using the hours specified in this option and subtracting anywhere from 0 to 20 percent of the hours specified. This offset helps manage load. If the status is set to Enabled, you must specify the number of hours; if it is set to Disabled or Not Configured, AU will check for new updates every 22 hours.

- **Allow Automatic Update Immediate Installation** This option specifies whether AU should automatically install updates that do not interrupt Windows or need a reboot. If you enable this option, AU will auto-install such updates; if you disable it, they will not be immediately installed.

- **Delay Restart for Scheduled Installations** This setting defines the amount of time AU will wait before executing a scheduled reboot. If this setting is enabled, the scheduled restart will happen after the number of minutes you specify. If this setting is disabled or not configured, the default waiting period is five minutes.

- **Re-prompt for Restart with Scheduled Installations** If this setting is enabled, a scheduled restart will occur in the specified number of minutes after the prompt for restarting was postponed by the user. If this setting is disabled or not configured, the scheduled restart will take place 10 minutes after the first prompt.

- **Allow Nonadministrators to Receive Update Notifications** If this setting is enabled, all users can receive notifications that updates are ready for download and/or installation. If this setting is disabled or not configured, AU will notify only logged-on administrators that pending update action is necessary.

- **Remove Links and Access to Windows Update** If this setting is enabled, end users cannot get updates from a Windows Update Web site that has not been approved. If this policy is not enabled, the Windows Update icon remains in place for local administrators to visit. Such local administrators can install unapproved updates.

Allow 10 to 15 minutes for the changes to the domain's policy to replicate among all domain controllers. To manually initiate detection of these client machines, open a command prompt on the client and type *wuauclt.exe/detectnow*.

One added benefit of using group policy to configure the AU client is the ability to spread the load of patch management over several different WSUS servers based on your Active Directory structure. By creating GPOs and linking them to different organizational units (OUs) and sites within AD, you can configure different options for the AU client, including target update locations, update behavior, reboot settings, and any of the other settings described earlier in this section. The only difference in procedure from the preceding example is that instead of creating a GPO based on the Default Domain Policy, you should create the GPO at the appropriate level. Remember, the mnemonic for the application of GPOs—LSDOU—means that local policies will be applied before site policies, and then domain policies, and then organizational unit policies, with the last setting applied winning.

Best Practices According to Microsoft

- Use Group Policy to enable AU functionality and to configure each client computer to contact the WSUS server for updates.
- Ensure that users have a seamless update experience by removing user access to Windows Update for managed computers.
- Use client-side targeting to reduce some of the tedium of administering computer groups on the WSUS server console.

Local Group Policies

To adjust the Group Policy on a machine that is not managed by Active Directory, you must load the appropriate templates into the Microsoft Management Console using the following steps:

1. Click **Start**, select **Run**, and type *GPEDIT.msc* to load the Group Policy snap-in.

2. Expand **Computer Configuration and Administrative Templates**.

3. Right-click on **Administrative Templates**, click **Add/Remove Templates**, and then click **Add**.

4. Enter the name of the AU ADM file, which can be found in the INF subdirectory within your Windows root, or in the INF subdirectory within the WSUS server machine's Windows root (see Figure 5.11).

5. Click **Open** and then click **Close** to load the *wuau.adm* file.

Figure 5.11 Policy Templates

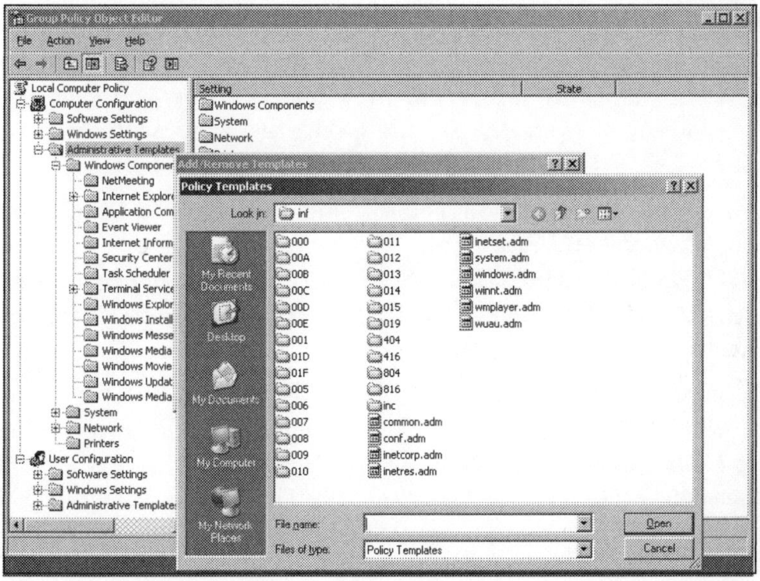

You can now adjust the policy settings as described in the previous section.

Finally, to adjust some of these behavior settings through Registry changes, use the appropriate key for each of the following settings:

■ To enable or disable AU, create the value **NoAutoUpdate** in the *HKEY_LOCAL_MACHINE\SOFTWARE\Policies\Microsoft_Windows\Windows Update\AU* key. The value is a DWORD with possible values 0 (enabled) or 1 (disabled).

■ To configure the update download and notification behavior, create the value **AUOptions** in the *HKEY_LOCAL_MACHINE\SOFTWARE\Policies\ _Microsoft\Windows\WindowsUpdate\AU* key. The value is a DWORD that includes integers 2 (notify of download and notify before installation), 3 (automatically download but notify before installation), 4 (automatically download and schedule the installation), and 5 (let the local administrator choose the setting).

- To schedule an automated installation, create the values *ScheduledInstallDay* and *ScheduledInstallTime* in the *HKEY_LOCAL_MACHINE\SOFTWARE\Policies\Microsoft\Windows\Windows Update\AU* key. The value for each is a DWORD. For *ScheduledInstallDay*, the range is from 0 to 7, with 0 indicating every day and 1 through 7 indicating the days of the week, Sunday through Saturday. For *ScheduledInstallTime*, the range is from 0 to 23, signifying the hour of the day in military time.

- To specify a particular WSUS server to use with the AU client, create the value *UseWUServer* in *HKEY_LOCAL_MACHINE_SOFTWARE\Policies\Microsoft\Windows\Windows Update\AU* key. The value is a DWORD; set it to 1 to enable the custom WSUS server name. Then, create the values *WUServer* and *WUStatusServer* in the same key, of types *Reg_SZ*, and specify the name (with the *http://*) as the value.

- To specify how long to wait before completing a missed installation, create the value *RescheduleWaitTime* in the *HKEY_LOCAL_MACHINE_SOFTWARE\Policies\Microsoft\Windows\Windows Update\AU* key. The value is a DWORD that ranges from 1 to 60, measured in minutes.

- To specify whether to restart a scheduled installation with a currently logged-in nonadministrative user, create the *NoAutoRebootWithLoggedOnUsers* value in the *HKEY_LOCAL_MACHINE\SOFTWARE\Policies\ Microsoft\Windows\WindowsUpdate\AU* key. The value is a DWORD that can be 0, which indicates that a reboot will take place, or 1, which indicates the reboot will be postponed while a user is logged on.

Shortcuts...

Monitoring the Client Computer System

Sometimes you may wonder what is going on behind the scenes on your client systems when they are attempting to download and install updates. Fortunately, WSUS and the AU client provide several event templates that are written to the system event log to describe the current status of the update process, any errors

Continued

that are encountered, and a brief notation of what updates were successfully installed. You can program an event-log monitoring tool to monitor for certain event IDs that are specific to WSUS. This tool will give you a picture of your network's health regarding updates. Use the following list to decode the events that appear within the event log and to determine what's happening with your client machine.

- **16, Unable to connect** The client cannot connect to either the Windows Update site or the WSUS server, but will continue trying indefinitely.

- **17, Install ready; no recurring schedule** Updates have been downloaded and are to be installed, but an administrator must log on and manually start the installation process.

- **18, Install ready; recurring schedule** Updates have been downloaded and are ready to be installed. The date this install is scheduled to occur is listed in the event description.

- **19, Install success** Updates have been successfully installed and have been listed.

- **20, Install failure** Some updates didn't install correctly and have been listed.

- **21, Restart required; no recurring schedule** Updates have been installed, but a reboot is required. Until this reboot is complete, Windows cannot fetch more updates for installation. Any user can reboot the machine.

- **22, Restart required; recurring schedule** Updates have been installed, but a reboot is required and has been scheduled within five minutes.

Summary

Remember that as you increase the number of WSUS servers on your network, you must give consideration to how each of the servers will be managed and how each of the machines falls into your overall patch management structure.

- Remember to use chain mode to make update distribution easier.
- Consider the different models of management supported by WSUS.
- Make use of bandwidth management features, such as deferred downloading, express installation, and update filtering.
- Use computer groups to target updates to different sets of machines.
- Deploy AU software using Group Policy, to quickly and easily get your client machines in tune with WSUS.

Solutions Fast Track

Installing Multiple Servers

- ☑ To save bandwidth, use chain mode to download updates from the Internet and then distribute those updates to branch offices with downstream servers.
- ☑ Use chain mode to move updates closer to the point where they will be deployed, thereby making network traffic more efficient.
- ☑ Use only three levels of hierarchy when establishing a chain.
- ☑ Use central management if your network is contained within one site.

Deploying WSUS Client Software

- ☑ When your client computers first contact the WSUS server, the latest Automatic Updates (AU) software installed on your client computers self-update to the latest version.
- ☑ The version of AU included with the initial release of Windows XP (the so-called gold RTM version without any service packs) cannot update itself automatically.
- ☑ Because the client installation program is in the form of an MSI, you can easily push the program to clients by using Group Policy if your clients are joined to a Windows-based domain

Managing Bandwidth Concerns

☑ Use the deferred downloading feature to save network bandwidth and make downloading of updates and accompanying metainformation more efficient.

☑ Limit downloading updates localized for languages that do not exist on your network. There's no need to waste network throughput and disk storage space for a foreign version of a security update when all of your users are native English speakers.

☑ If you change language options after having downloaded updates, you should manually synchronize such updates between a master server and its subordinate replica members.

☑ Use Express Download on busy internal networks, but only if you can afford significantly larger initial downloads over the Internet from Microsoft Update.

Using Computer Groups

☑ Create computer groups to target updates to different sets of machines on your networks.

☑ If you are using a replica group, make sure that you create a sufficient number of groups on the master server for all computers that will be managed by WSUS, even if they are not managed directly by the master server.

Creating Group Policies

☑ Use Group Policy to enable AU functionality and to configure each client computer to contact the WSUS server for updates.

☑ Ensure that users have a seamless update experience by removing user access to Windows Update for managed computers.

☑ Use client-side targeting to reduce some of the tedium of administering computer groups on the WSUS server console.

Frequently Asked Questions

The following Frequently Asked Questions, answered by the authors of this book, are designed to both measure your understanding of the concepts presented in this chapter and to assist you with real-life implementation of these concepts. To have your questions about this chapter answered by the author, browse to **www.syngress.com/solutions** and click on the **"Ask the Author"** form.

Q: Is centralized management better for me, or should I consider distributed management?

A: If you have a network that is primarily contained within one site, you will find management is much easier by configuring your WSUS deployment to use the centralized management scheme. If you are the only administrator on your network, choose central management so that you can spend less time deploying each server. The distributed management model is mainly designed for university networks and subsidiary businesses that are run separately.

Q: In what situations does the Express Download feature excel?

A: If you have a lot of traffic on your internal network, or your client computers that are targeted for updates are connected to your WSUS servers over a really slow, high-latency wide area network (WAN) connection, the Express Installation feature will be a godsend, since it can cut the size of the actual patches sent to clients themselves by up to three-quarters. If you have a normally loaded, reasonably fast-switched network, you are not going to see a lot of difference over the traditional methods of updating.

Q: Some of the computers I manage run simulations overnight, during the prime hours for unattended patching. What can I do to prevent these machines from restarting after they install an update that requires a reboot?

A: Previous versions of Windows 2000 and XP did not support this type of functionality, but it was introduced to both platforms in the latest service packs for each. Once you have updated the clients, you can enable the **Auto-restart for Scheduled Automatic Updates Installations** option in Group Policy.

Chapter 6

Administering WSUS Servers

Solutions in this chapter:

- **Downloading and Synchronizing Updates**
- **Managing Updates**
- **Backing Up and Restoring WSUS Servers**

☑ **Summary**

☑ **Solutions Fast Track**

☑ **Frequently Asked Questions**

Introduction

Without some type of patch management software, keeping computers up to date can be a full time job. Windows Server Update Services (WSUS) eases a lot of that burden, but is not free of administration. After installing WSUS, you must configure it to synchronize with Microsoft's Update servers. Once synchronized, you must go through all of the updates and decide which ones to deploy to your clients. After everything is working as expected, back up your WSUS server so that you do not have to repeat all of this work again.

Downloading and Synchronizing Updates

Before you can update clients, you must synchronize with Microsoft's servers. The default installation of WSUS does not contain any client updates; therefore, until you perform your first synchronization, there will be no updates to approve. This initial synchronization will take some time and consume a fair amount of bandwidth on your Internet connection. As a precaution, you may want to perform this task during non-peak hours.

There are five tasks that should be completed to allow WSUS to synchronize for the first time.

1. Schedule a time for WSUS to synchronize or perform a manual synchronization.

2. Configure WSUS for Internet access.

3. Tell WSUS where to store updates.

4. Configure WSUS to download updates in the correct language.

5. Choose which products and classifications WSUS will download.

Navigating to the Synchronization Options

All of the synchronization options covered in this section are configured in the same place. We will now walk you through navigating to the "Synchronization Options" window. Unless mentioned otherwise, the remaining examples and exercises start here.

1. Navigate to the WSUS administration console by typing *http://wsus_server_name/wsusadmin* (where *wsus_server_name* is the name of your WSUS server). (See Figure 6.1.)

Shortcuts

Accessing the WSUS Administration Console

If you forget the Uniform Resource Locator (URL) to manage your WSUS server, there is a link to it on the WSUS server. Go to the Start menu and navigate to Administrative Tools. The shortcut labeled Microsoft Windows Server Update Services will open the WSUS Web console.

Figure 6.1 Opening the WSUS Administration Console

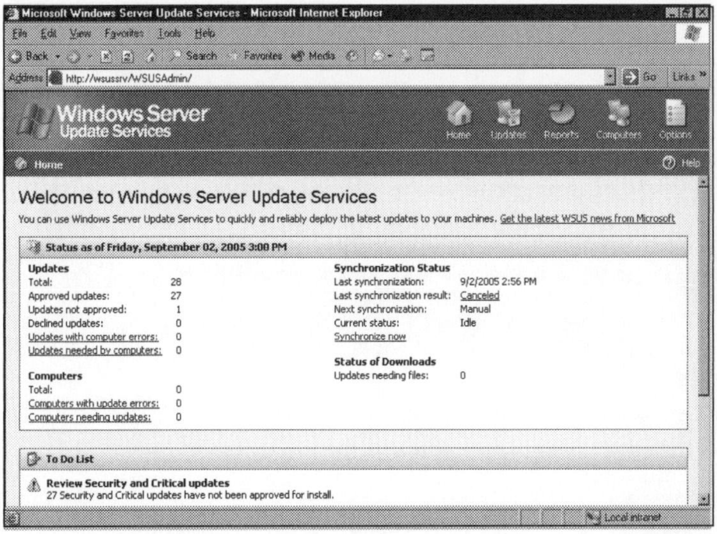

2. Click the **Options** button in the upper right-hand corner of the administration console. This takes you to the Options window shown in Figure 6.2.

3. From the Options window click on the **Synchronization Options** button. This will take you to the Synchronization Options window shown in Figure 6.3.

Figure 6.2 Navigating to Options

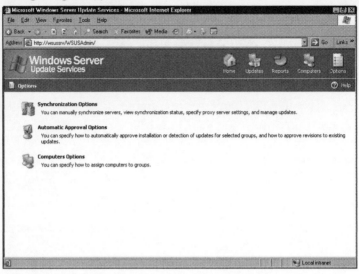

Figure 6.3 Configuring Synchronization Options

Scheduling Synchronization

By default, WSUS is set for manual synchronization, which means you must click the **Synchronize now** button every time you want WSUS to synchronize. This works fine for your initial synchronization, but you should automate it for future synchronizing. One of the main reasons for deploying WSUS is to automate client updates. Leaving your WSUS server in a state where synchronizations are manual does not help automation.

You can schedule WSUS for daily updates at any half-hour increment from the Synchronization Options page shown in Figure 6.3. Select the radio button next to **Synchronize daily at** and choose the time you want WSUS to synchronize. Remember, WSUS does not necessarily start the download at the time specified. It uses a random 30-minute offset, meaning it will start somewhere between the time you specified and up to 30 minutes later. Microsoft does this so that those who set their WSUS server to download at a given time (e.g., 3:30 A.M.) do not start downloading at exactly the same time. The random offset spreads the load between 3:30 A.M. and 4:00 A.M.

BEST PRACTICES ACCORDING TO MICROSOFT

Perform your first WSUS synchronization when it will have the least impact on your network. Always synchronize during non-peak hours.

The synchronization status of your WSUS server can be found by looking at the Synchronization Status section on the Synchronization Options page (see Figure 6.3), or on the WSUS Home page (see Figure 6.4). To open the WSUS Home page type ***http://wsus_server_name/wsusadmin*** (where *wsus_server_name* is the name of your WSUS server). From here you can see the last time your server attempted to synchronize, whether its last attempt was successful, when it is scheduled to synchronize again, and its current state (idle or synchronizing).

Figure 6.4 Viewing the Synchronization Status from the WSUS Administration Console Home Page

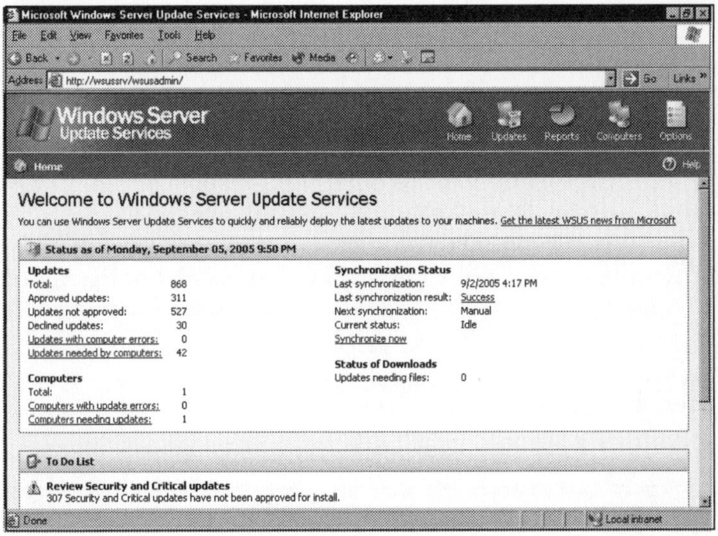

Click the link next to Last Synchronization Result: Success to view a detailed report of the last synchronization attempt (see Figure 6.5). From this report you will see the start and end time of your last synchronization, the total number of new updates, the total number of revised updates, the total number of expired updates, a list of any errors, and a list of all downloaded updates complete with product title and classification. This is the first place you should look if you suspect any errors during WSUS downloading updates. It is also an easy way to see what new updates have been released.

Figure 6.5 Viewing the Synchronization Results Status Report

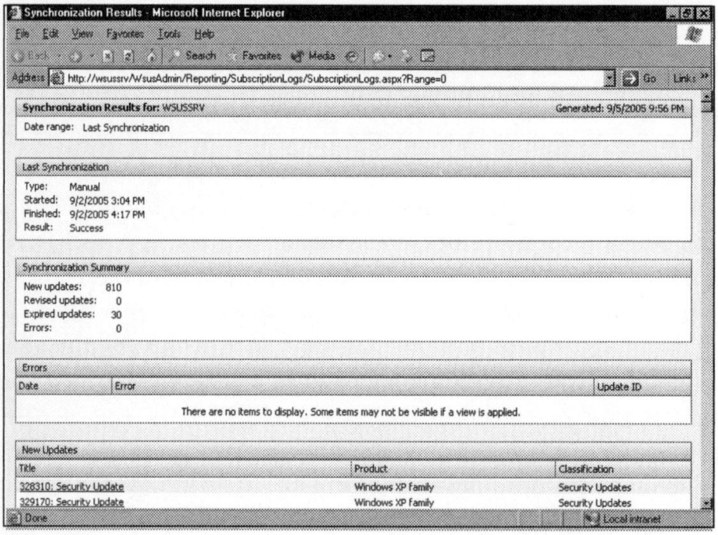

Configuring Internet Access

Your WSUS server must be configured to either synchronize with Microsoft's Update Servers or with another WSUS server. This section focuses on installing a single WSUS server and synchronizing it with Microsoft. In order to access Microsoft's servers, your WSUS server must have Internet access.

If you are not using a proxy server, you need to configure your WSUS server with the correct default gateway and make sure your firewall allows outgoing traffic from the WSUS server. If you do not want to enable the WSUS server to get to all Web sites, you can allow explicit access to the sites used for Microsoft Windows Updates. Table 6.1 lists all the Web sites required for a WSUS server to synchronize.

Table 6.1 Allowing Internet Access to the Site Required for WSUS

Sites Needed for WSUS

http://windowsupdate.microsoft.com
http://*.windowsupdate.microsoft.com
https://*.windowsupdate.microsoft.com
http://*.update.microsoft.com
https://*.update.microsoft.com
http://*.windowsupdate.com
http://download.windowsupdate.com
http://download.microsoft.com
http://*.download.windowsupdate.com
http://wustat.windows.com
http://ntservicepack.microsoft.com

If you are using a proxy server, you must configure WSUS to use the correct proxy settings to get to the Internet. This is accomplished from the Synchronization Options window shown in Figure 6.6. If your proxy server does not require authentication, then you just need to enter the Server name and Port number. If your proxy server requires authentication, you must also fill in a User name, Domain, and Password. Depending on the authentication settings of your proxy server, you may or may not have to enable basic authentication. Remember, when you use basic authentication your credentials are passed in clear text.

Figure 6.6 Configuring Proxy Settings

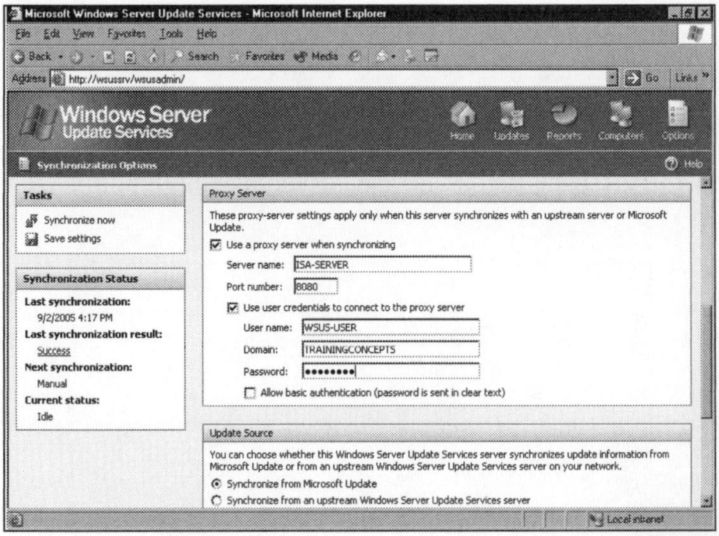

Update Files and Languages

At this point you can synchronize your WSUS server; however, before starting the first synchronization it is a good idea to verify that WSUS is downloading updates in the correct language. You also need to choose where WSUS will store updates, when it will download updates, and the types of update files to be used.

Language support is configured from the Synchronization Options page shown in Figure 6.7. Scroll down to the section labeled Update Files and Language and click the **Advanced** button. This gives you the window shown in Figure 6.8.

Figure 6.7 Updating Files and Language Support

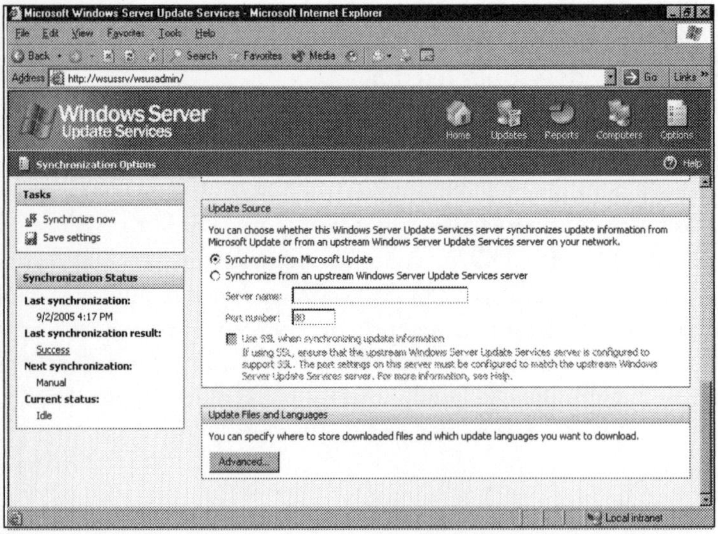

Figure 6.8 Configuring File and Language Support

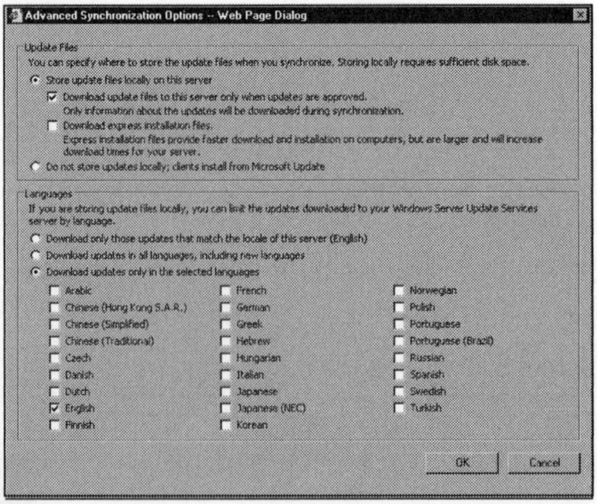

By default, WSUS will download only updates that match the locale of the WSUS server. If all of your clients use the same language as the WSUS server, you have nothing else to configure. If you are using multiple languages, you have two choices available: configure WSUS to download all updates in all languages or specify exactly which languages to download. It is recommended that you specify the languages so that you are not downloading unnecessary updates.

Storing Updates

All updates consist of two parts—*update files* and *metadata*. The update files are the actual files used to update a client computer and the metadata is the information about the update. Keeping the metadata separate from the actual update files reduces synchronization time with Microsoft's servers. Since WSUS only has to synchronize the information about the updates and not the updates themselves, it can finish initial synchronizations much quicker. This gives you all of the information you need about an update such as its purpose, its End User Licensing Agreement (EULA), and which platforms are supported by the update, without having to download the update first.

WSUS stores each of these parts in separate locations. The metadata is stored in the WSUS database and the update files are either stored locally on the WSUS server or they are left on Microsoft's servers. If you choose to leave the update files on Microsoft's servers, your WSUS server will only download the metadata for updates. When you set these updates to install on client machines, each machine will go directly to Microsoft Windows Update Servers and download the update. This requires each machine to have access to the Internet. This is not the preferred method for storing updates, as you will have a lot of unneeded Internet traffic. Instead of just downloading updates once from the Internet to the WSUS server, updates will be downloaded every time they are deployed. If you want your clients to install from Microsoft's servers, select the radio button next to **Do not store updates locally; clients install from Microsoft Update** in the Advanced Synchronization Options window shown in Figure 6.8.

The preferred storage location for update files is locally on the WSUS server, which requires at least 6 gigabytes (GB) of free disk space to hold all of the updates. Microsoft recommends having at least 30GB free. If you are supporting several languages or if you are using express installation files, you can easily have more than 6GB of updates. If you want WSUS to store its updates locally, select the radio button next to **Store update files locally on this server** in the Advanced Synchronization Options windows shown in Figure 6.8. When storing files locally, WSUS only downloads the metadata until the update is approved for installation. If you want WSUS to download the metadata and the update files at the same time, uncheck the box next to **Download update files to this server only when updates are approved** in the Advanced Synchronization Options windows shown in Figure 6.8.

Express Installation Files

Updates contain new versions of files that already exist on the client machines. Express installation files look at things from a binary perspective. There are a lot of similarities between the original file and the updated file. Express installation files pinpoint the exact differences between each file version and only update the differences (also called deltas). Once the differences are changed in the original file, you are left with the new updated file. This approach uses much less bandwidth between the client and the WSUS server because less data has to be pushed to the client. The trade-off is that express installation files are much larger than standard installation files. The reason for this is that, instead of just containing the new updated file, they must contain all possible variants of the files they will update.

Express installation files provide quicker update deployments to client machines. They are, however, much larger than standard updates. It is common for an express update file to be two to four times larger than the file being updated. If you are running low on disk space (less than 30GB), Microsoft does not recommend using express installation files; however, if you have the disk space, this is the preferred method of deploying updates.

You must store updates locally to take advantage of the Express Installation files; however, if you are storing your updates on Microsoft's servers, this feature is not available to you. By default, Express Installation files are not used by WSUS. If you want WSUS to download express installation files, check the box next to **Download express installation files** in the Advanced Synchronization Options windows shown in Figure 6.8.

SOME INDEPENDENT ADVICE

If you are updating computers over a slow network, be sure to enable Express Installation Files. Think of it this way: you have to download it from Microsoft only once, but you have to deploy it across your network every time.

Changing the Local Storage Location

The day may come when you will need to change the hard disk used by WSUS for storing updates. This is easy to do if you started with the minimum of 6GB. Microsoft also provides a command line tool called *WSUSUtil.exe* that can be used to move the location of our update files.

WSUSUtil.exe is located in the Program Files\ Updates Services\Tools directory on the drive where WSUS is installed. To use *WSUSUtil.exe*, you must have administrative rights on the WSUS server. This tool must be run locally; it will not work across the network from another server. Before running *WSUSUtil.exe*, you should install the new drive and create the desired folder structure. You can then use the *movecontent* switch of *WSUSUtil.exe* to move all of the updates to the new location. Table 6.2 explains all of the options for *WSUSUtil.exe*.

Table 6.2 Understanding the Syntax of WSUSUtil.exe

Switch	Purpose
Export	Exports update information in the database to a package file. Does not export update approvals, update files, or server settings.
Import	Imports update information from a package file into the database.
migratesus	Migrates updated approvals from Software Update Services (SUS) to WSUS.
movecontent	Changes the location WSUS uses for update files. Copies update files from old location to new.
Reset	Checks that every update entry in the database has a matching update file stored on the WSUS server. If files are missing, WSUS will download them again.
deleteunneededrevisions	Deletes the update information in the database for unneeded updates.
listinactiveapprovals	Shows inactive approvals due to a change in language support on WSUS.
removeinactiveapprovals	Removes inactive approvals due to a change in language support on WSUS.

Moving the Location of WSUS Update Files

We will now use *WSUSUtil.exe* to move the WSUS update files to a new hard drive. In this example, we use the *movecontent* switch to move the data from the *c:* drive to the *e:* drive.

1. Click the **Start** button.
2. Click the **Run** bottom from the Start Menu. The Run dialog box will appear (see Figure 6.9).

Figure 6.9 Opening the Command Prompt

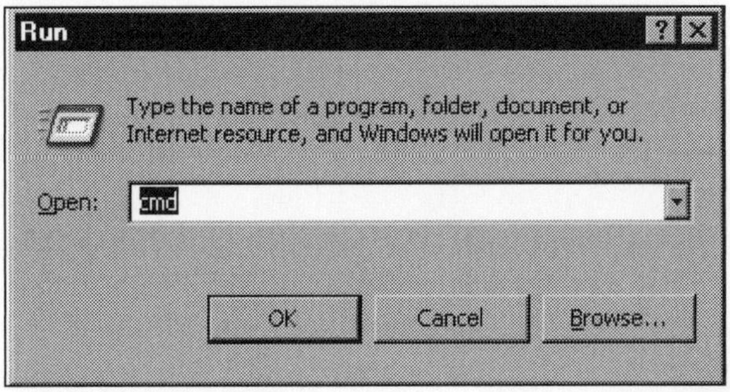

3. Type **CMD** into the Open box.

4. Click **OK**. The Command Prompt window will appear (see Figure 6.10).

5. Change to the WSUS directory (defaults to *c:*) by typing **CD c:\program files\update services\tools**.

6. Type in the following command and press **Enter**:

```
wsusutil.exe movecontent newpath logfile [-skipcopy]
```

In this example *newpath* is the new location to store the update files and *logfile* is the location of the log file.

For example, to move the update files from the *c:* drive to the *e:* drive and to store the log on the root of e: in a *wsusmove.log* file, use the following command:

```
wsusutil.exe movecontent E:\WSUS1\ E:\move.log
```

Figure 6.10 Using the Command Prompt Tool *WSUSUtil.exe*

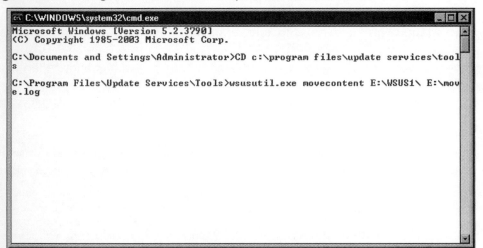

Managing Updates

WSUS administrators spend most of their time managing updates, which are broken down into three general phases—viewing updates, approving updates, and testing updates. These phases follow a logical progression: view which updates are available, approve WSUS to detect which machines need updating, and have WSUS update your test machines followed by your production machines.

The viewing updates phase is where you look at which updates have been released. You can view all available updates or you can filter your view to make it easier to find the updates you need. WSUS can be intimidating if you look at all of the updates at once. It is better to start off with a small number and work your way up from there.

After viewing the updates and getting a feel for what is available, you are ready to approve the updates. Initially, you will have to manually approve client updates, whereas updates for WSUS itself are automatically approved. You can continue to use manual approvals or you can configure WSUS to automatically approve updates for clients. Depending on how far you are willing to go with configuring automatic updates, you can have WSUS automate everything for you.

The next phase is optional, but highly recommended. The testing updates phase involves approving updates for a small pilot of machines to see how the updates affect your environment. This pilot should mimic your production environment. If testing goes well, you can approve the updates for all of your machines. If updating your test machines causes problems, you can fix the issue and test again. This way you will minimize the risks to your production environment.

Classifying Updates

WSUS updates are separated by product family, product, and update classification. A product family is a grouping of products (e.g., Microsoft Office). Products are the different versions of an application or operating system within a given product family (e.g., Microsoft Office 2003 and Microsoft Office XP are separate products within the Microsoft Office product family). Update classifications define the type of update. Each product has many different classifications of updates. For example, the Microsoft Windows XP product includes critical updates, service packs, and security updates classifications (to name a few). Table 6.3 explains the different products and product families supported by WSUS. Table 6.4 explains all of the update classifications.

Table 6.3 Understanding the Products and Product Families of WSUS

Product Family	Product
Exchange	Exchange 2000 Server
Exchange	Exchange Server 2003
Office	Office 2002/XP
Office	Office 2003
SQL	WMSDE
Windows	Windows 2000 family
Windows	Windows Server 2003 family
Windows	Windows Server 2003, Datacenter Edition
Windows	Windows XP 64-bit Edition Version 2003
Windows	Windows XP family
Windows	Windows XP x64 Edition

Table 6.4 Understanding the Update Classifications of WSUS

Update Classifications	Explanation
Connectors	Software components to support connections between different software.
Critical Updates	Fixes for specific problems relating to critical bugs not related to security issues.
Development Kits	Software to help when writing new applications. Typically contains an editor, compiler, and visual builder.
Drivers	Software components to support hardware.
Feature Packs	Adds new functionality to an existing product.
Guidance	Technical guidance such as scripts and sample code to aid in the deployment and use of a product.
Security Updates	Fixes for security related issues.
Service Packs	Contains all the critical updates, security updates, and updates released for a product. May also contain new features, although these are typically deployed through feature packs.
Tools	Utilities for performing a specific task.
Update Rollups	Contains critical updates, security updates, and updates in one easy-to-deploy package. Update rollups are usually geared towards one area or component (i.e. security, Exchange, Internet Information Server [IIS)].
Updates	Fixes bugs not related to security issues or considered a critical update.

Understanding the different types of updates is critical to properly utilizing WSUS for your environment. It is easy to get confused when reading the difference between updates, security updates, and critical updates. Also, sometimes update rollups and service packs appear to be the same.

Technically speaking, updates, security updates, and critical updates all serve the same purpose, which is to update a product. Instead of grouping all updates together, Microsoft breaks them down into three categories—Critical updates, Security updates, and Updates. These fix a known problem that should not be left in its current state. Security updates (still considered critical in most cases) only fix security-related issues. Updates are where Microsoft puts the remaining updates that are not considered critical or security related. At a minimum, you should apply all critical updates and security updates.

Update rollups and service packs do similar things. They both group together critical updates and security updates into one easy-to-deploy package. What is the difference?

Service packs are used to deliver a large number of updates and new features in between product releases. Because of the high volume of updates contained in service packs, most customers have to do extensive testing before deployment. On the other hand, update rollups do not contain as many changes as service packs and typically require less testing. Service packs cover every component of a product. Update rollups are usually geared towards a particular component, such as IIS. Update rollups make it easy to keep your systems up to date between service packs without having to install each individual update.

Configuring Products and Update Classifications Supported by WSUS

We'll now discuss the steps used for choosing which products and update classifications will be supported by WSUS. In this example, we configure WSUS to download all update classifications, and we will choose to only support Exchange Server 2003, Office 2003, and the Windows Server 2003 family.

1. From the Synchronization Options page, scroll down to the Product and Classifications section shown in Figure 6.11.

Figure 6.11 Choosing Products and Classifications

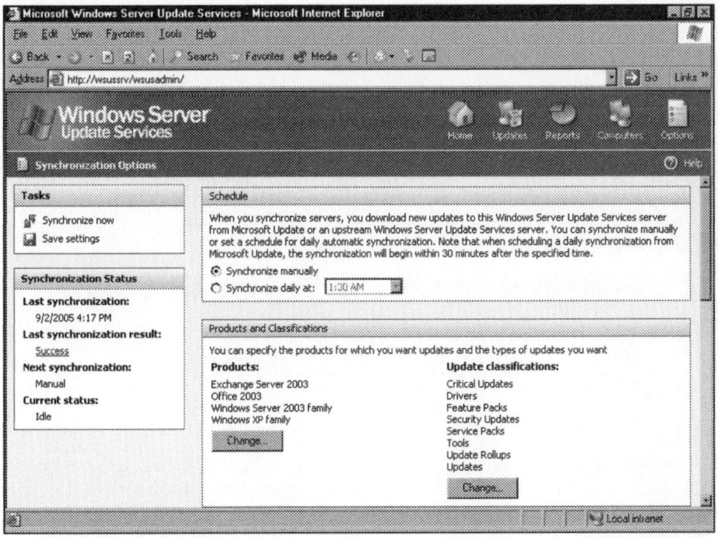

2. Click the **Change** button underneath Products. The Add/Remove Products window will appear (see Figure 6.12).

Figure 6.12 Adding and Removing Products

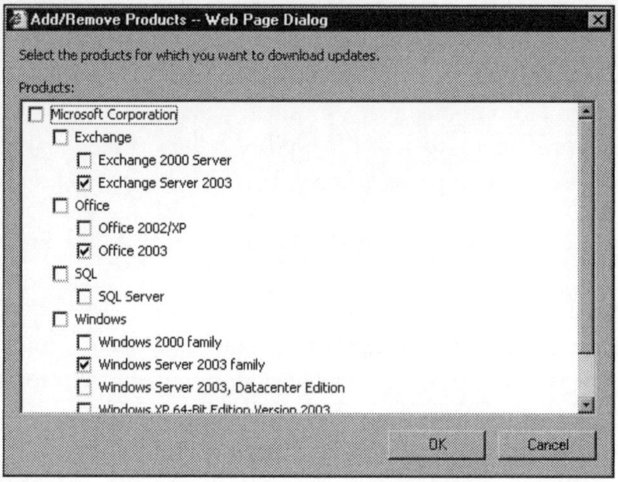

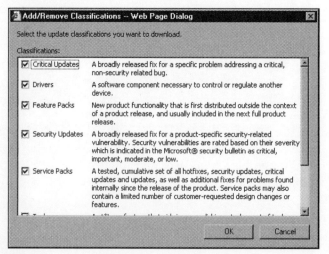

3. Select the boxes next to the products you want updated by WSUS. If you want to choose all products, check the box next to Microsoft Corporation. To select all of the products within a product family, check the box next to the product family.

4. After selecting the desired products, click **OK** to continue. This takes you back to the Synchronization Options window shown previously in Figure 6.11.

5. Click the **Change** button underneath Update classifications. The Add/Remove Classifications window will appear (see Figure 6.13).

Figure 6.13 Managing Update Classifications

6. Select the boxes next to the classifications you want WSUS to manage.

7. After selecting the desired classifications, click **OK** to continue. This will take you back to the Synchronization Options window shown previously in Figure 6.11.

8. Click the **Save settings** button. Once your changes have been saved, you will see the notification window shown in Figure 6.14.

9. Click **OK** to close the notification window.

Figure 6.14 Saving Settings

Viewing Updates

After configuring WSUS to download the correct updates and synchronize with Microsoft's servers, you are ready to view your updates. The home page for the WSUS administration console provides a summary of the total number of updates on your server (see Figure 6.15). It shows you how many updates are approved, not approved, and declined. It also shows you how many updates your computer needs and how many total computers are missing updates. The home page allows you to look at a glance to see where you stand with updates.

Figure 6.15 Using the Home Page of the WSUS Administration Console

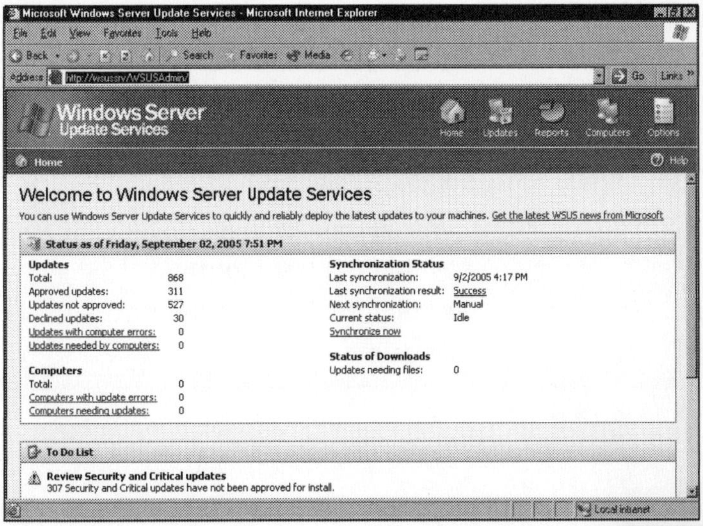

To view all updates, click the **Updates** button on the home page of the WSUS administration console (see Figure 6.15). The Updates window will appear (see Figure 6.16). From there, you can view the complete list of updates. This window is separated into three sections—the Update Tasks section, the View selection section, and the Filtered View section. The Update Tasks section is covered later in this chapter. For now we focus on the View selection and Filtered View sections.

If you do not want to see all of the updates at once, filtering your view is recommended. A standard deployment of WSUS has close to 1000 updates. As you can imagine, it is difficult to navigate through this many updates at one time. Once you modify your filter, WSUS will use the new settings every time you return to the Updates page.

You can filter based on products and classifications, approval status, or synchronization dates. Table 6.5 lists all of the filter options. Once you apply your filter, WSUS will refresh the screen with only the matching updates. You can then sort these updates by title, classification, release date, or approval status. You can also search all updates for keywords. This makes it very easy to find the update you need without having to scroll through all of the possible updates.

Table 6.5 Understanding Update Filters

Category	Criteria
Products and classifications	Critical and security updates
Products and classifications	All updates
Products and classifications	WSUS updates
Products and classifications	Custom
Approval	Install
Approval	Detect only
Approval	Remove
Approval	Decline
Approval	Any approval
Approval	Not approved
Approval	All updates
Synchronized	Within the last week
Synchronized	Within the last month
Synchronized	Within the last two months
Synchronized	Any time

Figure 6.16 Viewing the Updates

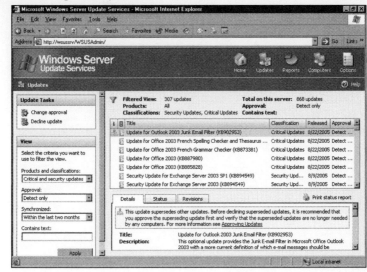

Now that you know how to narrow down your list of updates, let's look at the properties of an update using the Update for Outlook 2003 Junk Email Filter (KB902953) as an example. The first thing you notice is that the title of the update includes the Microsoft knowledge base number, which makes it very easy to read upon the update. You can find knowledge-based articles by going to http://support.microsoft.com and typing the KB number into the "search field". The filtered view also lets you quickly see what type of update it is (critical update), when it was released (August 22, 2005), and its approval status (Detect only).

If you want more information about the update without actually going to the Internet and reading the KB article, read the details at the bottom of the Filtered View section. Figure 6.17 shows the Details tab of this update, which contains details such as description, does the update require a reboot, does the update require user input, and so on. Table 6.6 explains the information listed on the Details tab.

Figure 6.17 Viewing the Details of Update KB902953

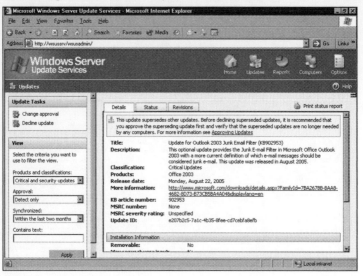

Table 6.6 Understanding the Details Tab

Detail	Explanation
Title	Shows the name of the update
Description	Explains the purpose of the update
Classification	Tells which classification the update falls under (i.e., security update, critical update, service pack)
Products	Lists for which products this update is recommended
Release date	Shows when the update was made available
More information	A URL to Microsoft's Web page about the update
KB article number	Shows the knowledge-based article released for this update
MSRC number	Lists the Microsoft Security Response Center number for this update
MSRC severity rating	Shows the Microsoft Security Response Center rating for this update
Update ID	Displays the Globally Unique Identifier (GUID) assigned to this update
Removable	Indicates if update can be removed after installation
May request user input	Tells if the update requires user interaction

Continued

Table 6.6 continued Understanding the Details Tab

Detail	Explanation
Must be installed exclusively	Indicates if the update must be installed by itself
Includes	Lists other updates contained in this update
Included by	Lists other updates that contain this update
Supersedes	Shows which update(s) this update replaces
Superseded by	Shows which update(s) replaced this update
Languages supported	List the languages supported by this update
EULA	Tells if this update has an End User License Agreement (EULA)

The Status tab is the tab you would use to see which machine in your environment was missing a particular update (see Figure 6.18). It shows the status of the file, such as if the file has been downloaded or not. It tells you the approval status of the update and indicates if a deadline has been set for installing the update. It also shows the status of the update for each of your computer groups. The status can be *installed*, *needed*, *not needed*, *unknown*, or *failed*.

A status of *installed* indicates the update was successfully installed. A status of *needed* means the machine needs the update but had not installed it yet. *Not needed* tells you the machine does not match the criteria for installing the patch (e.g., a patch for Windows XP would not be needed on Windows 2000). *Unknown* means WSUS does not know the status of the update for a given machine. These usually occur when WSUS knows about a new update, but the client machine has not checked in yet. *Failed* is the one option you hope not to see. It indicates that the machine needed the update, but was not able to install it.

The Revisions tab is shown in Figure 6.19. It displays the revision number, title, release date, and approval status for the update. This tab can be used to determine if you are installing the latest version of an update. For each of these tabs, click the **Print status report** button to print out the information shown on the screen.

Figure 6.18 Using the Status Tab

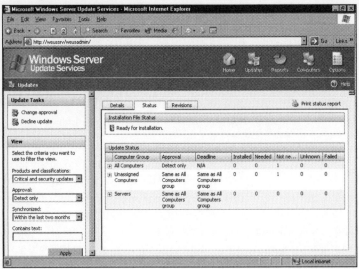

Figure 6.19 Using the Revisions Tab

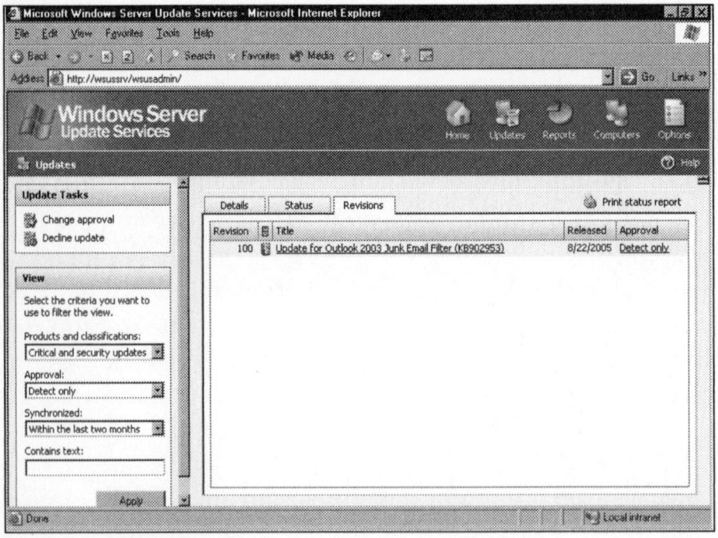

Approving Updates

After downloading and viewing your updates, you need to approve them. Until you approve your updates, WSUS will not do anything with them. The term "approve updates" is a little misleading. When you hear "approve updates," you probably assume that you are allowing WSUS to install an update. As logical as this may sound, it is incorrect. Approving an update just means you are telling WSUS what action to take with the update. Installing the update it just one of the possible approved actions.

You have four choices when approving updates—Decline, Remove, Detect only, and Install. Until you choose one of these, updates (other than Critical Updates and Security Updates) are set to not approved, meaning WSUS will do nothing with the update. Critical Updates and Security Updates are always set to Detect only. Setting an update to Decline will instruct WSUS to not install the update and to remove it from the list of available updates. Only set an update to decline if you are certain that none of your machines need or will need this update. Configuring an update to Remove will cause WSUS to uninstall the update from the client machine. This option is not supported on all updates. As with declining an update, you must make sure your client machines no longer need the update before you set it to Remove.

Setting an update to Detect only, tells WSUS not to install the update but to check and see if the machine needs the update. When the client computer checks in with the WSUS server, WSUS will scan the machine to see what updates are installed. If the machine is compatible with and needs the update, then WSUS will make a note of it on the Updates page and in the Status of Updates report. Figure 6.20 shows the WSUS administration console home page. Look at the Computers section underneath the Status section. It says Computers needing updates. If you click on this link it will load the Status of Computers report shown in Figure 6.21.

Figure 6.20 Looking for Updates on the Home Page

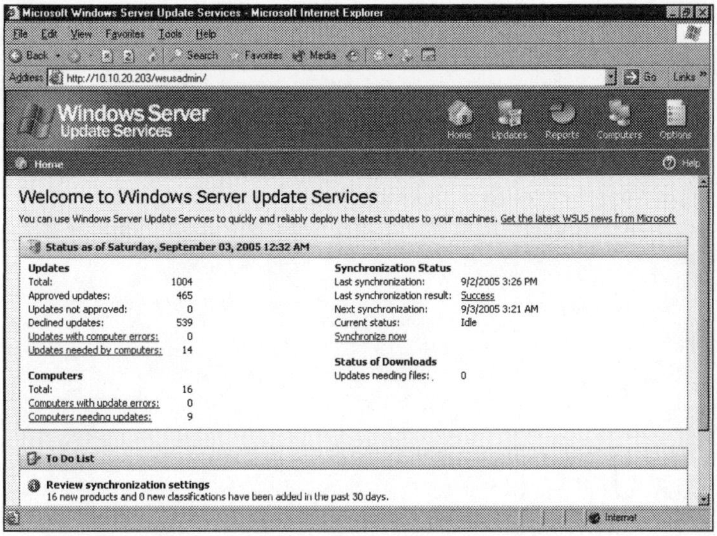

From the Status of Computers report on this WSUS server, you can see there are nine machines needing updates. The first machine, *ctoddpc.tc.ads*, needs six updates. It was last updated on September 2, 2005. No updates have ever failed or come back with an unknown status. It lets you know that WSUS is successfully talking to the client machines and that the client machine has been successful in downloading updates from WSUS.

Figure 6.21 Viewing the Status of Computers

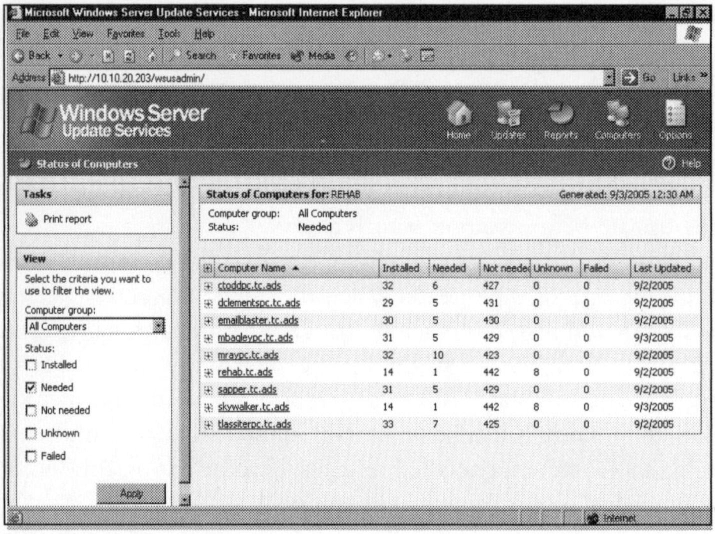

When you expand the *ctoddpc.tc.ads* entry it shows the name of each needed update along with its approval level and status (shown in Figure 6.22). In this example, you can see that the updates for *ctoddpc.tc.ads* have been approved for install, but they haven't been installed yet. Once the installation time set through group policy for the client machine is reached, the update will be installed.

Figure 6.22 Looking at Needed Updates

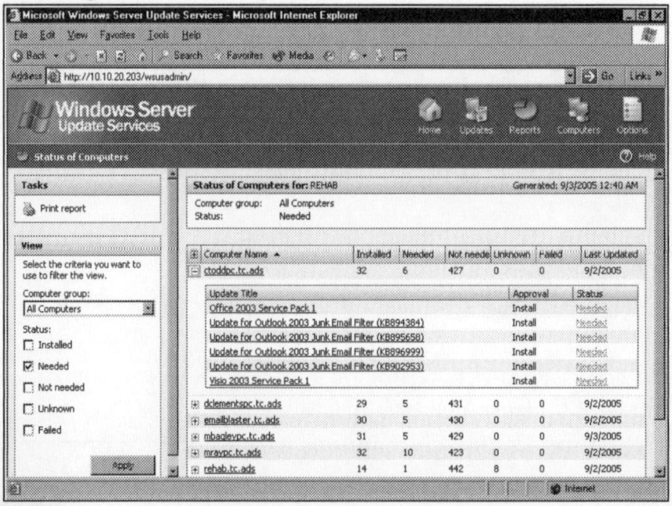

When you set an update to *Install*, it is installed on the client machine at the next scheduled interval. By default, exactly when it is installed depends on the choices you made when setting up the group policies for WSUS; however, you can set a deadline for the installation. This allows you to set exact dates and times when the update will be installed. Deadlines override any settings on the client machine.

If you want to have an update installed immediately the next time the machine checks back in with WSUS, you can set a deadline with a date in the past. Since the date has already passed, WSUS will think it missed it the first time and force the update to start installing. Please note that you cannot use deadlines for updates that require user interaction. Using deadlines on these updates will cause the installation to fail. This can be determined by looking at the *May request user input* field in the Details tab of an update (shown previously in Figure 6.17).

Approving an Update for Installation with a Deadline

You will now see how to use a deadline to force an update to be installed at a certain time. In this section, we are going to install the Update for Outlook 2003 Junk Email Filter (KB902953). We are going force the install to occur on September 9, 2005 at 5:00 P.M.

1. Open the WSUS administration console by typing *http://wsus_server_name/wsusadmin* (where wsus_server_name is the name of your WSUS server), as shown in Figure 6.23.

2. Click on the **Updates** button in the upper right-hand corner of the administration console. The Updates window will appear (see Figure 6.24).

Figure 6.23 Using the Home Page

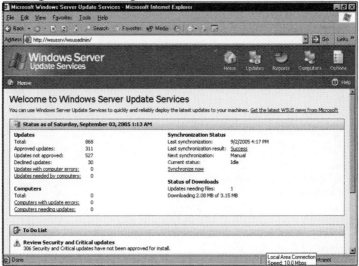

Figure 6.24 Changing the Approval of Updates

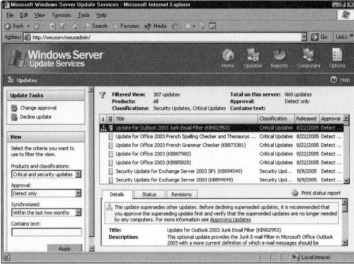

3. Select the update you wish to approve for installation.

4. Click on the **Change approval** button underneath Update Tasks. The Approve Updates window will appear (see Figure 6.25).

Figure 6.25 Selecting Install

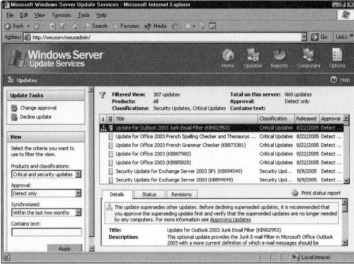

5. Click the drop-down arrow next to **Approval**.

6. Select **Install** from the list.

7. Click **None** next to Deadline. The Edit Deadline window will appear (see Figure 6.26).

Figure 6.26 Choosing a Deadline

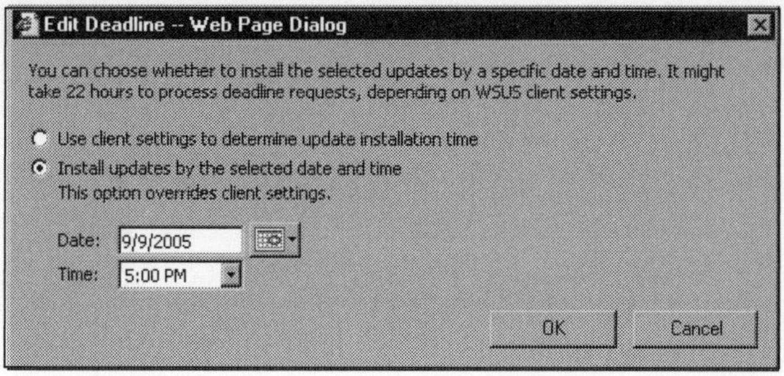

8. Type in the date or click on the calendar button to choose the date from the calendar shown in Figure 6.27.

9. Type in the time when you want the update to be installed.

10. Click **OK** to save your deadline changes. You'll go back to the Approve Updates window shown in Figure 6.25.

11. Click **OK** to save your changes. The update approval status will now change to Install, as shown in Figure 6.28.

Figure 6.27 Picking the Month and Day

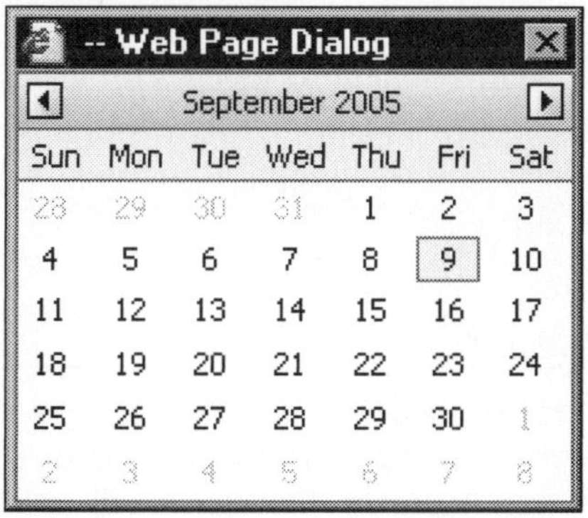

Superseding and Superseded Updates

Some updates are meant as replacements for other updates. Notice that the Update for Outlook 2003 Junk Email Filter (KB902953) supersedes the other updates for each tab (see Figure 6.28). An update may supersede another update for many reasons. The most popular reasons are enhancements or improvements to the original update. Just because a superseding update is released, don't assume you should automatically decline the previous update. The superseding update might not work with all operating systems. For example, a new Windows XP update might replace an older update that worked on both Windows XP and Windows 2000. However, the newer update may not run on Windows 2000. Declining the older update would leave your Windows 2000 machines at risk.

Figure 6.28 Verifying the Change

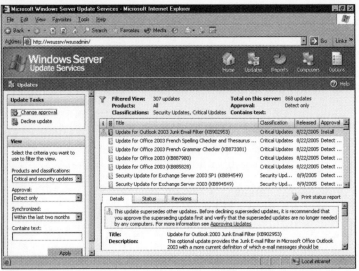

You can tell that an update supersedes a previous update by the symbol next to the update (see Figure 6.28). The symbol next to Update for Outlook 2003 Junk Email Filter (KB902953) looks like a flow chart with one blue rectangle at the top and three grey rectangles at the bottom. This same symbol is put next to older updates that have been superseded by newer updates.

BEST PRACTICES ACCORDING TO MICROSOFT

Microsoft recommends not declining superseded updates unless you are 100 percent sure it is no longer needed. The WSUS documentation gives the following examples of when you may need to install a superseded update:

- If a superseding update supports only newer versions of an operating system, and you are running older versions of the operating system in your environment.
- If a superseding update has more restricted applicability than the update it supersedes.
- If an update no longer supersedes a previously released update due to new changes. Because of changes made with each update release, an update may not supersede an update that it superseded in a previous version. However, WSUS will still show the earlier update as a superseded update.

SOME INDEPENDENT ADVICE

You may find it easier to follow the simple rule of not declining updates that you previously approved. This way, both the newer and older updates are available just in case. No harm can come from leaving the older update approved for installation.

Automatic Approvals

So far, you have learned how to manually approve updates. WSUS also supports setting updates for automatic approval. Using automatic updates allows you to put WSUS on autopilot. It will keep your machines up to date without your interaction. This is the preferred way to use WSUS as it removes the potential for human error. You do not have to worry about forgetting to approve updates.

WSUS allows you to set automatic approvals differently for each machine group. This allows you to use automatic updates without having to update all of your machines (e.g., you may want to automatically approve all updates for your workstations, but not for your servers). By dividing your machines into two separate computer groups you can put both servers and workstations on their own update routine.

You can set WSUS to automatically approve updates for detection or installation based on the classifications of the update. For instance, you may want all security updates and critical updates to automatically be installed, and drivers and service packs to only detect which machines need the update. This allows you to keep your servers secure without having to load all available updates.

NOTE

If you ever have conflicting settings between detection rules and installation rules, the installation rules will always take precedence.

WSUS can also be configured to automatically approve revisions to already approved updates (enabled by default). There are many reasons an existing update might be revised. Perhaps the update has expired. Maybe it has been tweaked to add or remove certain features. Sometimes the update itself has not changed, but the EULA has. If you disable this feature, WSUS will deploy the old version of the update until you manually approve the new version.

Configuring WSUS to Use Automatic Approvals

You will now learn how to configure WSUS to automatically approve critical updates and security updates for a "servers" computer group. Notice as you proceed through the steps that WSUS is configured by default to automatically approve the latest revision of already approved updates and to automatically approve updates to WSUS.

1. Navigate to the WSUS administration console by typing in **http://wsus_server_name/wsusadmin** (where *wsus_server_name* is the name of your WSUS server) (See Figure 6.29.)

Figure 6.29 Opening the WSUS Administration Console

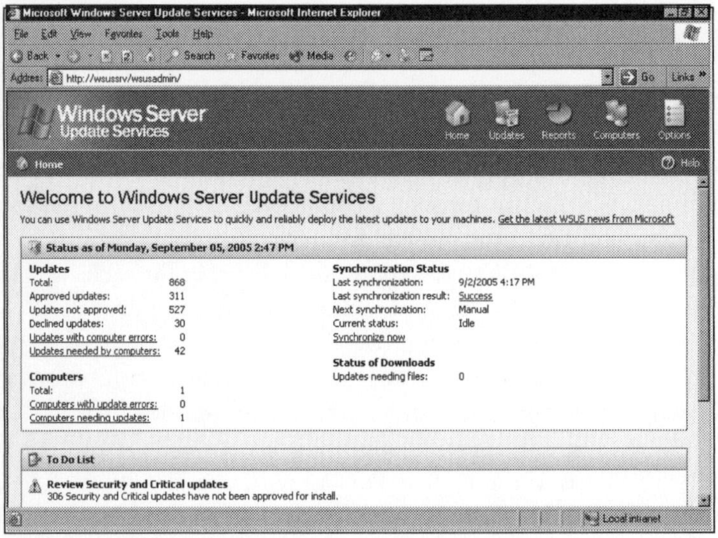

2. Click the **Options** button in the upper right-hand corner of the administration console. The Options window will appear (see Figure 6.30).

Figure 6.30 Using WSUS Options

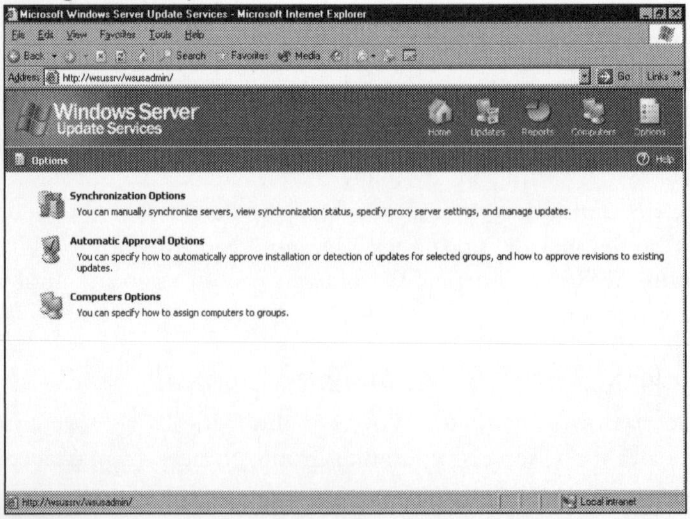

3. Click the **Automatic Approval Options** button. The Automatic Approval Options window will appear (see Figure 6.31).

Figure 6.31 Setting Automatic Approval Options

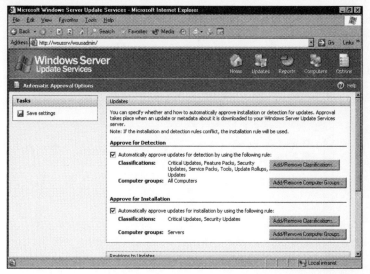

4. Check the box next to **Automatically approve updates for installation by using the following rule** under the Approve for Installation section.

5. Click the **Add/Remove Classification** button. The Add/Remove Classifications window will appear (see Figure 6.32).

Figure 6.32 Selecting Classifications

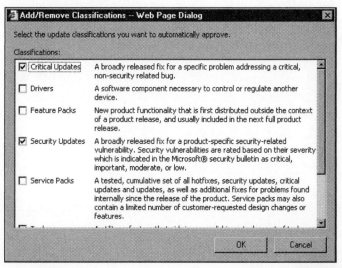

6. Choose the classifications that you want to automatically be approved. For this exercise, check the boxes next to Critical Updates and Security Updates.

7. Click **OK** to save your classification choices and return to the Automatic Approval Options window shown in Figure 6.31.

8. Click the **Add/Remove Computer Groups** button to go to the Computer Groups window shown in Figure 6.33.

Figure 6.33 Choosing Computer Groups

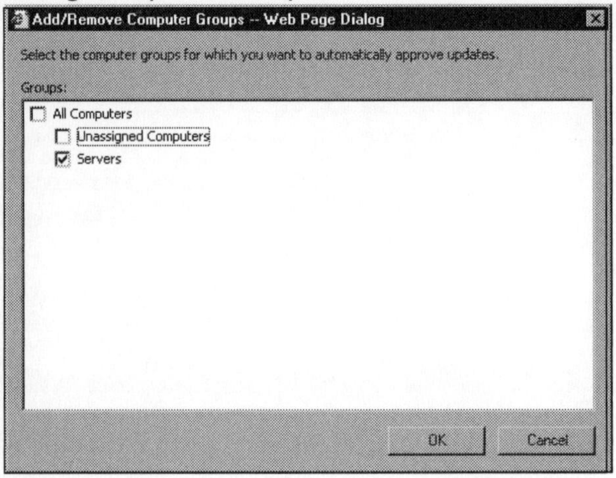

9. Select the groups you want WSUS to automatically update. For this exercise, choose the **Servers** group.

10. Click **OK** to continue.

11. From the Automatic Approval Options window, scroll down and verify that the radio button next to **Automatically approve the latest revision of the update** is selected under the Revisions to Updates section, as shown in Figure 6.34.

12. Verify that the checkbox next to **Automatically approve WSUS updates** is selected under the WSUS Updates section (also Figure 6.34).

13. Click the **Save settings** button under Tasks. This will give you the window shown in Figure 6.35.

Figure 6.34 Verifying Revisions and WSUS Updates

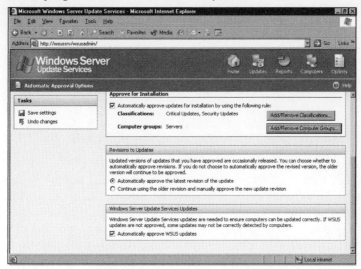

Figure 6.35 Saving Settings

14. Click **OK** in the notification window. WSUS is now configured to automatically approve updates.

Testing Updates

Obviously, it is important to keep your machines up to date. If not, you wouldn't be reading a book about WSUS. However, you must also protect your company's uptime by not haphazardly pushing out every update that comes along. There is a fine line between not patching enough and overdoing it.

The reason we patch machines is to make them secure and stable so we can improve our uptime. We must make sure that the updates themselves do not cause downtime. This can be accomplished by testing updates before rolling them out to production machines. Microsoft recommends having a test environment that closely mimics your production environment.

The easiest way to do this is to create separate WSUS computer groups for production and testing. Configure the test group to automatically install updates. Have the production group detect only needed updates. After you have updated your test machines and given them enough time for problems to occur, you can approve the updates for installation to your production group.

Shortcuts...

Minimizing the Risk of Patch Management

Depending on the size of your environment, you may want several stages of testing. First, you can roll updates out to the machines in your test lab. If there are no problems, you may roll them out to the Information Technology (IT) department. If the update works for IT, push them out to a few other departments before you update all of your machines. By gradually updating your machines you are reducing the risk associated with patch management.

Backing Up and Restoring WSUS Servers

Microsoft does not provide a specific tool for backing up or restoring WSUS. However, you can use the backup program built into Windows (*ntbackup*) to get the job done. You can use a third-party backup product if you prefer. The backup software does not have an extra component or agent to back up WSUS like it would for Exchange or Structured Query Language (SQL). As long as it can back up the file system, it will work

When backing up WSUS, you must be sure to back up everything you may need in case of a disaster, including the metadata and the update files. Backing up the metadata will allow you to restore information about your clients, information about synchronized updates, and the configuration information of your WSUS server. Without the metadata, you would have to completely reconfigure your WSUS server if it failed. Backing up the update files will keep you from having to download all of the updates again in case of a failure. If you are storing updates on Microsoft's servers, you will not have any local update files to backup; however, you should still back up the metadata.

BEST PRACTICES ACCORDING TO MICROSOFT

Always try to keep an offsite copy of your backups. This way, in the case of a disaster in your data center, you will still have access to the tapes.

Using *NTBackup* to Back Up WSUS

We will now walk you through using *NTBackup* to backup WSUS. In this example, we will back up the *c:\WSUS\MSSQL$WSUS* folder and the *e:\WSUS\WsusContent* folder.

1. Click the **Start** button.

2. Select **Run** from the Start menu.

3. Type **ntbackup** into the Open box.

4. Click **OK** to open *ntbackup*. The Backup Utility window will appear (see Figure 6.36).

Shortcuts...

Using NTBackup without Wizard Mode

NTBackup runs in Wizard mode by default. This is fine if you need to back up or restore a file. If you just want to view the files that have been backed up or you want to schedule a backup, you may find it easier not to use wizard mode. To exit Wizard mode, uncheck the box next to use Wizard mode and close **NTBackup**. The next time you open *NTBackup* it will be in normal mode.

Figure 6.36 Using NTBackup

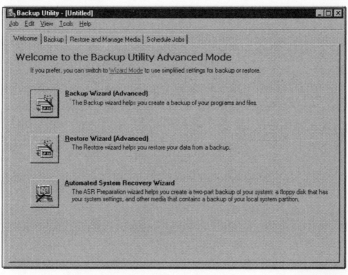

5. Click the **Backup** tab. This will take you to the window shown in Figure 6.37.

Figure 6.37 Selecting the Metadata

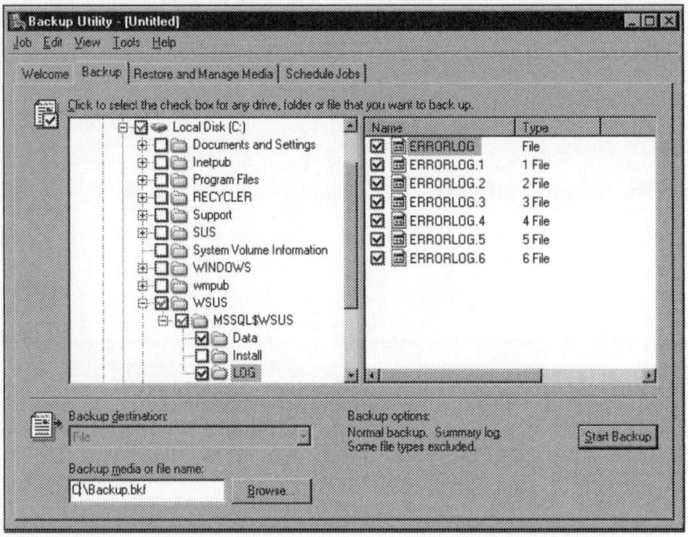

6. From here you must select which files to back up.

    ■   To back up the metadata, navigate to *c:\WSUS\MSSQL$WSUS* and select the **Data** and **LOG** folders, as shown in Figure 6.37.

    ■   To back up the update files, navigate to the **WSUS** folder on the drive that holds the update files and select the **WsusContent** folder, as shown in Figure 6.38.

Figure 6.38 Selecting the Update Files

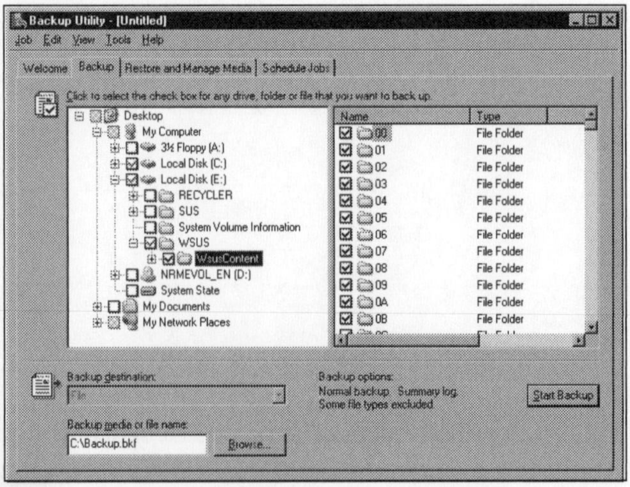

SOME INDEPENDENT ADVICE

When you are selecting folders to be backed up, make sure you see a blue check and not a grey check. The blue check indicates you are backing up all files and subfolders. The grey check means you are only backing up some of the files.

7. Choose the location where you want to store the backup. For this exercise, the backup will be stored on the *c:* drive in a file named *Backup.bkf.*

8. Click the **Start Backup** button. The Backup Job Information window will appear (see Figure 6.39).

Figure 6.39 Configuring the Backup Job

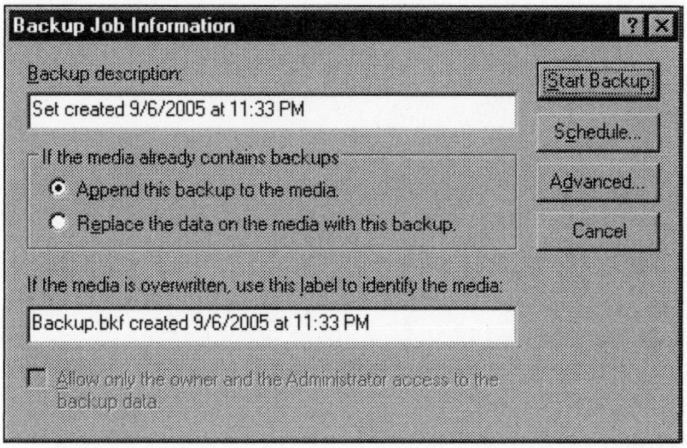

9. Type in a name for the backup description and click the **Advanced** button. The Advanced Backup Options window will appear (see Figure 6.40).

10. Check the box next to **Verify data after backup** to have *NTBackup* verify that the backup worked.

Figure 6.40 Verifying the Data After Backup

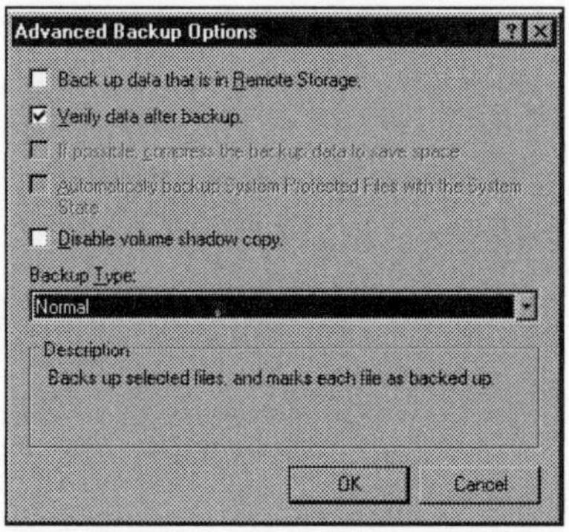

11. Make sure the backup type is set to **Normal**.

12. Click **OK** to continue. This will start the backup and display the progress window shown in Figure 6.41.

Figure 6.41 Watching the Backup Progress

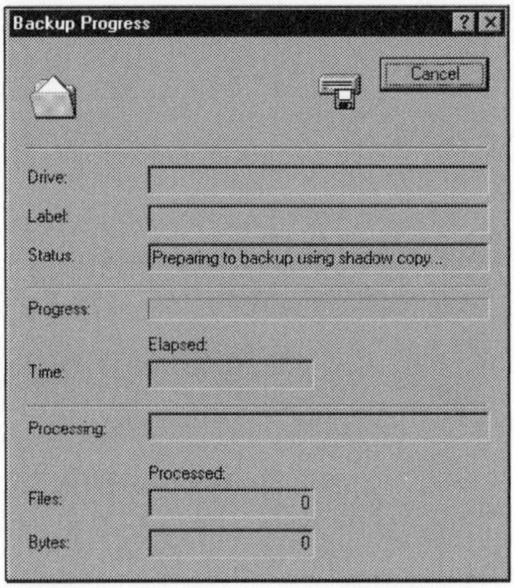

13. Once the backup is complete, the Backup Progress window will show a report button as shown in Figure 6.42. Click **Close** to exit the backup job or click **Report** to view the details of the backup.

Figure 6.42 Completing the Backup

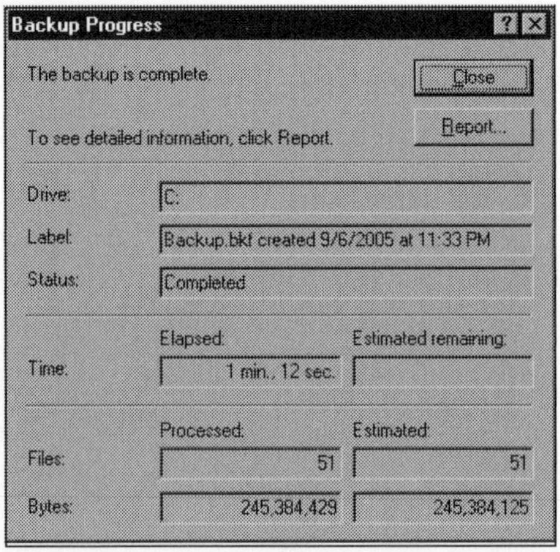

Using NTBackup to Restore WSUS

Now that we have backed up WSUS, we will show you how to restore it using
NTBackup. We will restore the *c:\WSUS\MSSQL$WSUS* folder and the
e:\WSUS\WsusContent folder to their original location.

1. Click the **Start** button.

2. Select **Run** from the Start menu.

3. Type *ntbackup* into the Open box.

4. Click **OK** to open *ntbackup*.

5. Click on the **Restore and Manage Media** tab as shown in Figure 6.43.

Figure 6.43 Restoring from Backup

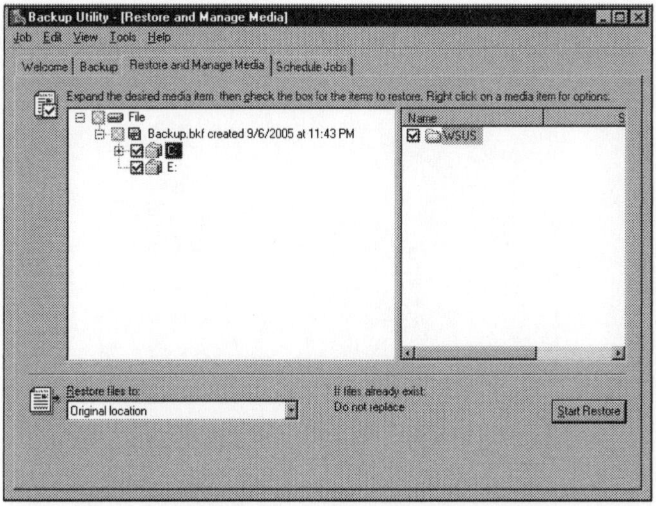

6. Select the folders where WSUS is stored (e.g., *c:* and *e:* for this example).

7. Click the **Start Restore** button. The Confirm Restore window will appear
   (see Figure 6.44).

8. Click **OK** to start the restore.

9. As your data is restored, you can see its status in the Restore Progress window
   shown in Figure 6.45. Once the restore is complete, the Restore Progress
   window will show a report button (see Figure 6.46). Click **Close** to exit the
   restore job or click **Report** to view the details of the restore.

Figure 6.44 Confirming Restore

Figure 6.45 Watching Restore Progress

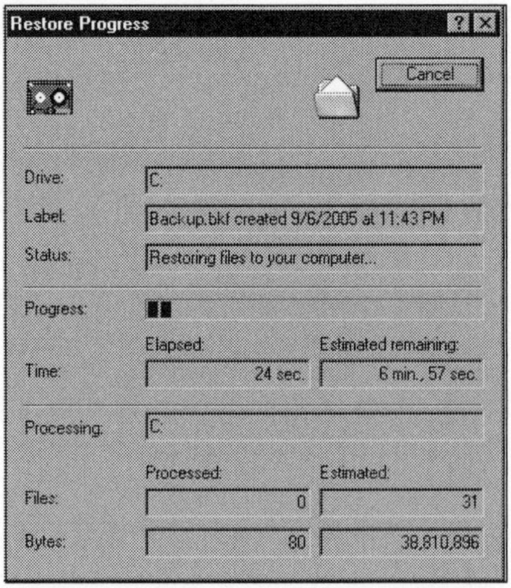

Figure 6.46 Completing the Restore

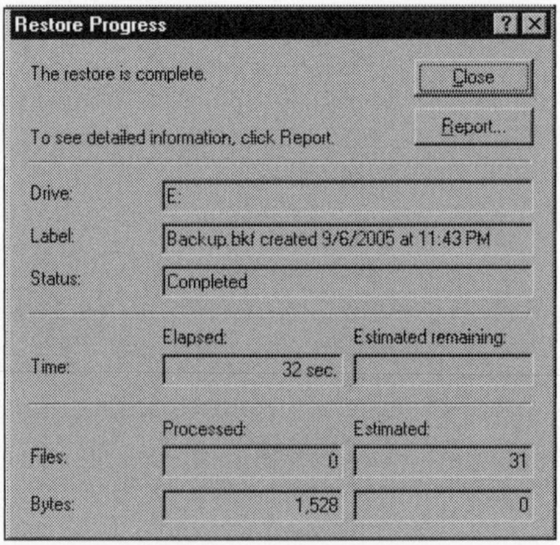

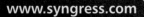

Summary

A lot more work goes into administering WSUS servers than some people realize. You must configure WSUS for daily downloads and synchronizations. After synchronizing, you must view all of the possible updates and decide what to do with them. If you decide to install the updates, you must properly test them to make sure they work in your environment. After all this, you must be sure to backup your WSUS server in case of failure.

When configuring WSUS for downloading and synchronizing you must do the following:

- Choose a time for WSUS to perform daily synchronizations.

- Allow WSUS to access the Internet.

- Select where WSUS will store updates—locally or on Microsoft's servers.

- Choose the languages supported by WSUS.

- Select which products WSUS will update.

- Choose which update classifications will be downloaded by WSUS.

Managing updates involves:

- Viewing which updates are available. You can filter this view to make it easy to find what you need.

- Approving updates for clients. You can set an update to Decline, Remove, Install, or Detect only.

- Testing updates before rolling them out to production. You can use WSUS computer groups to target your testing.

When backing up and restoring WSUS you need to be familiar with the following:

- The storage location of the updates and metadata
- Using backup software to back up the local file system
- Using backup software to restore the local file system

Solutions Fast Track

Downloading and Synchronizing Updates

☑ You must synchronize your WSUS server before it will update clients.

☑ Before synchronizing, you should configure WSUS for Internet access, tell WSUS where to store updates, choose which products to support, and select which update classifications and languages to download.

☑ WSUS can be configured to automatically download updates at half-hour increments or configured for manual synchronizations.

☑ By default, WSUS downloads updates that match the locale of the WSUS server.

☑ Updates can be stored locally or on Microsoft's servers.

☑ When storing updates on Microsoft's servers, all clients must download their own copy of the updates from the Internet.

☑ When storing updates locally, WSUS downloads the updates once. In turn, the clients download the updates from WSUS.

☑ When storing updates locally, you have the option to use Express installation files.

☑ Express installation files deploy quicker, but take longer to download initially.

☑ You can use command line tool *WSUSUtil.exe* to change the storage location for locally stored WSUS updates. This is useful when you outgrow your existing drive.

Managing Updates

☑ Managing updates consists of three main areas—viewing updates, approving updates, and testing updates.

☑ Update classifications break the updates into categories. Each category serves a slightly different purpose.

☑ There are 11 different update classifications, with the most common ones being critical updates, security updates, service packs, and update rollups.

☑ WSUS currently supports 11 different products spread across four product families.

☑ Product families (such as Exchange) group together products (i.e., Exchange 2000 Server and Exchange Server 2003).

☑ When you view updates in WSUS, you can filter your view to only show certain classifications or products.

☑ When approving updates, you are telling WSUS what action to take with a given update.

☑ Do not assume that approving an update means it will be installed.

☑ There are four possible choices for update approval—Decline, Remove, Detect only, and Install.

☑ Setting an update approval to Decline means the update will not be installed. It will be removed from the list of available updates. Only decline an update if you are sure none of your clients will need it.

☑ Approving an update for Detect only will instruct WSUS to locate all machines in need of an update. This is the default setting for critical and security updates.

☑ Setting an update to Remove will cause the update to be uninstalled from client machines. Not all update support being removed.

☑ Configuring updates to Install will cause the updates to be installed on client machines in need of the update.

☑ Properly test all updates before deploying them to your production network.

☑ The easiest way to test updates is to approve the update for a small group of machines and see if there are any adverse reactions.

Backing Up and Restoring WSUS Servers

☑ WSUS does not contain a separate tool for performing backups and restores.

☑ Backups are performed using *ntbackup* or another third-party backup solution.

☑ You must backup both the metadata and the update files.

☑ By default, the metadata is stored in the WSUS database in the *c:\WSUS\MSSQL$WSUS* directory.

☑ The update files are stored in the *WSUS\WsusContent* directory on the drive selected to hold updates.

☑ If your client's are pulling updates from Microsoft's servers, you will not have any local update files to backup.

Frequently Asked Questions

The following Frequently Asked Questions, answered by the authors of this book, are designed to both measure your understanding of the concepts presented in this chapter and to assist you with real-life implementation of these concepts. To have your questions about this chapter answered by the author, browse to **www.syngress.com/solutions** and click on the **"Ask the Author"** form.

Q: Are all updates automatically downloaded to my WSUS server? Won't this use a lot of disk space?

A: Yes. This would require a lot of space. However, by default, WSUS only downloads an update once it has been approved for installation. This way you only have to store updates you will be using.

Q: Can I add my own updates to WSUS?

A: No. WSUS only supports updates originating from Microsoft Update servers.

Q: When is a good time to have my WSUS server synchronize?

A: WSUS should be scheduled to synchronize during off-peak hours. You want WSUS to synchronize when it will not put a burden on your Internet connection. Typically, this is at night between 1:00 A.M. and 4:00 A.M.

Q: Why do express installation files take so much longer to download?

A: Express installation files aren't just a copy of the update itself. Express installation files work by only pushing the differences between an updated file and non-updated file. This requires the express installation files to contain every possible variation of the file they are updating, so they can calculate the differences. Containing these extra files is what makes them so large.

Q: Which products does WSUS update?

A: Microsoft may update the list at any time. The plan is for WSUS to eventually update all of Microsoft's corporate software. At the time this book was written, WSUS supported the following products:

- Exchange 2000 Server
- Exchange Server 2003

- Office 2002/XP

- Office 2003

- SQL Server

- Windows 2000 family

- Windows Server 2003 family

- Windows Server 2003, Datacenter Edition

- Windows XP 64-Bit Edition Version 2003

- Windows XP family

- Windows XP x64 Edition

Q: Which languages are supported by WSUS?

A: WSUS supports all languages supported by all versions of the Windows operating system.

Q: Is it true that WSUS uses the Microsoft Baseline Security Analyzer (MBSA) to scan machines to determine needed updates?

A: No. Microsoft created a separate scanning engine for WSUS. It does not use MBSA.

Q: Can I deploy updates across multiple domains in the same forest by using one WSUS server?

A: Yes. WSUS is not dependent on your domain structure. As long as WSUS has network communication with all of the machines it will work.

Q: Why should I back up my WSUS server? Can't I just download all of the updates again?

A: Yes. You can download all of the updates again. What you cannot download is your WSUS configuration. This configuration includes things such as the approval status of your updates and WSUS synchronization settings. By backing up your WSUS server, you won't have to reconfigure your WSUS server if it crashes.

Q: Do I have to use Microsoft's backup software to backup WSUS?

A: No. Everything you need to recover WSUS is backed up at the file-system level. Any functional third-party backup software will work.

Chapter 7

Configuring and Administering WSUS Clients

Solutions in this chapter:

- **Using Active Directory**

- **Using Local Settings**

- **AU Client**

- **Using WSUS to Update Clients and Servers**

- **AU Client Investigation**

☑ **Summary**

☑ **Solutions Fast Track**

☑ **Frequently Asked Questions**

Introduction

Windows Software Update Services (WSUS) has a client-server relationship; therefore, client software must be configured and rolled out in order for clients to properly communicate and eventually become updated by the server. Clients can be rolled out to your target audience in a few different ways. The differences in topology, Active Directory design, and layout, whether to use Active Directory or not, and the physical location of clients are factors in deciding how to activate client machines in your WSUS environment. This chapter focuses on the different options you have for configuring your clients for automatic updates, and once configured, updating these clients at regular intervals. We touch on the actual mechanics of the client software piece, called the Automatic Update (AU) client, and its job in the updating process. We offer insight into some of the steps and processes it takes to update your clients and servers, pointing out some of the "gotchas" we have seen in the WSUS community. We point out some of the new functionality WSUS has included over its predecessor, System Update Services (SUS), offering not only operating system (OS) updates for a number of versions of Windows, but also Microsoft Office products such as Word and Excel as well as the server products from Microsoft (e.g., Structured Query Language [SQL] Server and Exchange). Lastly, we discuss several different measures you can take when investigating client connectivity and troubleshooting updating issues.

Using Active Directory

Active Directory is the most efficient way to implement WSUS in your environment, especially if you have a lot of client machines to update. One of Active Directory's key features is its ability to help administrators push out client changes to multiple machines quickly and effectively using Group Policy. Group Policy is Active Directory's central mechanism for making changes and distributing them in a global fashion. By design, its architecture is one to many, which is our focus for defining the client-server relationship between AU clients and WSUS.

BEST PRACTICES ACCORDING TO MICROSOFT

- Microsoft recommends that you use the power of the Group Policy Object (GPO) when rolling out WSUS to multiple computers. It also recommends that you refrain from editing your default domain or default domain controller GPO to make these changes.
- Use the Group Policy Management Console (GPMC) when creating and managing GPOs. To obtain the latest GPMC, go to *microsoft.com/downloads* and search for GPMC Service Pack 1.

Some Independent Advice

- Consider using separate GPOs when dealing with computers that fall into different WSUS computer groups due to computer function or application software. This way, you only affect one computer group when making GPO changes for installation and reboot times.
- In a complex environment, you may have to create many computer-specific GPO's to accommodate varying client types and the different ways in which you want them updated and rebooted. With this in mind, try to organize your organizational unit (OU) structure in such a manner that all the objects in that OU will apply that GPO, and refrain from using GPO filtering. By default, when you create a GPO and link it to an OU, all the objects in that OU will apply to that GPO. To have that same GPO apply only to a specific set of objects in an OU, you can use GPO filtering and only apply the GPO to objects you specify in the Access Control List (ACL) of that GPO. This is not recommended.

Group Policy

Active Directory Group Policy is used as a means for administrators to make policy changes in a single GPO and then deploy that policy to multiple machines (e.g., work-stations, servers, or domain controllers). In order for any Group Policy to have content, it must contain what are known as Administrative Template (ADM) files, which are stored with an *.adm* file extension. WSUS is no different, having its own template file consisting of all the settings needed to configure and schedule automatic client updates. The WSUS template file is called *wuau.adm* and is discussed in the next section.

The *wuau.adm* File

The WSUS *wuau.adm* file is the core of all WSUS client configuration settings. This template can be configured globally via Group Policy, or locally via local machine policy. Windows 2000 Server, Server 2003, and XP class operating systems all ship with this file, located under the *%windir%\inf* directory. This file may be different for each Windows client; however, as clients check into the WSUS server the first time, they are updated to the latest AU client as well as the latest local template file. At this point, the template file will contain *only* the settings specific to the particular OS version and Service Pack level. When using Active Directory Group Policy, the local client *wuau.adm* template files remain un-configured, as the policy is actually coming from the *wuau.adm* template configuration on the Domain Controller (or Controllers) and is saved in the client local registry. Only when clients are configured directly by means of local Group Policy is this local template file used. This is discussed in more detail in the "Using Local Settings" section of the chapter. Regardless of how clients are configured (Active Directory GPO or local GPO), the settings are the same. Tables 7.1 and 7.2 identify the settings contained within the computer and user portions of the *wuau.adm* ADM, as well as the OS level required to support them.

WSUS is limited to the client OS and service pack version; therefore, we have listed the OS requirements for successful interaction with your WSUS server. Note that down-level clients such as Windows NT, Windows 98, and Windows ME do not contain and cannot use the *wuau.adm* template file because it is not compatible with WSUS. If you are still using older clients, you should look at deploying a more secure and supported OS such as Windows XP that can actively participate in your patch update deployment strategy:

- Microsoft Windows 2000 Server, Advanced Server, and Professional with Service Pack 3 (SP3) or greater
- Microsoft Windows Server 2003 Standard, Enterprise, Datacenter and Web Edition with any Service Pack
- Microsoft Windows XP Professional with any Service Pack

Table 7.1 *wuau.adm* File Computer Configuration Settings and Requirements

Policy Setting	OS Requirements
Do not display the *Install Updates and Shut Down* option in the Shut Down Windows dialog box	Windows XP SP2
Do not adjust the default option to *Install Updates and Shut Down* in the Shut Down Windows dialog box	Windows XP SP2
Configure the AUs	Windows Server 2003, XP SP1, 2000 SP3
Specify the intranet Microsoft update (MU) service location	Windows Server 2003, XP SP1, 2000 SP3
Enable client-side targeting	Windows Server 2003, XP SP1, 2000 SP3
Reschedule the AUs scheduled installations	Windows Server 2003, XP SP1, 2000 SP3
No auto-restart for scheduled AU installations	Windows Server 2003, XP SP1, 2000 SP3
AU's detection frequency	Windows Server 2003, XP SP1, 2000 SP3
Allow AU's immediate installation	Windows Server 2003, XP SP1, 2000 SP3
Delay the restart for scheduled installations	Windows Server 2003, XP SP1, 2000 SP3

Continued

Table 7.1 continued *wuau.adm* File Computer Configuration Settings and Requirements

Policy Setting	OS Requirements
Re-prompt for restart with scheduled installations	Windows Server 2003, XP SP1, 2000 SP3
Allow non-administrators to receive update notifications	Windows Server 2003, XP SP1, 2000 SP3

Table 7.2 *wuau.adm* File User Configuration Settings and Requirements

Policy Setting	Minimum OS Requirement
Remove access to all Windows Update features	Windows XP, Windows Server 2003
Do not display the *Install Updates and Shut Down* option in the Shut Down Windows dialog box	Windows XP SP2
Do not adjust the default option to Install Updates and Shut Down in the Shut Down Windows dialog box	Windows XP SP2

SOME INDEPENDENT ADVICE

Although all of the *wuau.adm* template settings state that the required OS version level for Windows XP is Service Pack 1 (SP1) or higher, Windows XP with no Service Pack is supported; however, it requires extra work in order to be compatible with WSUS. The AU client version 5.4.26x that ships in the out-of-the-box Windows XP bits is not compatible with WSUS because it is at a version level that cannot *self-update*, which is required in order to obtain the needed AU client version that enables your clients to successfully interact with your WSUS server. As mentioned earlier, a self-update happens the first time a compatible AU client checks in with your WSUS server to update to the latest WSUS AU client version. Thus, for Windows XP clients with no Service Pack installed, you must manually update to at least the legacy Software Update Services client version 5.4.36x before it can automatically self-update itself to the AU client version necessary to work with your WSUS server (i.e., client version 5.8.x). It is highly recommended, however, that you at least install Windows XP SP1, if not Service Pack 2 (SP2), to bring your clients to a more secure and self-updateable OS. However, if you cannot install Windows XP SP1, you can download and install the latest WSUS AU client from *microsoft.com/downloads* and push it out via Group Policy or another third-party deployment solution. The latest client distribution is called WindowsUpdateAgent20-x86.exe version 2.0, which can be

downloaded at *http://go.microsoft.com/fwlink/?Linkid=43264.* As an alterna-
tive, you can configure these clients to point to the public Windows or MU sites
and have them update the AU client in this way.

For advanced administrators, visit *http://msdn.microsoft.com/library/
default.asp?url=/library/en-us/wua_sdk/wua/updating_the_windows_update_
agent.asp* to learn more about using the *wuredist.cab* file to distribute the
latest version of the AU client using a signed installation package.

Note that if you are using Active Directory and GPOs to configure WSUS clients,
the local copy of the *wuau.adm* file is not used. This file is only used when configuring
local Group Policy on client machines in environments where Active Directory is not
used. This also means that if you make changes to the local template file and that computer is also subject to an Active Directory GPO, the Active Directory GPO will win
and overwrite the local settings.

Configuration

Configuring your Active Directory clients for WSUS updates is accomplished via
Windows Group Policy. The following steps will get you started with your first WSUS
GPO using the GPMC.

1. Click **Start | Run** and type *gpmc.msc* to open up GPMC. This is also acces-
   sible under your Administrative Tools menu item called Group Policy
   Management.

2. Expand your domain name and right-click on the **GPOs container**. Click
   New, and name your Group Policy WSUS AUs in the New GPO window's
   name field.

3. Click **OK** to create your new policy.

4. Right-click on the **WSUS AUs policy** and click **Edit**.

5. Expand Computer Configuration and highlight **Administrative Templates**.

6. Right-click **Administrative Templates** and choose **Add/Remove
   Templates** (see Figure 7.1).

Figure 7.1 Adding a Template to Your WSUS Group Policy

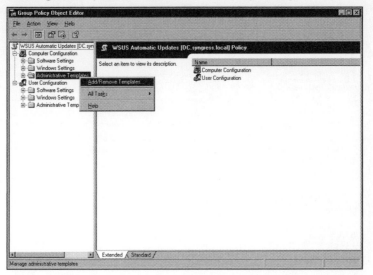

7. Highlight *wuau.adm* and click **Close (see Figure 7.2)**.

Figure 7.2 Adding the WSUS *wuau.adm* File to Your Template

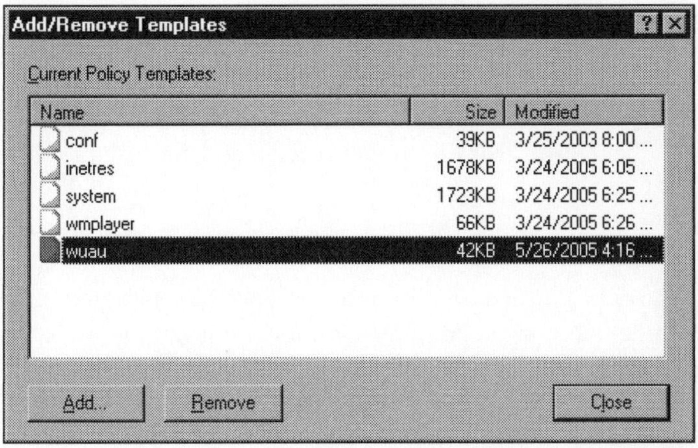

8. Under Computer Configuration, expand **Administrative Templates |
    Windows Components** and highlight **Windows Update**.

Figure 7.3 shows the configurable settings for your WSUS clients.

Figure 7.3 Configurable WSUS Client Settings

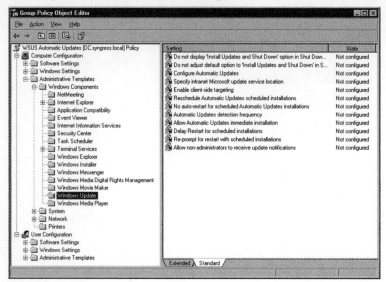

WSUS Client Settings

There is a chance that your WSUS clients do not all share the same update requirements. Different software installations, scheduled downtimes, and Service Level Agreements (SLAs) are all good reasons to have different WSUS client settings, which is why it is important to identify similar clients so that they can be grouped together to fit into similar WSUS Computer Groups. As the Computer Groups are assigned specific software updates, all clients in that group will receive updates based on the settings defined in the GPO.

Computer Configuration Settings

Group Policy consists of both computer- and user-specific configuration settings. The following list includes all of the Computer Configuration settings available in the *wuau.adm* administrative template. After loading the AU template into your GPO, these settings are located under **Computer Configuration | Administrative Templates | Windows Components | Windows Update**.

- **Do not display Install Updates and Shut Down' option** If this option is enabled, *Install Updates and Shut Down* from the shutdown dialog window options will be disabled. This is a workstation-only setting that can only be set on Windows XP SP2 machines. You may want to use this if you do not want your end users to physically install their own updates, but rather let WSUS do it for them.

- **Do not adjust default option to Install Updates and Shut Down in Shut Down Windows dialog box** By default, *Install Updates and Shut Down* will be the first choice on Windows XP SP2 machines after updates are downloaded and the users choose to shut down their machines. If you do not make this the default, but you do make it show up last in the shutdown dialogue window, you can enable this option. Remember, this setting has no effect if the *Do not display Install Updates and Shut Down* option in the Shut Down Windows dialog box is enabled.

- **Configure Automatic Updates** This is the on/off switch for WSUS client updates and is required if you are going to use a WSUS server. If enabled, you are required to choose one of the four automatic updating options (see Figure 7.4).

Figure 7.4 Configure AU Settings

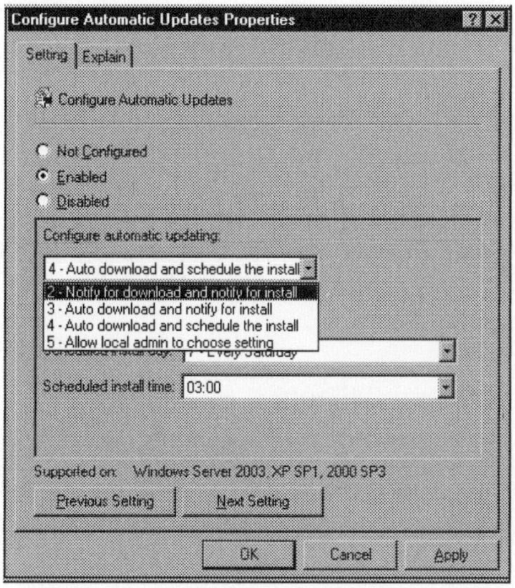

Table 7.3 Automatic Updating Setting Explanations

AU Setting	Explanation
2 - Notify for download and notify for install	This setting will *not* download or install any approved updates automatically, and will only notify you with the AU' task bar pop-up balloon when you logon to the machine. First, the updates are ready to be downloaded and then they are ready to be installed.

Continued

Table 7.3 Automatic Updating Setting Explanations

AU Setting	Explanation
3 – Auto download and notify for install	This setting *will* download approved updates automatically, but *will not* install them automatically. Instead, you will be notified by the AU task bar pop-up balloon when you logon to the machine (see Figure 7.5).
4 – Auto download and schedule the install	This setting will download approved updates automatically, as well as schedule them to be installed, based on your *Scheduled install day* and *Scheduled install time*. If you log on to the machine before the scheduled time, you will be notified by the AU task bar pop-up balloon that the updates are ready to be installed. It is up to you whether or not you want to install them on-demand prior to the scheduled time.
5 – Allow local admin the choose setting	This setting does not set any download or installation schedule for approved updates via Group Policy. Instead, it allows the administrator to make the settings locally on the machine. In this case, the AU Graphical User Interface (GUI) will not be grayed out, and will allow local changes.

Figure 7.5 AU Task Bar Popup Balloon

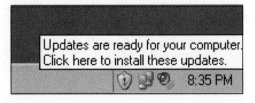

NOTE

If you select option 4, *Auto download and schedule install time*, you must also select the day and time that you want your updates to be downloaded and installed. Use the Schedule install day and Schedule install time drop-down boxes. You can choose to install either every day or one day during the week. Installation times are based *only* on the hour and can be scheduled anytime throughout the 24-hour clock.

- **Specify intranet Microsoft update service location** This is a required setting that specifies your WSUS server update and statistics update locations. Use standard Uniform Resource Locator (URL) heading syntax and type in the path to your WSUS server Web site (see Figure 7.6). If you are using Secure Sockets Layer (SSL) to encrypt traffic data, use *https://WSUSServer.* Remember that SSL is only used for encrypting the metadata while obtaining updates, and your WSUS server still requires that you have port 80 open for other communications.

Figure 7.6 WSUS Server Update and Statistics Location

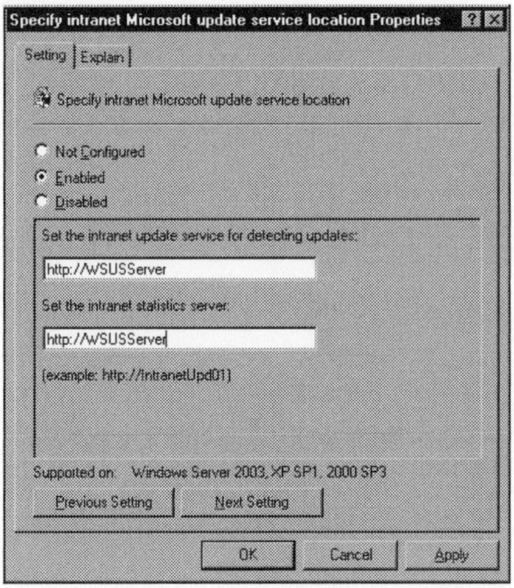

- **Enable client-side targeting** This setting is specific to how you set up your server. There are two ways of organizing clients as they connect and populate your WSUS server. On your WSUS server Admin webpage, under **Options | Computer Options** you have two choices (see Figure 7.7).

Figure 7.7 Computer Options

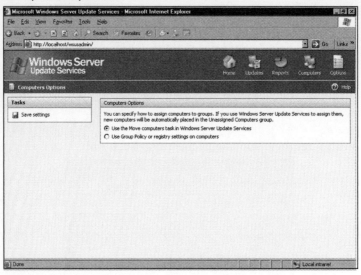

- **Use the Move computers task in Windows Server Update Services**
  This manual process is known as *server-side targeting*. You must move computers as they show up under Unassigned Computers into the Computer Group of choice. *Use Group Policy or registry settings on computers* is known as *client-side targeting*. With client-side targeting, destination Computer Groups must be created prior to enabling this setting in the policy. If it is not enabled, the computers will not show up in your WSUS console. Type your **Computer Group name** in the *Target group name for this computer* field exactly as it was entered in your WSUS Admin console under **Computers | Create a computer group** (see Figure 7.8). Note that client-side targeting uses a cookie on the local client to store group membership information. These cookies are refreshed every hour. If you move computers to different groups when using client-side targeting, it may take up to one hour to display in your WSUS console. Consider using the following command-line option to refresh the local cookie on a recently moved computer:

```
wuauclt.exe /resetauthorization /detectnow
```

Figure 7.8 Client-Side Targeting

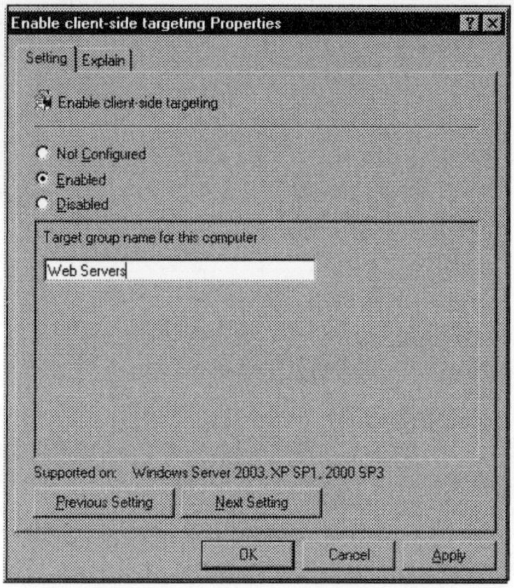

> **NOTE**
>
> You can use only one of these targeting methods. If you use client-side tar-
> geting and then switch to server-side targeting, remember to reconfigure your
> policies or you may have issues with clients checking in. Also note that if you
> are moving computers between computer groups, it may take up to one hour
> for that information to be refreshed in your WSUS Admin console.

- **Reschedule Automatic Updates scheduled installations** This setting
  refers to the amount of time your computer will wait after it has been restarted
  and has missed a previously scheduled installation. By default, this is set at 1
  minute. If you enable this policy, you can increase that time interval up to 1
  hour. Alternatively, if you disable this setting, your computer will not install
  missed scheduled updates until the *next* scheduled interval time specified in
  your "Configure Automatic Updates" setting. Also note that this setting
  requires that option 4 – "Auto download and schedule install time" be configured in your "Configure Automatic Updates" setting.

- **No auto-restart for scheduled Automatic Updates installations** *READ
  THIS CAREFULLY!* This setting *does not* mean that computer restarts are
  suppressed for *all* scheduled installations. If this setting is enabled, scheduled
  installations will *not* automatically reboot only if an Administrator is logged on,
  but will prompt the logged-on user that the computer *will* be automatically
  rebooted in 5 minutes. The user will have the option to suspend the reboot by

clicking the **Restart Later** button (see Figure 7.9), unless the scheduled installation was sent using a "deadline," in which case a mandated reboot will occur,
not giving the logged-on administrator an option to restart later. This goes
hand in hand with the option to enable "Re-prompt for restart with scheduled
installations." This setting allows you to delay the reboot with a time you
specify to re-prompt for reboot after the first prompt for reboot is suppressed.
Note also, that this setting requires that option 4, *Auto download and schedule
install time,* be configured in your Configure Automatic Updates setting.
Remember, if you do not reboot, the updates will not take affect. This is a
potential security risk and should be considered when designing your WSUS
scheduled updates and reboots.

Figure 7.9 AU Reboot and Restart Options

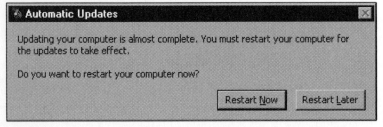

- **Automatic Update detection frequency** This setting determines the frequency that your computer will check in with your WSUS server to see if
  there is anything to download or install. By default, this is set to 22 hours.
  Based on the fact that many computers might be set with the same times, a
  randomization offset of 0 to 20 percent is subtracted from the time you specify.
  Consequently, if you choose a 10-hour update frequency, your computer will
  check in sometime between 8 to 10 hours apart.

- **Allow Automatic Updates immediate installation** This setting determines whether your computer will install updates that are non-intrusive to
  Windows and cause no interruption. This also means that there is no chance of
  the installation causing a reboot.

- **Delay Restart for scheduled installations** This setting decides whether
  you want to change the default reboot wait time of 5 minutes after a scheduled installation completes. Note that this setting requires that option 4 –
  "Auto download and schedule install time" be configured in your "Configure
  Automatic Updates" setting.

- **Reprompt for restart with scheduled installations** This setting is meant
  to allow a re-prompting for reboot for scheduled installations that happen
  while someone is logged onto a machine and suspend the initial prompt for
  reboot. The default wait time is set at 10 minutes.

NOTE

As long as a user stays logged on, they can suspend the reboot prompt on each appearance unless the scheduled installation was sent using a "deadline," which mandates a reboot. If this is the case, you will see a pop-up message (see Figure 7.10) with the Restart Later option grayed out. Also note that this setting requires that option 4, *Auto download and schedule install time*, be configured in your Configure Automatic Updates setting.

Figure 7.10 AUs Mandatory Restart

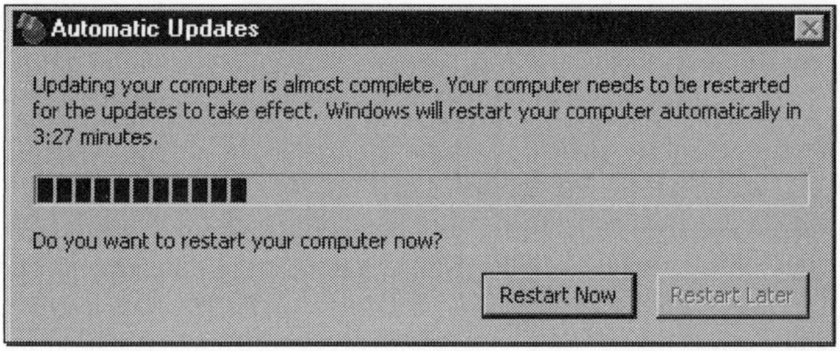

Automatic Updates

Updating your computer is almost complete. Your computer needs to be restarted for the updates to take effect. Windows will restart your computer automatically in 3:27 minutes.

Do you want to restart your computer now?

Restart Now   Restart Later

- **Allow nonadministrators to receive update notifications** If enabled, this setting will allow any user with rights to logon to a computer the ability to see the AUs notification pop-up balloons for download and installation updates. It is recommended that you leave this as the default and not enable it for your servers. Administrators see these notifications by default only. You may want to enable this for your end-users machines if they are not the local administrators of their own workstations; however, you still want them to see that their machines are being updated.

SOME INDEPENDENT ADVICE

There may be some confusion over the name of the public version of Microsoft's on-line update service. At the time of this writing, Microsoft is in a transition between the old version, Windows Update, and the new version, MU. MU updates the family of Microsoft products unlike its predecessor, Windows Update, and much like WSUS and SUS, respectively. The confusion arises over the inconsistent use of the old and new names. For example, the links to the online update service in Internet Explorer 6 is still entitled Windows Update; the link from the Start menu of Windows XP SP2 is MU. This confusion should be short-lived; however, an explanation may help clear things up until the transition is over.

User Configuration Settings

There are a few user-specific AU settings that primarily focus on the Microsoft's Internet version of WSUS called Windows Update or Microsoft Update. (See the preceding sidebar.) As the administrator of your patch deployment, you may want to use these settings to disable users' access to the public deployment site, so that you have complete control over what is approved for installation.

- **Remove access to use all Windows Update features** If enabled, this option disables all features of the Internet version of Windows Update located at *http://windowsupdate.microsoft.com*. If enabled, users will not be able access the AU Control Panel applet or the Windows Update shortcut link under **Start | All Programs | Windows Update**. In addition, users will not be able to access the Windows Update site when searching for driver updates. This setting is only compatible with Windows XP and Windows Server 2003 versions of the OS.

- **Do not display *Install Updates and Shut Down* option in Shut Down Windows dialog box** If you enable this option, you *disable* the display of 'Install Updates and Shut Down' from the shutdown dialogue window options. This is a workstation-only setting and can only be set on Windows XP SP2 machines. You may want to use this if you do not want your end users to physically install their own updates, but rather let WSUS do it for them.

- **Do not adjust default option to Install Updates and Shut Down in Shut Down Windows dialog box"** By default, *Install Updates and Shut Down* will be the first choice on Windows XP SP2 machines after updates are downloaded and the user chooses to shut down their machine. If you do not want to make this the default, but make it show up last in the shutdown dialog window, you can enable this option. Remember, this setting has no effect if the **Do not display Install Updates and Shut Down option in Shut Down Windows dialog box** is enabled. You may want to choose this option if you are worried about end users clicking on it by accident.

There is one more location that resembles the *Remove access to use all Windows Update features*. However similar, it differs owing to its compatibility with the Windows 2000 line of operating systems'. If you navigate to **User Configuration | Administrative Templates | Start Menu and Taskbar**, you will find a configuration setting called *Remove link and access to Windows Update*. If you enable this setting, AUs will be disabled for use with the public Windows Update site; however, it will still function with your WSUS server for approved updates only. Consider using this setting if you want to maintain complete control over your patch update deployment environment.

Most WSUS settings are configurable in the Computer Configuration portion of Group Policy. If you decide not to use any of the User Configuration settings, it is recommended that you disable this portion of the GPO. This will speed up client policy download and refresh times and improve network bandwidth utilization. To disable the User Configuration portion of your WSUS GPO follow these steps:

1. Click **Start | Run |** *gpmc.msc* to open your GPMC.

2. Navigate to and highlight your **WSUS specific GPO**.

3. Click the **Details** tab in the right-hand window.

4. At the bottom, click the drop-down box labeled GPO Status: and select **User Configuration settings disabled** (see Figure 7.11).

5. Click **OK** when asked, "Do you want to change the status for this GPO to User Configuration settings disabled?"

6. Click **File | Exit** to save your GPO.

Figure 7.11 Disabling User Configuration GPO Settings

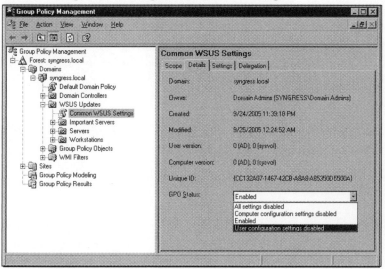

GPO Location and the Use of OUs

The use of OUs is critical for organizing your clients when designing how you want to deploy your WSUS updates. Remember that when you create a GPO and link it to a particular OU, all of the machines under that OU apply the settings in your GPO. This could become a potential problem if there are machines in the same OU requiring different installation and reboot schedules. To help design your GPO placement strategy in Active Directory, first separate your servers and your workstation clients into separate OUs, but make them both part of a similar sub-OU (see Figure 7.12).

Figure 7.12 WSUS OU Design

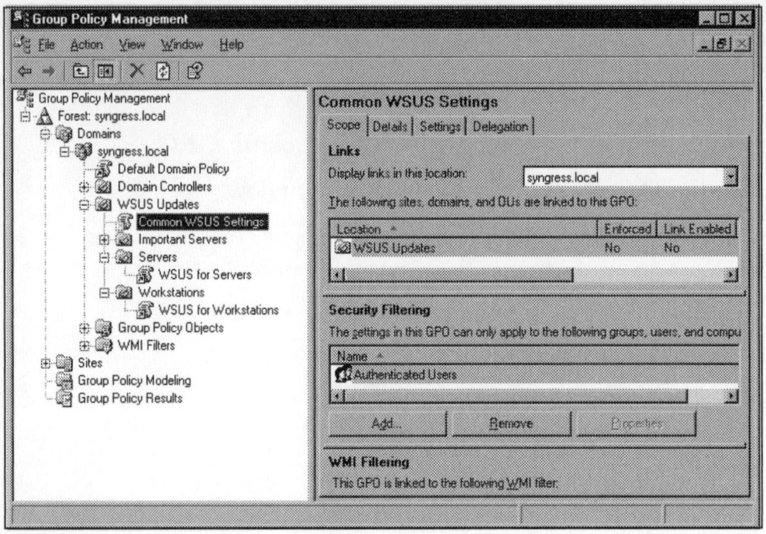

The underlying reason why you might want to design your OU structure like this is based on the fundamentals of GPO application order, shown in its acronym form Active Directory Group Policy application order (LSDO).

- Local Policy
- Site Policy
- Domain Policy
- OU Policy
- Sub-OU

Group Policy is applied in the order shown in the preceding list of bullets, with the last policy taking precedence over previous policy settings; therefore, you should make all common WSUS settings on your parent OU. For example, if all of your servers and workstations point to the same WSUS server, have the same detection frequency interval, allow immediate installation of non-intrusive updates, and require that a restart not happen if an administrator is logged on, you could configure each of the following policy settings in a GPO linked to the parent OU.

- Specify intranet MU service location
- AU detection frequency
- Allow AU immediate installation
- No auto-restart for scheduled AU installations

All machines under your parent OU will receive those settings. The other policy settings that must be different for servers as opposed to workstations, can be configured in GPO's linked to the root of the Server's OU and the Workstation's OU, respectively. The same rule applies if you have different needs for individual servers or individual workstations, keeping common settings at the root of the OU, and applying unique settings to a GPO linked to the OU that the physical computer object resides under. You can always use the Resultant Set of Policies (RSoP) feature of Windows XP and Windows 2003 to help you when troubleshooting the exact policy outcome a computer receives once all of your policies are in place. You can access this by clicking on **Start | Run |** *rsop.msc*. You can also use the GPMC's Group Policy Results Wizard to connect to a remote machine. The Windows 2000 OS does not support either the Group Policy Results Wizard or RSoP. For these older clients, you must obtain a copy of the Windows 2000 Resource Kit Supplement 1, and use a utility called *gpresult.exe*, which will display all of the group policies that a machine has applied.

One thing you may notice about using Group Policy is the delay in time between your policy changes and the time it takes your WSUS clients to recognize and adhere to those changes. By default, machines in an Active Directory Domain refresh their Domain Group Policy settings once every 90 minutes, with a random offset of 30 minutes. It is typically a good idea to keep these default settings in an effort to reduce the network traffic of hundreds, maybe thousands of machines refreshing and downloading their policies all the time; however, there may be instances where you need those policies to be refreshed immediately. This is possible although it varies depending on client OS version. For Windows XP and Windows 2003 machines, issue the following command-line syntax to force a Group Policy update:

```
gpupdate.exe /force
```

As noted earlier, you can also update only the portion of the GPO you want to refresh. For example, if you just wanted to update your computer-specific GPO settings you would type:

```
gpupdate /target:computer /force
```

For Windows 2000 machines, issue the following command:

```
secedit /refreshpolicy machine_policy /enforce
```

Using Local Settings

When faced with machines that are not part of an Active Directory forest, that sit in a workgroup, that are offset in a more secure part of your network like a Demilitarized Zone (DMZ), or have random one-off stand-alone machines that facilitate a third-party application, local settings are your best bet for configuring WSUS client updates. Even if your machines sit in a legacy Windows NT 4.0 domain, an Active Directory WSUS server can still deploy updates to these machines as long as they have the correct local policy settings:

- Local Group Policy
- Local Machine Registry
- System Policy
- Control Panel

BEST PRACTICES ACCORDING TO MICROSOFT

- When using local settings to set your WSUS server location, Microsoft recommends using the fully qualified domain name of your server to insure correct name resolution (e.g., use http://WSUSServer.syngress.local instead of http://WSUSServer).
- If your non-Active Directory clients refer to a different Domain Name Server (DNS) or a DNS server without a zone for the domain name your WSUS server resides in, consider using a local hosts file for name resolution.
- Using the local Group Policy Editor, WSUS settings are saved and read from the policy section of the registry located under the following hive and key HKEY_LOCAL_MACHINE\Software\Policies\Microsoft\Windows\WindowsUpdate\.
- When using the AU User Interface (UI) or the Local Group Policy Editor, you may notice that WSUS changes happen immediately. Although the same key is manipulated when using tools like *regedit.exe* and *regedt32.exe*, to edit the local registry directly, the AU Client may need to be restarted to read those settings into memory.

SOME INDEPENDENT ADVICE

All methods for updating WSUS clients that use local settings are indirectly used to obtain the settings entered directly into the registry. This is where the AU client looks when deciding how it is supposed to be set.

Both Local Group Policy and Local Machine Registry settings can be tedious when you have to roll them out to a host of machines, because they typically require a manual visit to each client machine, whether via the console or using some type of remote connection software like Microsoft's Remote Desktop. This is one of the reasons Microsoft recommends you use Active Directory as much as possible. Being an administrator, however, you know that this is not always a reality. Consequently, you will be able to use the following basic guidelines for configuring and administering these settings.

Local Group Policy

Although Local Group Policy is last in the priority order when discussing LSDO, it is the highest in priority when dealing with non–ACTIVE DIRECTORY clients. Since there are no Site or Domain-specific GPO's on a stand-alone machine, the Local Group Policy is the one place to set and manage your WSUS policy settings.

To configure your stand-alone clients for WSUS updates, follow these steps using your local machine GPO Editor (formally known as the Group Policy Editor in Windows 2000):

1. Click **Start | Run** and type *gpedit.msc* to open up your GPO Editor.

2. Expand **Computer Configuration | Administrative Templates | Windows Components.**

3. Click on **Windows Update** and in the right-hand side of the window you will notice most of the same WSUS configurable settings, shown previously in the domain GPO Group Policy settings, depending on OS type and version. See Figure 7.13 for the local Group Policy configuration settings for a Windows XP SP2 machine.

Figure 7.13 Windows XP SP2 Local Group Policy

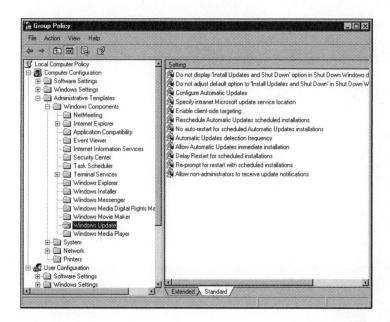

Once you configure settings in the local Group Policy of a client machine, those settings become effective immediately, because they are locally configured and there is no waiting for Group Policy update intervals to take place. However, this does not mean that the client will automatically contact your WSUS server; this depends on your detection interval setting. The default detection interval setting is every 22 hours, plus a random offset (discussed in more detail later in this chapter). To force your stand-alone client to check in with your WSUS server after a manual configuration change using local Group Policy, do one of the following.

To initiate a manual detection from the client to the WSUS server:

1. Click on **Start | Run** and type in **wuauclt.exe /detectnow**.

2. Click **OK.**

Stopping and starting the AU client will automatically force the WSUS AU client into a detection state, and thus will check in with its configured WSUS server.

1. Click on **Start | Run** and type **cmd** to take you to a Command Prompt window.

2. Type **net stop wuauserv** or **net stop "Automatic Updates"** to stop the AU client.

3. Type **net start wuauserv** or **net stop "Automatic Updates"** to start the AU client.

All of the settings previously discussed in Using Group Policy are the same settings that are available when using the local GPO Editor. Although the editing location is different, the configured registry keys are all the same.

Local Machine Registry

Regardless of the front end, almost all software configurations ultimately end up manipulating the Windows registry for final client configuration commitments. That being said, you can edit the registry directly to configure your WSUS-specific client configuration needs. In situations where Group Policy is not available due to the lack of an active Directory domain and where configuring local policy becomes too tedious because of each "logical" machine visit, a few scripting techniques might help you roll out the needed registry keys.

As mentioned, both Group Policy and Local Policy place their settings in the registry hive and keys shown here:

-   *HKEY_LOCAL_MACHINE\SOFTWARE\Policies\Microsoft\windows\WindowsUpdate*

-   *HKEY_LOCAL_MACHINE\SOFTWARE\Policies\Microsoft\windows\WindowsUpdate\AU*

Table 7.4 and Table 7.5 outline each of the possible registry key combinations, their possible key partners (if necessary), the registry key data type, and the corresponding Group Policy and Local Policy. The tables are divided to show you each key separately, the first showing the WSUS client environment variables and the latter showing the AU client's own configuration options.

Table 7.4 Windows Update Agent Environment Registry Keys

Key Name	Values	Data Type	Matching Group Policy
ElevateNonAdmins	Range = 1| 0		
	1 = Non-administrators are allowed to approve or disapprove updates.	Reg_DWORD	Allow non-administrators to receive update notifications.
	0 = Only users in the Administrators user group can approve or disapprove updates.		
TargetGroup	This is the name of the computer group to which you want your computer to belong (e.g., Exchange Servers.) This policy is paired with TargetGroupEnabled.	Reg_String	Enable client-side targeting.
TargetGroupEnabled	Range = 1 | 0 1 = Use client-side targeting.	Reg_DWORD	Enable client-side targeting.
	0= Do not use client-side targeting. This policy is paired with TargetGroup.		
WUServer	Hypertext Transfer Protocol (HTTP)/ Hypertext Transfer Protocol Secure Sockets (HTTPS)URL of your WSUS server used by your AU client. This policy is paired with		

Continued

Table 7.4 continued Windows Update Agent Environment Registry Keys

Key Name	Values	Data Type	Matching Group Policy
	WUStatusServer; both must be set to the same value in order for them to be valid.	Reg_String	Specify intranet MU service location.
WUStatus	HTTP/HTTPS URL of the server to which reporting information will be sent by AU's client. This policy is paired with WUServer; both must be set to the same value in order for them to be valid.	Reg_String	Specify intranet MU service location.

Table 7.5 AU Configuration Registry Keys

Key Name	Values	Data Type	Matching Group Policy
AUOptions	Range = 2 | 3 | 4 |5 2 = Notify before download. 3 = Automatically download and notify for installation. 4 = Automatically download and schedule installation (valid only when used with ScheduledInstallDay and ScheduledInstal Time values). 5 = AU is required, but local administrators can configure its settings.	Reg_DWORD	Configure AU.

Continued

Table 7.5 continued AU Configuration Registry Keys

Key Name	Values	Data Type	Matching Group Policy
AutoInstallMinor Updates	Range = 0 | 1 0 = Treat minor updates like other updates and use scheduled times. 1 = Silently install minor, non-intrusive updates.	Reg_DWORD	Allow AUs immediate installation.
DetectionFrequency	Range= 1 -22 Time between AU client detection cycles with your WSUS server. The default is set at 22.	Reg_DWORD	AUs detection frequency.
DetectionFrequency Enabled	Range = 0 | 1 1 = Enable detection frequency. 0 = Disable custom Detection Frequency, which means use the default.	Reg_DWORD	AUs detection frequency.
NoAutoRebootWith LoggedOnUsers		Reg_DWORD	
NoAutoUpdate	Range = 0 | 1 0 = Enable AUs 1 = Disable AUs	Reg_DWORD	Configure AUs.
RebootRelaunch Timeout	Range = 1–1440 (minutes) This is the time to wait before the AU client will re-prompt to restart after a scheduled restart has been issued.	Reg_DWORD	Re-prompt for restart with scheduled installations.

Continued

Table 7.5 continued AU Configuration Registry Keys

Key Name	Values	Data Type	Matching Group Policy
RebootRelaunch TimeoutEnabled	Range = 0 | 1 1 = Enable RebootRelaunch Timeout. 0 = Disable custom RebootRelaunch Timeout and use default value of 10 minutes.	Reg_DWORD	Re-prompt for restart with scheduled installations.
RebootWarning Timeout	Range = 1–30 (minutes) This configures the number of minutes you want your computer to wait before rebooting after a scheduled installation. The default is 5 minutes.	Reg_DWORD	Delay restart for scheduled installations.
RebootWarning TimeoutEnabled	Range = 0 | 1 1 = Enable Reboot WarningTimeout. 0 = Disable custom RebootWarning Timeout value and use the default.	Reg_DWORD	Delay restart for scheduled installations.
RescheduleWaitTime	Range = 1–60 (minutes) This is the amount of time your AU client should wait during a computer startup to install previously scheduled missed updates.	Reg_DWORD	Reschedule AU scheduled installations.

Continued

Table 7.5 continued AU Configuration Registry Keys

Key Name	Values	Data Type	Matching Group Policy
RescheduleWait TimeEnabled	Range = 0 | 1 1 = Enable RescheduleWaitTime. 0 = Disable RescheduleWaitTime (reschedule installation will be attempted at next scheduled interval).	Reg_DWORD	Reschedule AUs scheduled installations.
ScheduledInstallDay	Range = 0 | 1 | 2 | 3 | 4 | 5 | 6 | 7 0 = Every Day 1–7 = The days of the week starting with Sunday through Saturday. Paired with AUOption and only valid if option is equal to 4.	Reg_DWORD	Configure AU.
ScheduledInstallTime	Range = 1 – 23 Representing hours in the day using a 24-hour format. Paired with AUOption and only valid if option is equal to 4.	Reg_DWORD	Configure AU.
UseWUServer	Range = 0 | 1 0 = Don't Use WUServer. 1 = Use WUServer paired with WUServer. WUServer will not be used if this set to = 1	Reg_DWORD	Configure AU.

SOME INDEPENDENT ADVICE

When you use your Registry Editor to make WSUS changes, the UI shows those settings as "grayed out" and unchangeable, as do both Group Policy and Local Policy. The UI simply shows the changes that have been made. Be aware that because you cannot lock these down with Group Policy, anyone with the correct permissions can use the UI to change settings.

To give you an example of what a registry looks like after configuring the most common AU client requirements, the root of the *WindowsUpdate* key was exported.

Sample AU Client Registry Export

```
Windows Registry Editor Version 5.00

[HKEY_LOCAL_MACHINE\SOFTWARE\Policies\Microsoft\windows\WindowsUpdate]
"WUServer"="http://WSUSServer"
"WUStatusServer"="http://WSUSServer"
"ElevateNonAdmins"=dword:00000000

[HKEY_LOCAL_MACHINE\SOFTWARE\Policies\Microsoft\windows\WindowsUpdate\AU]
"UseWUServer"=dword:00000001
"NoAutoRebootWithLoggedOnUsers"=dword:00000001
"AutoInstallMinorUpdates"=dword:00000001
"DetectionFrequencyEnabled"=dword:00000001
"DetectionFrequency"=dword:00000006
"RescheduleWaitTimeEnabled"=dword:00000001
"RescheduleWaitTime"=dword:0000000f
"NoAutoUpdate"=dword:00000000
"AUOptions"=dword:00000004
"ScheduledInstallDay"=dword:00000006
"ScheduledInstallTime"=dword:00000003
```

Shortcuts…

Using the REG Command for a Quick Display of Client Setup

The quickest way to identify WSUS client settings is to create a simple script file that can be used to query the registry keys you are interested in, and pipe them to the console for quick review. This can be used for troubleshooting purposes or for random audits of your WSUS clients, to make sure that you are not having GPO inheritance, blocking, or conflict problems. To remotely query your WSUS computer's registry, you need the **reg.exe** command-line utility, which is part of the Windows Server 2003 and Windows XP source codeof. It is also part of the Windows 2000 Resource Kit Supplement 1 for Windows 2000 machines. The version included in Windows Server 2003 and XP can be used on Windows 2000 machines. The following code quickly enumerates the values of the HKEY_LOCAL_MACHINE\SOFTWARE\Policies\Microsoft\windows\WindowsUpdate registry key and its AU subkey and values. From a command prompt window, type the following (note that WSUSClient is the Network Basic Input/Output System (NetBIOS) name of your WSUS client host).

```
Reg.exe query
\\WSUSClient\SOFTWARE\Policies\Microsoft\windows\WindowsUpdate /s
```

The /s switch at the end of the command signifies that you want to retrieve all of the subkeys. The results of this query are as follows:

```
C:\>reg query \\WSUSClient\
HKLM\SOFTWARE\Policies\Microsoft\windows\WindowsUpdate /s

! REG.EXE VERSION 3.0

HKEY_LOCAL_MACHINE\SOFTWARE\Policies\Microsoft\windows\WindowsUpdate

    WUServer    REG_SZ   http://WSUS

    WUStatusServer     REG_SZ   http://WSUS

    ElevateNonAdmins    REG_DWORD       0x0

HKEY_LOCAL_MACHINE\SOFTWARE\Policies\Microsoft\windows\WindowsUpdate\
AU

    UseWUServer REG_DWORD       0x1

    NoAutoRebootWithLoggedOnUsers        REG_DWORD        0x1
```

Continued

```
   AutoInstallMinorUpdates       REG_DWORD          0x1

   DetectionFrequencyEnabled     REG_DWORD          0x1

   DetectionFrequency  REG_DWORD           0x6

   RescheduleWaitTimeEnabled     REG_DWORD          0x1

   RescheduleWaitTime  REG_DWORD           0xf

   NoAutoUpdate        REG_DWORD           0x0

   AUOptions    REG_DWORD           0x4

   ScheduledInstallDay REG_DWORD           0x6

   ScheduledInstallTime          REG_DWORD          0x3


C:\>
```

To simplify the command, program the keys that you want to randomly query as permanent environment variables on your workstation, so you do not have to retype them every time. For example, from the command line type the following:

```
Set WU=HKEY_LOCAL_MACHINE\SOFTWARE\Policies\Microsoft\windows\
WindowsUpdate

Reg.exe query \\WSUSClient\%WU% /s
```

Use **reg.exe** with the /v switch followed by y the value name if you just want to query a particular value. For example, if you want to query for the *DetectionFrequency* of a particular client, type the following:

```
Reg.exe query \\WSUSClient\%WU%\AU /v DetectionFrequency
```

Determining the client WSUS settings is easy once you are familiar with each of the value codes. You must be an administrator of the machines you are querying. If you are running these scripts from an Active Directory workstation against machines in a DMZ, make sure you authenticate with those machines first. You can use the **net use** command to authenticate to \\machinename\ipc$:

```
Net use \\machinename\ipc$ /user:username password
```

If you want to audit all of your machines, use the following script to pipe everything to a text file. All you need to do is populate the **machines.txt** file with a list of the clients you want to audit and use the internal Windows FOR command.

```
@ECHO OFF

Set WU=HKLM\SOFTWARE\Policies\Microsoft\windows\WindowsUpdate

If exist c:\wsusaudit.log del c:\wsusaudit.log

for /F %I in (c:\machines.txt) do @echo WSUS Results for %I >>
```

Continued

```
c:\wsusaudit.log & reg.exe query \\%I\%WU%\AU /s >> c:\wsusaudit.log
& @echo. >> c:\wsusaudit.log
```

View the **wsusaudit.log** on the c:\ root for the results. These examples give you the basis for quick and easy registry query information for your WSUS clients. In addition, for any machines that you need to configure using the registry, consider using the **reg.exe** command with the ADD or DELETE parameters to add, modify, or delete WSUS client registry keys in single or bulk fashion.

The registry seems like a very complex set of codes; however, once you learn its structure, maneuvering about and searching for keys and values becomes second nature. It cannot be stressed enough that the registry must be taken seriously. Misconfigurations and possible key and value deletions can quickly result in a non-working system.

SOME INDEPENDENT ADVICE

Remember, using the registry to configure WSUS clients is primarily for non-Active Directory machines. The power of Group Policy in both a management and a security perspective is far superior to using the local registry to make global settings.

System Policy

If you are one of the unfortunate administrators stuck maintaining a large legacy NT 4.0 domain and are worried about automating updates, stop worrying. WSUS can still provide a means of controlling and automating the updates to clients that are in your NT 4.0 domain and that meet the WSUS client requirements (i.e., Windows XP, XP SP1, XP SP2, Windows 2000 SP3, and Windows 2000 SP4. Windows Server 2003 does not support legacy system policies. Although you can use one of the previously discussed methods, a simpler method is to use the *wsus.adm* file and import it into your domains *ntconfig.pol* file, which resides in your domain controllers */Netlogon* share. Although Windows 2000, Windows XP, and Windows 2003 machines process Group Policy in an Active Directory environment, they can also process a *ntconfig.pol* file if one exists in a down-level domain. Although lowest in the pecking order in Active Directory, it is the highest in an NT 4.0 domain and will suffice in distributing WSUS client settings.

You can use System Policy to manipulate local registry settings by means of a policy in an NT 4.0 domain. System Policy is the legacy policy distribution method of NT 4.0 domain controllers. When computers boot up in an NT 4.0 domain, they check their authenticating domain controllers' */Netlogon* directory share for a file called *ntconfig.pol*. If one exists, they load it into memory and apply it to their local registries. If any user- or computer-specific settings are defined for the logged-on user or machine, they are *tattooed* into the registry permanently. The System Policy configuration tool is called Policy

Editor (*poledit.exe*) and can be obtained by installing the *adminpak.msi* file on the Windows 2000 Server source CD under */i386*. Once installed, *poledit.exe* is located in the */WINNT* directory.

Using System Policies is not limited to an NT 4.0 domain. If you have stand-alone machines, you can configure them to look for their system policy locally, or to an accessible remote share. First, create a network share on one of your stand-alone machines and configure it so that all of your WSUS-capable machines have *Read* access. Next, use Policy Editor to import your custom ADM file and create a *ntconfig.pol* file with all of the necessary WSUS settings. Following that, place the *ntconfig.pol* file in the accessible file share. Lastly, configure all of the machines to look at your centrally located policy file. This is done by setting the *UpdateMode* that is part of the *system.adm* ADM file.

Specifying a Path to Your System Policy

1. Click on **Start** | **Run** | *poledit.exe* to open Policy Editor.

2. Click **Option** | **Policy Template File** | **Add**.

3. Browse to the *%windir%\system32\inf* directory and click on **system.adm** (you need to turn on the ability to see system and hidden files in order to see the */inf* directory).

4. Click **Open** and **OK**.

5. Click **File** | **Open Registry** to open the local registry of the computer.

6. Double-click **Local Computer** and expand **Network** | **System policies update**.

7. Highlight **Remote update** and click to check the **Option** button.

8. Under **Settings for Remote update** | **Update mode**, click on the drop-down box, and choose **Manual** (use specific path).

9. In the field labeled *Path for manual update*, type in the path to the share that you created containing your *ntconfig.pol* file (see Figure 7.14).

Figure 7.14 System Policy Update Mode

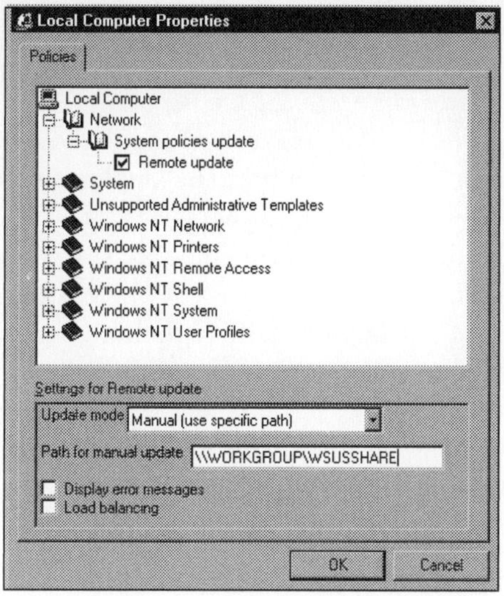

If you are a former NT 4.0 administrator, you may be familiar with configuring custom ADM files for policy deployment. If not, you may be interested in learning how a custom ADM file can be useful in a Windows Server 2003 Active Directory domain. Although confusing at first, creating custom ADM files to use with Policy Editor can be useful in a legacy environment that needs to support policies for applications such as WSUS. For more information on how to get started learning about and creating custom ADM files, see Knowledge Base article "225087" at http://support.microsoft.com.

SOME INDEPENDENT ADVICE

If you are using the predefined *wsus.adm* file with the System Policy Editor, remember to first re-save the file in a non-uniform format for compatibility. For more information, see Microsoft's knowledge-based article "KB325909."

Control Panel

Most people have probably heard of and possibly configured AU by means of the AU UI in the control panel. Newer Windows products such as Windows XP and Windows 2003 have the ability to configure AU by going to **My Computer** and clicking on the **Automatic Updates** tab. Although this may seem like a logical place to configure AU for your WSUS server, the only real way to configure WSUS server communication is by using one of the following four options:

- Group Policy
- Local Policy
- Local Registry
- NT 4.0 Policy

If no other changes are made, the control panel applet is used for configuring AU using Microsoft's online Windows Update or MU Web sites. The only way that the control panel can be used to configure download and installation times from a WSUS server environment is when it is used in conjunction with one of the three aforementioned configurations. As you may recall, one of the four option choices when choosing the **Configure Automatic Updates** policy setting was the *Allow local admin to choose* setting. When using this option along with the policy setting *Specify intranet MU service location*, the local computer administrator can control download and installation days and times using the control panel applet. They will not, however, be able to disable AU.

AU Client

The AU client is the piece of code responsible for understanding each client setting, communicating with the WSUS server on a scheduled basis, and ultimately keeping your client up to date. Each supported Microsoft OS ships with its own version of the AU client; however, in order to work properly with WSUS it needs to be updated to the latest version. This is done when the client machine first contacts your WSUS server. The following sections provide a brief description of the AU client version history, and explains all of the AU client settings, what they are used for, and how they function with the different settings that are applied.

BEST PRACTICES ACCORDING TO MICROSOFT

- Microsoft recommends that you set your WSUS server to automatically approve WSUS updates. This is to ensure that your clients receive the latest version of the WSUS client files and any other components critically related to the WSUS automatic update process. These may include:
  - The AU Client
  - The Windows Installer
  - The Background Intelligent Transfer Service (BITS)
  - These components are the default settings for the WSUS server, and are located on the WSUS server administrative Web page under **Options | Automatic Approval Options | Windows Server Update Services Updates | Automatically approve WSUS updates**.

SOME INDEPENDENT ADVICE

If your company deploys client machines using any type of imaging software, it is highly recommended that you also use a separate Security Identifier (SID) re-generator after the image is created. This is to avoid any issues with your AU client reporting the same SID to your WSUS server as another cloned machine. This can cause new cloned machines to not show up in the WSUS console, or previously reported machines to not check in for a number of days. Microsoft has its own utility called *sysprep*, which you can use with the *–reseal* switch to accomplish this task. *Sysprep* is available as part of the *deploy.cab* file on all Windows source media, under the */support/tools* directory.

Client Version History

The AU client is made up of a few different files. For the purpose of this discussion, we concentrate on the three core AU files and their functions:

- *wuauclt.exe* (WSUS Auto Update Client)
- *wuaueng.dll* (WSUS Auto Update Engine)
- *wuaserv.dll* (WSUS Auto Update Service)

On a healthy AU client, all of these files are the same version; however, not all clients have the same file versions. The AU client has gone through some upgrades, mostly to help improve the process and work more efficiently with continuing versions of the Microsoft Update (MU) server line of products (see Table 7.6).

Table 7.6 OS Version vs. AU Version

OS Version	AU Version
Windows 2000 SP3	5.4.3628.1
Windows 2000 SP4	5.4.3630.2554
Windows XP	5.4.2600.0
Windows XP SP1	5.4.3790.2182
Windows XP SP2	5.8.0.2469
Windows 2003	5.4.3790.0
Windows 2003 SP1	5.8.0.2469

AU client version 5.4 is compatible with the older SUS, which ships with Windows XP, XP SP1, Windows 2000 SP3, and Windows 2003. This is the client that was responsible for communicating with Microsoft's flagship online Windows Update v4 and Windows Update v5. Figure 7.15 shows what the AU client UI looks like for an out-of-the box installation of Windows XP with no Service Pack. Figure 7.16 shows the typical SUS client AU interface. If you find an AU client with version 5.7, you have run across a client involved in a beta test of WSUS' predecessor, Windows Update Services (WUS). This version of the AU client was only used for beta purposes and changed, along with the name of the server piece, when it went to release candidate (RC). When Microsoft released WUS, they realized that it was a poor name choice and changed it to WSUS. Version 5.8 of the AU client was released with the RC of the WSUS, and stayed with that version until the final release to manufacturing (RTM). Version 5.8 of the AU client is compatible with WSUS and backwards compatible with older SUS servers. It is also the client used to communicate with the newer Windows Update v6 and the latest combination of Windows Update and Office Update called Microsoft Update (see Figure 7.17).

Figure 7.15 AU Client Shipped with Windows XP Out of the Box

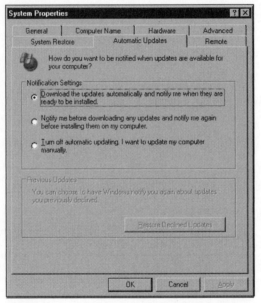

Figure 7.16 AU Client Used with SUS Server

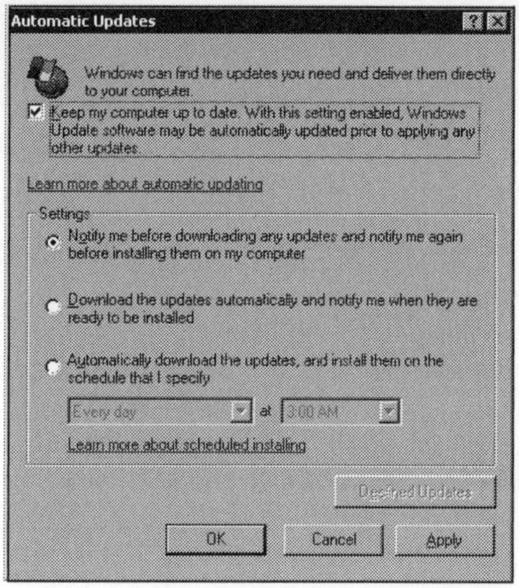

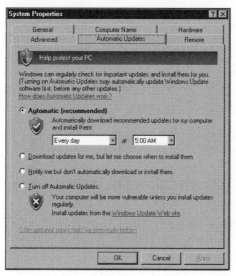

Figure 7.17 AU Client UI Used with WSUS Server

Selfupdate

Just as Microsoft took us from SUS to WSUS, they plan to further improve and increase the functionality of WSUS as we know it today. This means that when new versions of WSUS come out or newly supported features for WSUS are integrated, clients may need an updated client version to be compatible. As discussed earlier, most of the AU clients have the ability to Selfupdate themselves to the latest version. Each WSUS-compatible

AU client is configured to look at what is called the *self-update tree* on the WSUS server. Upon each scheduled detection interval, the AU client looks for this tree at a predefined virtual directory of your WSUS Web server, located at *http://WSUSServer/selfupdate* (see Figure 7.18). Here, a custom Web page enables the download and upgrade of the latest library and executable files that create the AU client.

Figure 7.18 WSUS Selfupdate Virtual Directory

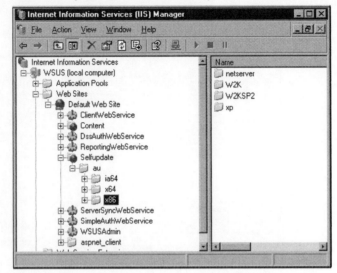

Continued Patch Support

Microsoft is determined to make sure that consumers are running the latest, most productive and secure OS that they offer. To help insure that this mission is accomplished, Microsoft retires its older product based on a predefined scheduled timeline. Along with product retirement comes patch production retirement, meaning that Microsoft will stop producing patches for these older, nonsupported operating systems. To help better organize your OS upgrade strategy, the following is Microsoft's patch support timeline for the supported WSUS client base (see Table 7.7).

Table 7.7 WSUS Client Patch Support Timeline

OS Version	Windows Update Support
Windows Server 2003 with SP1	Ongoing
Windows Server 2003	No new updates offered after June 2007
Windows XP with SP2	Ongoing
Windows XP with SP1	No new updates offered after September 2006; previous updates available
Windows XP	No new updates offered after September 2004; previous updates available
Windows 2000 with Service Pack 4	Ongoing
Windows 2000 with SP3	No new updates offered after June 2005; previous updates available
Windows 2000	No longer supported

Using WSUS to Update Clients and Servers

There are many different ways to configure AU clients for WSUS updates. If you were an administrator of the predecessor to WSUS called Software Update Services (SUS) or the more popular online *WindowsUpdate.com* site, you know that both of these update mechanisms only allow you to update Windows-specific software updates. What is unique and possibly the biggest change in the release of Microsoft's WSUS, is its ability to update not only the Windows OS, but also specific Microsoft product line suites. The following sections briefly discuss and show how to update your Windows clients, and also touches on some specifics that deal with updating products such as Microsoft Office, Exchange, and SQL Server.

Updating Windows Clients

Once your policies are in place and you have chosen your client configuration method, the next step is to begin updating your clients. Updating WSUS clients requires a few steps. First you must choose the updates that target your current environment (e.g., what type of updates and for what products). This is accomplished by choosing the **Products and Classifications** configuration page in your WSUS Admin console under **Options | Synchronization Options**. There you will find the following two categories:

- Products
- Update Classifications

Tables 7.8 and 7.9 show the different combination of product versions and their updated classifications.

Table 7.8 WSUS Products and Product Versions

Products	Versions
Exchange	Exchange Server 2000 and 2003
Office	Office 2000, XP and 2003
SQL	SQL Server
Windows	Windows 2000, Windows Server 2003, Windows Server 2003 Datacenter Edition, Windows XP, Windows XP x64 Edition, and Windows XP 64-Bit Edition Version 2003

Table 7.9 WSUS Update Classifications

Classifications	Description
Critical Updates	A broadly released fix for a specific problem addressing a critical, non-security related bug.
Drivers	A software component necessary to control or regulate another device.
Feature Packs	A new product functionality that is first distributed outside the context of a product release, and is usually including in the next full product release.
Security Updates	A broadly released fix for a product-specific security-related vulnerability. Security vulnerabilities are rated based on their severity, which is indicated in the Microsoft security bulletin as critical, important, moderate, or low.
Service Packs	A tested, cumulative set of all hotfixes, security updates, critical updates, and additional fixes for problems found internally since the release of the product. Service packs may also contain a limited number of customer-requested design changes or features.
Tools	A utility or feature that aids in accomplishing a task or set of tasks.

Continued

Table 7.9 continued WSUS Update Classifications

Classifications	Description
Update Rollups	A tested, cumulative set of hotfixes, security updates, critical updates, and updates packaged together for easy deployment. A rollup generally targets a specific area such as security, or a specific component of a product such as Internet Information Services (IIS).
Updates	A broadly released fix for a specific problem addressing a non-critical non-security-related bug.

Trying to decipher what you may need and what might fall into what category may be overwhelming. Once downloaded, you have the option to sort by product and update classification type on the Updates menu of your WSUS admin console. Go to the **Updates** option in your WSUS admin console page. In the left-hand windows pane, under **View**, drop the box down that says **Products and classification:** and choose **Custom**. Click on the **Change Custom View** hyperlink and choose both product type and update classification as a filter (see Figure 7.19). Type a descriptive name under **Custom view name:** and click **Save**. This search option will now be available to you for future searches.

Figure 7.19 Customizing Downloaded Products and Classifications

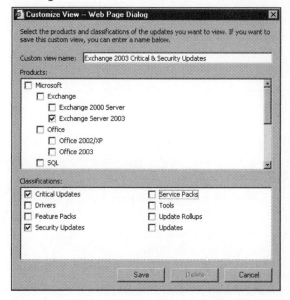

You can also choose to use the **Contains text:** field for a more defined search, if you know specifically what you are looking for.

SOME INDEPENDENT ADVICE

If you are looking for an update to deploy that Microsoft released but are unable to find it in your downloaded updates, reconfirm the product types and update classifications you have selected for your environment on the **Options | Synchronized Options** console page.

After all of your required products and classifications are set and your updates are downloaded, you can start approving and deploying updates. The following sections focus on two of the most commonly misused and misconceived aspects of the updating process: using deadlines and understanding how to approve or decline superseded updates.

Using Deadlines

Deadlines are WSUS' mechanism for allowing administrators to mandate that updates be installed by a particular date and time with no exceptions. When approving updates for the All Computers group or any other pre-defined computer group, you will see two configurable options: *Approval* and *Deadline*. Until you choose the Approval setting *Install*, the Deadline option will not be configurable and will show *N/A* for Not Available. The good thing about this is that you would not have to set a deadline for anything that is not scheduled for installation.

To set a deadline for an update that you have approved for installation, click on the specific update. Next to the group you have chosen for the update installation, you will see a hyperlink called None under the Deadline column. Click this hyperlink and you will be presented with Figure 7.20.

Figure 7.20 Setting Deadlines For Update Installations

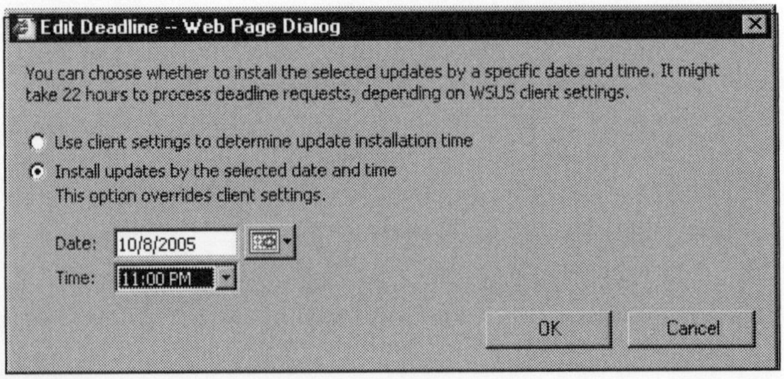

Choose the **Install updates by the selected date and time** option. By selecting a Date and Time and clicking **OK**, you are essentially saying the following:

1. Download the update *immediately* (depends on your clients next scheduled detection cycle).

2. Depending on your WSUS client settings, the update will be available to install, and will automatically *force* the client to install on the date and time you have configured.

SOME INDEPENDENT ADVICE

Deadlines can only be scheduled to install at the beginning of the hour. The ability to schedule a deadline in 5 minutes or 30 minutes is not possible. However, if you wish to install an update without waiting for the top of the next hour, you can schedule the deadline for a past date and time, telling the client to immediately download and install the update the next time it checks in with your WSUS server.

These generate a lot of questions and confusion in online WSUS forums and news-groups. The following sections explain what you have to do to complement these settings, and what happens if you choose this deployment method.

Immediate Installation

Choosing a deadline means that you are mandating that a particular update be installed no later than on that specific date and time. Essentially, you are *forcing* an installation. Deadlines overwrite any client settings you previously configured. The beauty of using deadlines is that there is no need to re-configure GPOs or local client settings in order to *immediately* and automatically tell your clients to pull and install a needed critical or security update. The word *immediately* is the key to the WSUS. Administrators ask, "After setting deadlines for updates, clients are not being updated immediately. Why not?" The main reason is that WSUS does not have the ability to notify or wake up client computers. All communications initiate from the client side through the detection frequency, which is the amount of time before your WSUS clients check in with your WSUS server; the default setting is 22 hours. The following hypothetical situation explains detection frequency in more detail.

An auditor is scheduled to be onsite early Saturday morning to make sure all of your client machines are updated with the latest Microsoft security updates. Friday night at midnight, a detection interval occurred for your WSUS clients. As the administrator, you configure a recently released critical update and a deadline date of yesterday noon, essentially telling the clients that they missed it and must immediately install the update. You then go home and go to bed, assured that all of your clients will be successfully updated.

You wake up to your manager calling you with the bad news he got from the audit report. What happened?

The WSUS clients had not yet reached their next detection frequency cycle and thus had no idea that an update was available. The point of this illustration is: if you need an immediate installation of any update via WSUS, you must schedule a deadline for a past date and time, and force your WSUS clients to manually run a detection cycle. How can you do this? Consider writing a script that can kick off on all your clients and the client command for manual detection. Below are two sample scripts using the *psexec.exe* utility from *sysinternals.com*. One shows how to manually initiate a detection interval on a single computer, and the other shows how to manually initiate a detection interval for all of your machines, listing them in a file called *machines.txt*.

```
::Example for One Machine
@echo off
set DETECT=wuauclt.exe /detectnow
psexec.exe \\wsusclient %detect%
exit


::Example for Many Machines
@echo off
set DETECT=wuauclt.exe /detectnow
for /F %I in (c:\machines.txt) do psexec.exe \\%I %detect%
exit
```

Some Independent Advice

When using the *sysinternals.com psexec.exe* utility, error code 0 means the remote command was successful.

Forced Installation

When you use deadlines your WSUS client settings are overwritten; therefore, if your WSUS settings are configured to not reboot if an administrator is logged on, and to re-prompt every 30 minutes to remind the logged-on administrator to reboot the computer, this is overwritten. If the update requires a reboot, deadlines will set the WSUS clients to automatically reboot in 5 minutes, not allowing postponement (see Figure 7.21).

Figure 7.21 An Update Installed Using Deadlines Does Not Allow You to Restart Later

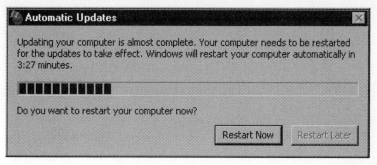

Make sure you schedule deadlines when you know the machines can be rebooted. Make sure to factor in your client's detection interval so that miscalculations will not cause unexpected reboots in the middle of the day. The following hypothetical situation explains deadlines in more detail.

Your WSUS client detection intervals are configured for 10 hours. On Sunday night at midnight, a detection interval occurred for your WSUS clients. As the administrator, you configure a recently released critical update and a deadline date of yesterday noon, essentially telling the clients that they missed it and must immediately install the update. You go home and go to bed assured that all of your clients will be successfully updated by Monday morning. Close to 10:00 A.M. Monday morning you start hearing a ruckus about users' workstations rebooting automatically without allowing them the option to *Restart Later*. What happened?

Your client detection interval did not kick in until approximately 10:00 A.M the next morning; only then were they informed of a mandatory deadline for the security update, which required a reboot.

SOME INDEPENDENT ADVICE

Use deadlines with caution and pay special attention when assigning deadlines to Computer Groups. Deadlines stick after they are set, meaning any computer that you later move into this group will see that deadline, usually from a past date and time, and immediately download and schedule the update installation. Consider removing deadlines after they have accomplished their immediate task and all of the computers have been updated successfully.

Superseding Gotchas

You may notice when approving updates for deployment that some updates mention *superseding*. Some updates may say, "This update is superseded by another update" (see Figure 7.22), whereas others may say, "This update supersedes other updates" (see Figure 7.23).

Figure 7.22 This Update is Superseded By Another Update

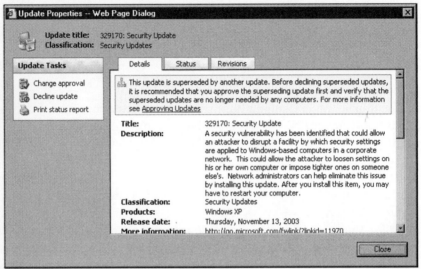

Figure 7.23 This Update Supersedes Other Updates

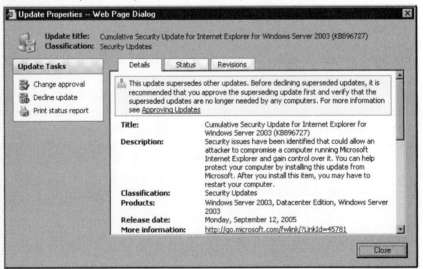

SOME INDEPENDENT ADVICE

When looking at the superseding status of many updates using the Updates page in your WSUS console, notice the icon symbol next to the update. The icon displays an organization chart-type tree. Superseding updates appear with the top organization chart box having a blue colored icon, symbolizing that the update is new and may replace older updates. Superseded updates show a similar icon; however, the blue organization chart box is at the bottom of the tree, symbolizing that this update has newer updates that may need to be approved.

Superseding means to "replace" or "take the place of," which may seem confusing when applied to WSUS and approving updates. It is best to take the common sense approach and approve all updates *superseding* other updates, and decline all *superseded* updates because they have been replaced. The following details when an update can *supersede* another update.

- If the update enhances, improves, or adds something to a previous update.

- If the update improves on the efficiency of the updates file package (e.g., the superseding update may no longer include files that are relevant to the fix or to the operating systems now supported by the new update; thus, the files have been removed).

- If the update updates a newer OS.

Pay close attention to the last two bullets. The first bullet is where newer superseding updates that enhance or improve previously released updates, are approved. However, this is not always the case concerning the last two bullets.

When superseding updates apply to different versions of the Windows OS, the earlier versions of these updates may still be relevant for older operating systems; however, these new superseding updates may not be packaged to update the older clients and thus, the superseded updates are still necessary. If you follow these simple rules when approving or declining updates that fall into these categories, you should be successful in ensuring that all of your clients receive the updates they need.

1. Start by approving the newer superseding updates and keeping tabs on the older updates it supersedes.

2. Once installed on your computers, verify which clients still require the older superseded updates and compare the differences in computers, type, OS, and so forth.

3. With the aforementioned information, you should be able to decipher whether the older update is needed and, if so, approve the older superseded update for those clients that still require it.

All aspects of approving updates, whether superseded, superseding, scheduled via deadline, or by using the more conventional WSUS client, apply across the board for any variety of products available through WSUS. These products include Windows OS updates, Microsoft Office Suite products, Microsoft Exchange, and Microsoft's Windows Microsoft SQL Server 2000 Desktop Engine (WMSDE) SQL server updates.

Updating the Microsoft Office Suite

WSUS supports updating the Microsoft Office suite of products, beginning with Office 2000, which includes all of the following products:

- Microsoft Word
- Microsoft Excel
- Microsoft PowerPoint
- Microsoft Outlook
- Microsoft Access
- Microsoft FrontPage
- Microsoft Visio
- Microsoft Project
- Microsoft Publisher
- Microsoft OneNote
- Microsoft InfoPath

This is a huge improvement over WSUS' predecessor, SUS. Before WSUS, you either made sure your client community was familiar with the public online Office Update Web site, you purchased a costly third-party patch deployment product, or you simply did not update your Microsoft Office line of products. The sheer number of Help Desk calls that are fixed with an Office Update or Service Pack installation is reason enough to use the free WSUS server functionality, ultimately reducing the total cost of ownership (TCO) for your company.

Updating Microsoft Server Family Products

The Microsoft marketing team decided to rename its BackOffice line of products to the Microsoft Server Family of products. The idea behind WSUS was to provide end-user administrators with a one-stop shop for all of their Microsoft Product update needs. Microsoft decided to start with Microsoft Exchange and Microsoft SQL Server, because they are both products that can be updated.

Microsoft Exchange

WSUS supports updating both Microsoft Exchange 2000 and 2003. Although critical- and security-related updates are currently supplied and downloadable from Microsoft, Service Packs for Exchange are not available via WSUS. In addition, Microsoft Exchange Server v5.0 and v5.5 are not supported. If you have been using Microsoft's Baseline Analyzer (MSBA) for security auditing, consider the following when you have a mixed Exchange WSUS/SUS environment: the newer MSBA v2.0 is completely compatible with WSUS and is required for scanning Exchange 2000 and 2003 server environments updated via WSUS. If you are looking at analyzing legacy Exchange 5.*x* products, you will still need to use the SUS complaint v1.2.1 of MSBA. If necessary, both versions can co-exist on the same machine.

Microsoft SQL Server

As of this writing, SQL server appears in the WSUS Server v2.0 SP1 (Build 2.0.0.2472) console, but does not download any SQL server-related updates; it simply lists SQL Server without any versions. Critical- and security-related updates for WMSDE are downloaded, with a version of SQL that Microsoft released to only be used by Windows components. This is different than the older MSDE version of SQL server, and is not limited to MSDE's 2-gigabyte (GB) database size. To date, there have only been two updates—one security and one critical?for this WMSDE.

- **Critical Update** Critical Update for SQL Server 2000 Desktop Engine (Windows) on Windows Server 2003 (KB899358)

- **Security Update** Cumulative Patch for SQL Server 2000 Desktop Engine (Windows) (KB815495)

The good news is the default SQL installation for WSUS is WMSDE; therefore, you can keep this up-do-date with critical- and security-related updates as they are released. Other popular Microsoft products also use the WMSDE version of SQL 2000, such as Microsoft's SharePoint Services product.

Updating Microsoft IIS

Microsoft IIS is a component of the Windows OS and subject to having its own vulner-abilities and required fixes. Microsoft releases IIS-specific updates via WSUS for all versions of Windows. Pay special attention when declining updates due to superseding. Although both of the IIS updates appear to be IIS Security Roll-up packages with the same knowledge base article number, they are different. Your first instinct may be to *decline* the older security update, released 7/22/2003, because you figure it is superseded by the later one released on 8/19/2003.

- **Security Update Windows 2000** Q327696: IIS Security Roll-up Package - Released 8/19/2003

- **Security Update Windows XP** Q327696: IIS Security Roll-up Package - Released 7/22/2003

When you look into the details of each update, you will see that they are for different operating systems, and that by declining the older one, you are leaving the Windows XP machines vulnerable.

Updating Microsoft Clusters

For many environments to keep up with tight uptimes and heavy redundancy requirements, Microsoft Clusters are becoming common. Whether you are clustering Exchange, SQL, or a file and print server, WSUS can be used to keep them up-to-date. Clustered servers are typically used to host one application on a multiple server in a failover-type of situation. They should not be set up to update and reboot at the same time. Separate the clustered servers in such a way that approving updates does not effectively bring all of the nodes down simultaneously, but spreads out the updates and reboots over time, thereby limiting production downtime. This can be accomplished using one of two methods:

- Group Policy
- WSUS Computer Groups

Using Group Policy, you can assign each clustered computer a different WSUS configuration—specifically different update and installation dates and times. Using this method means that you can group your clustered servers into the same WSUS Computer Group for ease of organization.

You can separate your WSUS cluster servers into different groups using WSUS Computer Groups. Approving updates can be based on Computer Group, and you can control which clustered Computer Group has the patch installed first. This method helps you maintain more control over your Group Policy.

A better solution, however, may be to choose to download but *not* install updates for your clustered server, and to control clustered update installations manually or via a custom script. This gives you the most control over clustered downtime and when and how clusters are updated. When deploying application updates via WSUS to a clustered server, those updates have to stop the cluster service on the installation node. You may want to deploy application-specific updates manually, and choose one of the prior methods for updating the Windows OS.

BEST PRACTICES ACCORDING TO MICROSOFT

- Configure your client computers to immediately install updates that do not require a restart and are non-intrusive to the OS, by choosing **Allow Automatic Updates immediate installation** in the WSUS administrator console.
- For maximum control of your servers and restart times, choose the download option, notify for installation, and reboot your servers on demand using a script for manual intervention.

SOME INDEPENDENT ADVICE

If you are using any type of clustering in your environment, we recommend that you use separate computer groups for each node so that you do not schedule updates for both of the nodes in a cluster that requires a reboot. By using separate groups, you can schedule the updates using deadlines and reboot the passive cluster nodes at your leisure.

Shortcuts...

Quick Client Update

Waiting for clients to run their scheduled detection rotations can seem to take forever. Fortunately, the AU client has a built-in utility that allows you to manually run a detection interval. You must be on the local command console of the machine in question, because there is no way to run this type of update from the WSUS administrative console. The following are reasons that you might want to force your AU client to re-check in with the server before its next scheduled detection time:

- You are eager to see a recently updated computer's update patch status in the WSUS reporting module for auditing purposes.
- You need to schedule a critical update with a deadline, and you are concerned that the deadline date and time falls short of the client's next detection interval.

There is a quick and easy remote execution that can be scripted to do this without a manual visit to the machine console or having to use Remote Desktop. By using a free utility from *sysinternals.com* called *psexec.exe*, you can remotely

Continued

execute the built in AU client manual detection call. Go to a command prompt and run the following command. A status code of *0* means that is was successfully run on the remote machine:

```
Psexec.exe \\wsusclient wuauclt.exe /detectnow
```

This command tells the client to immediately check in with the WSUS server, regardless of its configured detection interval time. It will update the WSUS server with its latest installation, reboot, or needed patches status.

SOME INDEPENDENT ADVICE

Microsoft releases critical security patches the first Tuesday of every month, which is known as Patch Tuesday. Be prepared to read over the related fixes and updates so that you can deploy them in your environment in an efficient manner, to ensure that your machines are as secure as possible.

AU Client Investigation

Are all of your clients configured for WSUS to appear automatically in your WSUS console? Do you use any type of disk-cloning software? Have all of your deployments and installations gone flawlessly? The following sections discuss some of the problematic client scenarios, and some of the valuable client investigation tools. These sections also discuss WSUS client logs, and details any Event log entries that you may find. They take you through some useful Group Policy utilities and finishes with pertinent online resources that you should have when investigating your AU client environment.

Log Files

Like most clients, the AU client generates its own log files, using them to track current computer settings, updated changes, scheduled downloads and deployments, client communication failures, installation failures, service restarts, and so on. The log files are the best place to start when troubleshooting AU client problems. The following sections discuss two log files and shows how to enable verbose logging when you want a lot more detail regarding troublesome issues.

WindowsUpdate.log

As it receives and executes requests from a WSUS server, the AU client continuously appends its working state to a *log file* called *WindowsUpdate.log*, which is located under the Windows installation folder at *%windir%\WindowsUpdate.log*. Do not confuse this with the other file called *Windows Update.log* (notice the space between Windows and

Update). This is a legacy log file that is used by older AU clients to connect to older version of Microsoft's online Windows Update site, and WSUS' predecessor, SUS. *Windows Update.log* can be deleted.

The *WindowsUpdate.log* file can be invaluable in determining AU client issues. The AU client logs the AU client version, the OS version, the computer type, the WSUS server path, all of the WSUS configuration options, and so on (see Figure 7.24).

Figure 7.24 Showing the *WindowsUpdate.log* File

Every process that the AU client executes on a machine is logged in this file. If there

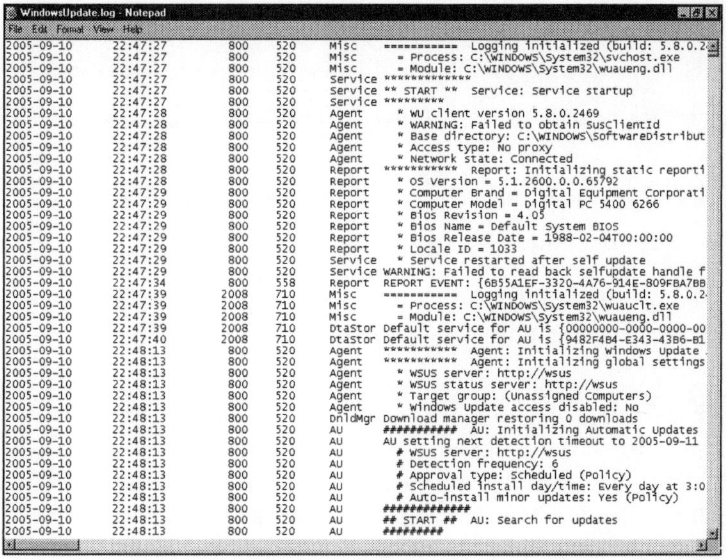

```
WindowsUpdate.log - Notepad
File Edit Format View Help
2005-09-10  22:47:27   800  520  Misc     ===========  Logging initialized (build: 5.8.0.2
2005-09-10  22:47:27   800  520  Misc       = Process: C:\WINDOWS\System32\svchost.exe
2005-09-10  22:47:27   800  520  Misc       = Module: C:\WINDOWS\System32\wuaueng.dll
2005-09-10  22:47:27   800  520  Service  *************
2005-09-10  22:47:27   800  520  Service  ** START **  Service: Service startup
2005-09-10  22:47:27   800  520  Service  *********
2005-09-10  22:47:28   800  520  Agent      * WU client version 5.8.0.2469
2005-09-10  22:47:28   800  520  Agent      * WARNING: Failed to obtain SusClientId
2005-09-10  22:47:28   800  520  Agent      * Base directory: C:\WINDOWS\SoftwareDistribut
2005-09-10  22:47:28   800  520  Agent      * Access type: No proxy
2005-09-10  22:47:28   800  520  Agent      * Network state: Connected
2005-09-10  22:47:28   800  520  Report   ***********  Report: Initializing static reporti
2005-09-10  22:47:28   800  520  Report     * OS Version = 5.1.2600.0.0.65792
2005-09-10  22:47:29   800  520  Report     * Computer Brand = Digital Equipment Corporati
2005-09-10  22:47:29   800  520  Report     * Computer Model = Digital PC 5400 6266
2005-09-10  22:47:29   800  520  Report     * Bios Revision = 4.05
2005-09-10  22:47:29   800  520  Report     * Bios Name = Default System BIOS
2005-09-10  22:47:29   800  520  Report     * Bios Release Date = 1988-02-04T00:00:00
2005-09-10  22:47:29   800  520  Report     * Locale ID = 1033
2005-09-10  22:47:29   800  520  Service    * Service restarted after self update
2005-09-10  22:47:29   800  520  Service  WARNING: Failed to read back selfupdate handle f
2005-09-10  22:47:34   800  558  Report   REPORT EVENT: {6B55A1EF-3320-4A76-914E-809FBA7BB
2005-09-10  22:47:39  2008  710  Misc     ===========  Logging initialized (build: 5.8.0.2
2005-09-10  22:47:39  2008  710  Misc       = Process: C:\WINDOWS\System32\wuauclt.exe
2005-09-10  22:47:39  2008  710  Misc       = Module: C:\WINDOWS\System32\wuaueng.dll
2005-09-10  22:47:39  2008  710  DtaStor  Default service for AU is {00000000-0000-0000-00
2005-09-10  22:47:40  2008  710  DtaStor  Default service for AU is {9482F4B4-E343-43B6-B1
2005-09-10  22:48:13   800  520  Agent    ***********  Agent: Initializing Windows Update
2005-09-10  22:48:13   800  520  Agent    ***********  Agent: Initializing global settings
2005-09-10  22:48:13   800  520  Agent      * WSUS server: http://wsus
2005-09-10  22:48:13   800  520  Agent      * WSUS status server: http://wsus
2005-09-10  22:48:13   800  520  Agent      * Target group: (Unassigned Computers)
2005-09-10  22:48:13   800  520  Agent      * Windows Update access disabled: No
2005-09-10  22:48:13   800  520  DnldMgr  Download manager restoring 0 downloads
2005-09-10  22:48:13   800  520  AU       ###########  AU: Initializing Automatic Updates
2005-09-10  22:48:13   800  520  AU       AU setting next detection timeout to 2005-09-11
2005-09-10  22:48:13   800  520  AU         # WSUS server: http://wsus
2005-09-10  22:48:13   800  520  AU         # Detection frequency: 6
2005-09-10  22:48:13   800  520  AU         # Approval type: Scheduled (Policy)
2005-09-10  22:48:13   800  520  AU         # Scheduled install day/time: Every day at 3:0
2005-09-10  22:48:13   800  520  AU         # Auto-install minor updates: Yes (Policy)
2005-09-10  22:48:13   800  520  AU       #############
2005-09-10  22:48:13   800  520  AU       ## START ##  AU: Search for updates
2005-09-10  22:48:13   800  520  AU       #########
```

is an error communicating with your WSUS server, it is logged in this file. If the AU client successfully downloads an update and schedules it for installation, it is logged. Every client detection interval is logged, and each update that is detected is logged. You should use this file often so that you become more familiar with AUs; don't be intimated by the mass of data contained in a log file. To help you better understand the mechanics of the *WindowsUpdate.log* file and how to further interpret its output, Microsoft has published a "Knowledge Base" article that is located at *http://support.microsoft.com* and search for KB902093.

If you are in a real bind and need even more information from the *WindowsUpdate.log* file, you have to enable *verbose logging*. To do this, you must make a change to the problematic machine's local registry to turn on *Extended Logging*. To do this, add an additional registry key and two values under the existing *Windows Update* registry key:

HKLM\SOFTWARE\Microsoft\Windows\CurrentVersion\WindowsUpdate.

1. Click **Start | Run** and type *regedit.exe* to open the Registry Editor.

2. In the left-hand pane of the window, navigate to
   **HKEY_LOCAL_MACHINE\
   SOFTWARE\Microsoft\Windows\CurrentVersion\WindowsUpdate** and high-
   light the **WindowsUpdate** key.

3. Right-click and select **New | Key**. Enter **Trace** as the key name.

4. Highlight **Trace**. Right-click and select **New | DWORD Value** and enter
   Flags as the name.

5. Double-click the **Flags** value and enter **7** under the Value data. Click **OK**.

6. Right-click again and select **New | DWORD Value** and enter **Level** as the
   name.

7. Double-click the **Level** value and enter **4** under the Value Data. Click **OK**.

8. Close Registry Editor.

Enabling the registry key creates a more verbose *WindowsUpdate.log* file, and allows
any attached debugger programs to trace the extended output.

ReportingEvents.log

If you want to know what the AU client has downloaded, installed, or scheduled for
installation, read the *ReportingEvents.log* file. If you want to know if the client successfully
downloaded an update, or if you want to clean up some updated files, the
ReportingEvents.log file is a good place to start.

Located under *%windir%\SoftwareDistribution*, the *ReportingEvents.log* file is a log file
that tracks, in detail, each downloaded update as well as whether that update has been
installed or is still pending an installation. The log file shows the date and time that
installations occurred, and whether or not they were successful. If they were successful
and you want to free up disk space, match the corresponding Globally Unique Identifier
(GUID) (*%windir%\SoftwareDistribution*) to where the actual updates are downloaded and
installed. To control disk space consumption, the AU client automatically expires and
purges all updates that have been installed for ten days. If you are not using express
installation files, and you have chosen to install many large patches, you may want to
delete the update files as soon as they are installed. For example, you could write a script
to parse through the *WindowsUpdate.log*, obtain the update GUID, match that to the corresponding Report Event in your *ReportingEvents.log* file, and look for the words *Success
Content Install Installation successful*. You could then generate a variable for the updated
GUID, match it to the corresponding directory under *%windir%SoftwareDistribution*, and
schedule purging the directory at a specified date and time.

Event Logs

The Windows Event Log is another useful place to go to for a quick investigation into AU installations, pending installations, or client reboots. The AU client logs everything to the System Event log under one of two Event Log sources:

- Windows Update Agent
- NtServicePack

Windows Update Agent

You can use your Event log file to filter by "source," and to show only one of the three event sources at a time. If you are filtering using Windows Update Agent, you will probably see many events relating to the successful installation of an update, and whether or not that update required a reboot. Figure 7.25 shows an Event ID 22 displaying a successful installation requiring a reboot, which will take place in the default setting of 5 minutes.

Figure 7.25 Computer Will Restart in 5 Minutes

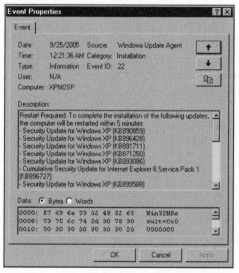

The Event ID is a good place to search when investigating a computer reboot. Another place to look for a computer restart is in the System Event log. Search for "Event ID 6006" in conjunction with "Event ID 6005," with significant time lapses in between. This event shows the stopping and starting of the Event log, and is always shown after a machine is restarted.

Event ID 18 shows that an update has been downloaded and is pending installation. It also shows the scheduled installation's date and time. Event ID 19 shows the successful installation of an update. Event 21 shows a successful installation that was unable to restart due to a logged-on administrator. This event warns you that until the computer is restarted, the updates have not taken effect and your computer is still vulnerable.

BEST PRACTICES ACCORDING TO MICROSOFT

- If you decide not to reboot your computers after you install critical- or security-related updates, your computer will not be patched yet and will still be vulnerable to bugs. Event ID 21 warns you if the computer is set to *not* reboot.
- It is recommended that reboots be scheduled after critical- or security-related installations occur, by using either the AU option to reboot or by generating a custom reboot script.

SOME INDEPENDENT ADVICE

Be forewarned when using the Deadlines feature for approving AUs for your clients. Although your servers may be set to download and install updates during downtime hours, if you schedule a deadline for an update in the middle of the day, that installation will override all client settings and possibly reboot your server during production hours. Be sure you have downtime approved before using Deadlines during production hours

If the AU client could not contact your WSUS server, you may see an Event ID 16 (see Figure 7.26), which may be an indication that there is a problem with that client's network card.

If you only see this error on one client, check the following:

- Make sure that the client has the correct WSUS URL for the WSUS server that is configured.
- Make sure that the client is pointed to the correct DNS server, and that it can successfully ping and resolve the WSUS server by name.
- Test to see if the client can get to any other servers or URLs.
- Use the *ClientDiag.exe* tool to troubleshoot further.

Figure 7.26 AU Client Unable to Connect to WSUS Server Error

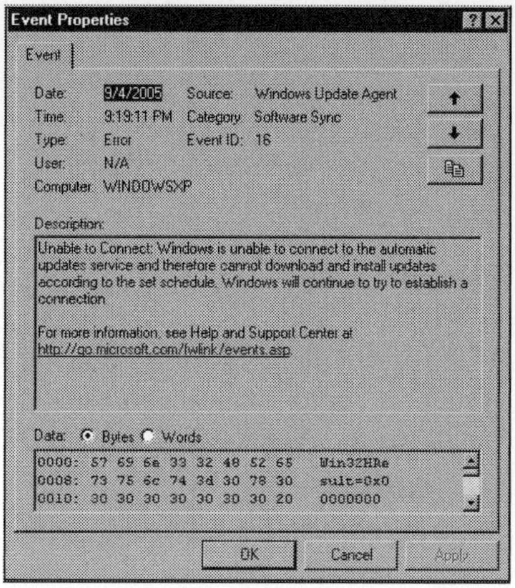

NtServicePack

The NtServicePack Event Source is used to show specific Microsoft *"hotfixes"* that have been successfully installed. Service Packs fall under this category and result in an Event ID 4363. Successful *hotfix* installations show Event ID 4377. The following are examples of a failed installation and the correlating Event IDs:

- **Event ID 4373** Signifies that a signature was not present in the subject of a particular *hotfix* installation.

- **Event ID 4367** Signifies a failed installation with a warning stating that the machine is only partially updating. A log file called *xpsp1htm.log* is created for more detailed investigation and can be located under the *%windir%* directory.

Command Line Tools

There are a few command-line tools that can help you identify problems, query for information, or speed up the detection update process. The following is a list of these tools:

- **WSUS Client Diagnostics Tool** (*ClientDiag.exe*) Downloadable from Microsoft's Web site.

- *Wuauclt.exe* Part of the Windows source code after an AU client is installed.

- **Gpudate.exe and Secedit.exe** *Gpupdate.exe* is part of Windows XP and Windows Server 2003 source code. *Secedit.exe* is built into Windows 2000 source code.

- **Gpresult.exe and RSoP.msc** *Gpresult.exe* is part of the Windows 2000 Resource Kit, Supplement 1, and RSoP (*RSoP.msc*) is part of Windows XP and Windows Server 2003 source code.

- **Regsvr32.exe** Part of all Windows source code.

- **Srvinfo.exe and Uptime.exe** Part of the Windows 2000 and 2003 Resource Kits.

- **Reg.exe** Part of the source code in Windows XP and Windows Server 2003, and part of the Windows 2000 Resource Kit, Supplement 1.

WSUS Client Diagnostic Tool

The WSUS Client Diagnostic Tool is a simple utility that provides the status of your AU client, its configuration, and its ability to connect to your WSUS server. The *ClientDiag.exe* utility has only one command-line parameter, which is used to dump the results to the *ClientDiag.log* log file in addition to displaying it on the screen. To run the diagnostic tool this way, type **ClientDiag.exe /t**. (A successful run of the utility is shown in Figure 7.27.) The WSUS server location in the registry was changed to show you what might happen if there is a problem resolving or contacting your WSUS server by name (see Figure 7.28).

Figure 7.27 Showing a Successful *ClientDiag* Output

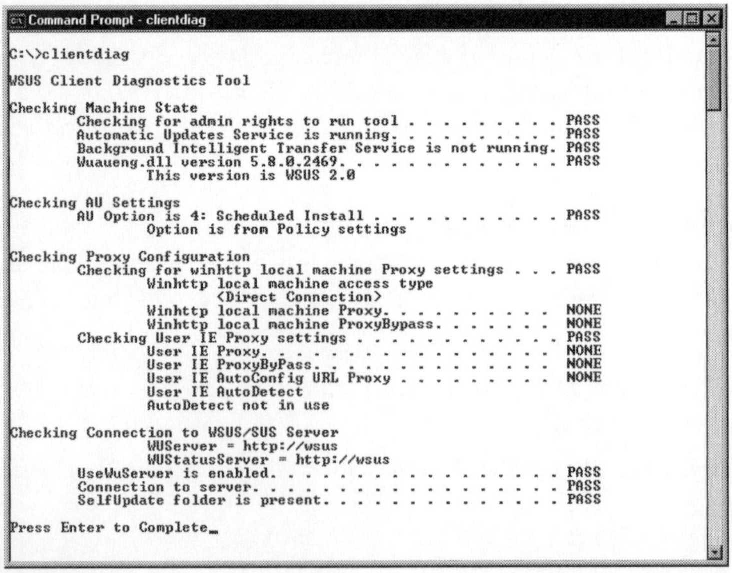

Figure 7.28 Showing a *ClientDiag* Error

```
C:\>clientdiag

WSUS Client Diagnostics Tool

Checking Machine State
        Checking for admin rights to run tool . . . . . . . .  PASS
        Automatic Updates Service is running. . . . . . . . .  PASS
        Background Intelligent Transfer Service is not running. PASS
        Wuaueng.dll version 5.8.0.2469. . . . . . . . . . . .  PASS
                This version is WSUS 2.0

Checking AU Settings
        AU Option is 4: Scheduled Install . . . . . . . . . .  PASS
                Option is from Policy settings

Checking Proxy Configuration
        Checking for winhttp local machine Proxy settings . . . PASS
                Winhttp local machine access type
                        <Direct Connection>
                Winhttp local machine Proxy. . . . . . . . .   NONE
                Winhttp local machine ProxyBypass. . . . . . . NONE
        Checking User IE Proxy settings . . . . . . . . . . .  PASS
                User IE Proxy. . . . . . . . . . . . . . . . . NONE
                User IE ProxyByPass. . . . . . . . . . . . . . NONE
                User IE AutoConfig URL Proxy . . . . . . . . . NONE
                User IE AutoDetect
                AutoDetect not in use

Checking Connection to WSUS/SUS Server
                WUServer = http://bogus
                WUStatusServer = http://wsus
                UseWuServer is enabled. . . . . . . . . . . .  PASS

VerifyWUServerURL() failed with hr=0x80072ee7

The server name or address could not be resolved

Press Enter to Complete_
```

The *ClientDiag.exe* utility can be downloaded from *Microsoft.com/downloads* or from the official home of WSUS at *http://www.microsoft.com/windowsserversystem/updateservices*.

Speeding Up Group Policy and Client Detection

By default, Group Policy is set to update clients every 90 minutes with a random offset. If you want to speed this up because you need to push out WSUS client configuration changes quicker, consider using the following commands to force a client policy update. To revisit commands that were run earlier, you can use both *gpudate.exe* and *secedit.exe* to force your clients to pull new Group Policy settings.

For Windows XP and Windows Server 2000 machines, run the following command:

```
gpupdate /target:computer /force
```

For Windows 2000 machines, issue the following command:

```
secedit /refreshpolicy machine_policy /enforce
```

To force a client detection update from your WSUS server, type the following built-in AU client command:

```
Wuauclt.exe /detectnow
```

Troubleshooting Group Policy Conflicts

When setting up large server environments, you usually end up with a very complex OU and Group Policy configuration. When different groups of servers have different downtime schedules, the development server clients need different WSUS client settings, productions servers, and so on. Consequently, you may find yourself with some GPO conflict. To show the final set of policies for your WSUS clients, and depending on the client version, you can use one of the following tools. *Gpresult.exe* is a command-line utility with switch options that print out all of the policies that the machine has applied or denied. Following is the syntax for this command:

```
usage:  gpresult [/V] [/S] [/C | /U] [/?]

        /V      Verbose mode

        /S      Super verbose mode

        /C      Computer settings only

        /U      User settings only
```

Use the */C* switch when troubleshooting GPO issues with your WSUS settings, to speed up the computation output.

Windows XP and Windows Server 2003 have a much richer graphical tool for displaying the RSoP Microsoft Management Console (MMC) snap-in console, which can be accessed by typing **Start | Run |** *rsop.msc* (see Figure 7.29).

Figure 7.29 Showing the Results of a WSUS Client's RSoP

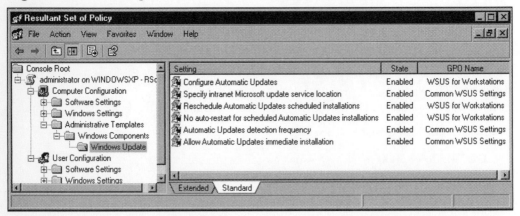

The snap-in looks like you are looking at the Group Policy Editor; however, only a subset of the components are displayed. The snap-in only shows what has been configured on the machine based on the policies pushed down to it. Where *gpresult.exe* is good for only showing polices that a client machine receives, the RSoP snap-in shows both of the settings that a client receives and the policy where the settings were obtained.

Miscellaneous Useful Commands

The following is a list of some miscellaneous commands that can be used for WSUS client troubleshooting and the day-to-day maintenance of a WSUS environment.

Regsvr32.exe is a Windows dynamic link library (DLL) registration utility. If your WSUS client does not seem to be functioning correctly, try unregistering and reregistering your AU client DLL file by running the following from a command-line window:

```
regsvr32.exe /u wuauclt.dll
regsvr32.exe /r wuauclt.exe
```

Srvinfo.exe and *uptime.exe* are two resource kit utilities that allow you to obtain system uptime from a remote command prompt. This is good for quickly checking whether a system that you expect to reboot after a patch update has in fact rebooted, and how long it has been up since its reboot. The following is the syntax for both commands:

```
srvinfo.exe \\remoteclient
uptime remoteclient
```

Notice that the *uptime.exe* utility does not require a prepending \\ like *srvinfo.exe* does.

Lastly, command utility *reg.exe* has been shown to be a very handy utility for querying remote registry keys. It can also be used in a massive batch file to quickly enumerate and audit an existing WSUS client environment for re-verification that all of the clients are set up correctly.

Disk Cloning Gotchas

WSUS uses the client SID or *ClientID* to register and monitor it as a unique member of its world. As you may know, when a machine is cloned, the SID stays the same. Although, when joined to the domain, the DomainSID of a computer will change, the local SID will not. It is highly recommended that you run a SID generator against newly cloned machines before deployment. Most cloning software companies have their own SID generation utilities. Microsoft has a free utility called *sysprep* that can be used with the *–reseal* parameter to prep disk images for future deployment. *Sysprep* is part of the Windows source code and is located in the *deploy.cab* file on your Windows CD under */Tools*. Although you can run *sysprep* after your image is deployed onto its destination machine, it is best to first *sysprep* the source image file so that it generates a new SID the first time it is booted on the destination machine, which is done by running a mini setup wizard upon first boot. To use *sysprep*, first build your pristine machine. Before shutting down to make the master image of that machine, run the following command, then shutdown your machine and image it for final deployment.

```
Sysprep -reseal
```

If you deployed WSUS before reading this book, and are running into issues with machines disappearing from your WSUS console, you now know why. The question is how to fix it? You could run *sysprep* on the problem machine, but if it already joined a domain you would have to disjoin and rejoin that domain, which is not the simplest solution. The simple answer is that first, you want to delete three registry keys, one of which is the suspect *ClientID* used by WSUS. Open your Registry Editor and navigate to the following key: *HKLM\SOFTWARE\Microsoft\Windows\CurrentVersion\ WindowsUpdate.*

If any of the following subkeys exist, delete them:

- AccountDomainID
- SusClientID
- PingID

After these are gone, you may need to run one more command if you are using *client-side* targeting for your client computer grouping. Regardless or whether you are or not, it does not hurt to run it anyway. Go to a command prompt window and type:

```
Wuauclt.exe /resetautorization /detectnow
```

This commands job is to expire the local cookie on the client-side targeting piece that the AU client creates, and then send a detection request to the WSUS server. The WSUS server and the AU client will regenerate another *ClientID*, ensuring your machine's uniqueness in WSUS' world. Another *AccountDomainID* will also be recreated; however, the *PingID* will not be recreated because it is a legacy key and no longer needed.

BEST PRACTICES ACCORDING TO MICROSOFT

Microsoft recommends using their *sysprep* utility when dealing with and creating master images using disk cloning software; otherwise, you could run into the problems discussed in knowledge base article KB55351.

SOME INDEPENDENT ADVICE

We have seen very similar issues when cloning machines from within VMWare's ESX product line. Microsoft's *sysprep* utility can also be integrated into the cloning ability of this platform to alleviate duplicate *ClientID* issues.

SOME INDEPENDENT ADVICE

If you wish to reset a *ClientID* remotely, consider using the *reg.exe* tool coupled with a freeware utility from *sysinternals.com* called *psexec.exe*. Use *reg.exe* to delete the registry keys, and *psexec.exe* to remotely run the reset command shown here:

Display potential keys to be deleted:

```
reg query \\pc\hklm\software\microsoft\windows\currentversion\windowsupdate
```

Remotely reset the cookie and send a detect to WSUS server:

```
psexec \\pc wauaclt.exe /resetauthorization /detectnow
```

Delete the registry keys:

```
reg delete \\pc\hklm\software\microsoft\windows\currentversion\windowsupdate
/v AccountDomainID /f

reg delete \\pc\hklm\software\microsoft\windows\currentversion\windowsupdate
/v SusClientID /f

reg delete \\pc\hklm\software\microsoft\windows\currentversion\windowsupdate
/v PingID /f
```

Resources

There are many resources available on the Internet to help you troubleshoot your AU client and WSUS. As you become more familiar with WSUS, some of the following sites can help you to start interacting with other WSUS administrators:

- **Official Home of Windows Software Update Services –**
  http://www.microsoft.com/windowsserversystem/updateservices

  The first official home for Microsoft WSUS products, and the first place to go for product updates and news on future releases.

- **Microsoft Communities WSUS Online Newsgroups –**
  http://www.microsoft.com/technet/community/newsgroups/topics/sus.mspx

  Microsoft supports a 24x7 online newsgroup called the *WSUS Community*, which is monitored by knowledgeable Microsoft Valued Professional (MVPs) who try to answer your questions and help you troubleshoot problems.

- **Unofficial WSUS Online Forum**
  http://www.wsus.info/forums

Another great resource is the *wsus.info* Web site forum, which is known as the unofficial WSUS forum in the industry, and is a great place to interact with other WSUS administrators that are troubleshooting issues and asking questions.

■ **Microsoft Help and Support—Online Knowledge Base**
http://support.microsoft.com

Once you feel you are knowledgeable installing, configuring and supporting WSUS and the AU client, why not go to the aforementioned newsgroups and forums and answer questions to help other newbie's?

Shortcuts...

Automatically Cleanup AU Client Downloads

Has 0x80070070 ever appeared as the error code under a failed attempt to download an update in your WSUS console? After researching the error and finding it to be disk space-related, the culprit was ironically the WSUS client itself, because the size of the temporary download and installation directory the AU client uses is enormous. By default, the AU client is supposed to auto purge used installation files that are older than 10 days old into its */Download* directory located under *%windir%\SoftwareDistribution\Download*. However, this does not always happen, thus leaving you with a potential risk for machines with smaller boot drive partitions. To make sure that your temporary downloads directory stays reasonably small, consider using a scheduled script to auto purge the files after a specific amount of time. The following is a script that was developed to accomplish this task. Two shareware utilities—*delold.exe* and *postie.exe*—are used to determine the age of the files and to physically delete them, where *postie.exe* is used as a command-line mail sender to e-mail the results of your clients to you after they run the cleanup job.:

```
:: Clean up of WSUS Download Directory
@echo off
delold /q /b /d /s /-c /n:15
%windir%\SoftwareDistribution\Download\*.*


if errorlevel == 1 goto success
if errorlevel == 0 goto fail
```

Continued

```
:success

postie -host:smtpmail.syngress.com -to:wsusadministrator@syngress.com
-from:"WSUSCleanUP@syngress.com" -s:"WSUSCleanup on %computername%
was SUCCESSFUL" -nomsg

goto eof


:fail

postie -host:smtpmail.syngress.com -to:wsusadministrator@syngress.com
-from:"WSUSCleanUP@syngress.com" -s:"WSUSCleanup on %computername%
FAILED" -nomsg


:eof

Exit
```

This script will quietly (*/q*) look in the */Download* directory (*%windir%\SoftwareDistribution\Download*.**), for anything with a creation date (*/b*) older than 15 days (*/n:15*), including directories (*/d*) and subdirectories (*/s*) and automatically purge them without asking for confirmation (*/-c*).

Delold.exe is available at http://www.savilltech.com/, and postie.exe can be found with a simple Google search.

Summary

Whether your clients exist in Active Directory, a workgroup, a stand-alone machine, and NT 4.0 Domain, or a secure DMZ, WSUS can be used as a centralized server to update them. By using Group Policy, Local Policy, or the registry or legacy System Policy, you can configure and deploy WSUS client settings quickly and easily. With the new *selfup-date* feature of WSUS, older SUS clients can automatically update their AU clients to be WSUS-compatible and to begin scheduling approved updates without any interruption. The new functionality in WSUS allows administrators the option to update a variety of Microsoft products, including the Microsoft Office Suite, Microsoft Exchange, and Microsoft SQL 2000 WMSDE, and so on. Troubleshooting and investigating WSUS client update behavior can be accomplished using various log files, downloadable diagnostic tools, and online support from WSUS administrators. WSUS is everything you need if you take the time to respect its capabilities and learn how to use it effectively and efficiently.

Solutions Fast Track

Using Active Directory

☑ By way of Group Policy, Active Directory is the core delivery mechanism for WSUS client configurations settings.

☑ The *wuau.adm* ADM is the brains of all WSUS configuration information.

☑ Try to design your OU structure around WSUS client update needs, enabling GPOs with common WSUS settings at the top level and using more client-specific WSUS GPOs closer to the clients home OU.

☑ Use and familiarize yourself with the GPMC to help you manage and troubleshoot your GPO infrastructure.

Using Local Settings

☑ Use local settings for WSUS client configuration only if Active Directory is not available, or you have one-off clients outside your Active Directory environment.

☑ Local settings *do not* override the Group Policy setting if you are configuring local settings on a client in Active Directory. Use the LSDO methodology when looking at your policy application order.

☑ Editing the local registry to make WSUS changes can be accomplished using various scripting methods with the help of the *reg.exe* command-line utility and does not require a local machine visit.

AU Client

☑ Different versions of Windows ship with different versions of the AU client; however the built-in *selfupdate* feature of WSUS allows clients to continuously update and stay compatible with its configured WSUS server needs.

☑ Windows XP without any service packs need its AU client updated manually to be able to use the *selfupdate* feature of the WSUS server. Pointing a Windows XP machine to the public Windows Update site will accomplish this task.

☑ Only the following Windows versions are compatible with WSUS: Windows XP any Service Pack, Windows Server 2000 with SP3 or later, and Windows Server 2003 with any Service Pack.

Using WSUS to Update Clients and Servers

☑ WSUS does not limit you to Windows only updates. WSUS allows you to update a host of Microsoft products including Microsoft Office, SQL, and Exchange.

☑ Updating WSUS clients can be an automatic or manual process, depending on your organizational needs. For example, you may have your client workstations set to update and reboot every night, whereas your server environment is a bit more controlled, using only the automatic downloading of updates and a manual installation process.

☑ When updating core enterprise applications such as SQL or Exchange on your servers, always perform the updates in a predefined test environment. Each production WSUS Computer Group should have a similar *test* Computer Group comprised of identically configured application servers.

AU Client Investigation

☑ Use the *WindowsUpdate.log* as a first place to troubleshoot quirky WSUS client activity.

☑ When investigating local client WSUS abnormalities, remember to use GPRESULT and the RSoP snap-in to get a concise answer of where your client is obtaining its settings

☑ If you are using disk cloning in your environment to roll out WSUS clients, remember to use a SID regenerator, such as Microsoft's *sysprep* utility, before final deployment, in a best effort to avoid duplicate WSUS *ClientIDs*.

☑ The WSUS Client Diagnostic Tools is a quick and easy way to first identify and troubleshoot client to server communication issues and shows you possible misconfigured client settings.

Frequently Asked Questions

The following Frequently Asked Questions, answered by the authors of this book, are designed to both measure your understanding of the concepts presented in this chapter and to assist you with real-life implementation of these concepts. To have your questions about this chapter answered by the author, browse to **www.syngress.com/solutions** and click on the **"Ask the Author"** form.

Q: When configuring Group Policy, I do not see any settings relating to AUs or WSUS. Am I in the right place?

A: Yes; however, you need to load the WSUS ADM called *wuau.adm* first. In your policy, right-click on **Administrative Templates** and select **Add/Remove Templates**. Choose **Add** and select *wuau.adm*. Click **Open** and **Close**. Your WSUS settings will be located under the following:

```
Computer Configuration\Administrative Templates\Windows Components\Windows
Update
```

Q: I created several WSUS Group Policies and have yet to see any clients show up in my WSUS Console. Is there any way to speed this up?

A: By default, Active Directory Group Policy updates clients every 90 minutes using a random offset. To speed this up from the client side, use the following command line:

```
Gpupdate.exe /force - Windows XP and Windows Server 2003
Secedit.exe /refreshpolicy machine_policy /enforce for Windows 2000
```

Q: I want to schedule my servers to download and install my approved updates once a week late at night during approved downtime. If one of our administrators is working on a server, I want to reboot it. Is this possible?

A: Yes. Using the *No auto-restart for scheduled Automatic Updates installations* GPO setting. This setting only specifies that it will *not* reboot if a local administrator is logged on, but will instead prompt that administrator whether he or she would like to *Restart Now* or *Restart Later*. Note, however, that if you are using deadlines, it will force a reboot.

Q: I have several Web servers located in a secure DMZ and outside of my Active Directory. Can I use my internal WSUS server to update them?

A: Yes. WSUS is not dependant on Active Directory in any way. You can use Local Policy or direct registry editing to configure your DMZ WSUS clients. You will, however, have to make sure your DMZ clients have port 80 (and 443 if using HTTPS) open inbound to your WSUS server for communication and download purposes.

Q: My non-Active Directory clients are not showing up in my WSUS console. How can I remotely check if my WSUS clients, set up in their own workgroup, are correctly configured with the required WSUS settings?

A: You can use built-in Windows command *reg.exe* to remotely query the computer's WSUS settings, using the following command. Consider scripting this for use with checking on multiple computers.

```
reg.exe query
\\WSUSClient\HKLM\SOFTWARE\Microsoft\Windows\CurrentVersion\WindowsUpdate /s
```

Q: Can I use WSUS to update my NT 4.0 clients in an NT 4.0 Domain?

A: No. WSUS only supports Windows XP, Windows 2000 SP3 or later, and Windows Server 2003.

Q: Can I use WSUS to update my NT 4.0 domain clients?

A: Yes, as long as they are either Windows XP, Windows 2000 SP3 or later or Windows Server 2003. You can use local policy, local registry entry, or NT 4.0 System Policy to deploy your WSUS server settings.

Q: I have a WSUS policy configured to apply to all of my Windows 2000 Professional client machines; however, I am not seeing any of them in my WSUS console. What do I do?

A: Make sure that all of your legacy Windows 2000 Professional clients meet WSUS' client compatibility specifications of SP3 or later.

www.syngress.com

Q: I have been using SUS for many years and have since introduced a WSUS server. Can my SUS clients be pointed to my WSUS server or will I have to roll out a newer WSUS AU client?

A: You can use Local or Group Policy to point your older SUS clients to the WSUS server. As long as your SUS clients are version 5.4.36x or later, they will use the built in *selfupdate* feature of WSUS and automatically update their clients. Older clients can be manually updated or pointed to the public Windows Update site for client updating.

Q: How can I configure my WSUS clients to *only* use WSUS and not be allowed to visit the Windows Update or Microsoft Update public update sites?

A: Although you could potentially configure this at your proxy or firewall, there is a custom GPO setting already available to block Microsoft's online update sites. Configure the following GPO setting:

```
Windows XP and Windows 2003
```

User Configuration\Administrative Templates\Windows Components\Windows Update**Remove Access to use all Windows Update features**

Windows 2000

User Configuration\Administrative Templates\Start Menu and Task Bar**Remove links and Access to Windows Update**

Q: I have approved several critical updates using the deadline option. The deadline time has passed and my clients have yet to show that they have downloaded or attempted to install my critical updates? What can I do?

A: Consider decreasing your Detection Time interval for your WSUS clients, or manually run a client detection using the following command:

```
wuauclt.exe /detectnow
```

Q: Can I force the installation of a critical update immediately?

A: Yes. Using the deadline option when approving updates will force an update installation on a specific date and time. You can specify a past date and time to force immediate installation; however, client detection must happen before they will recognize the approved deadline. Consider running the client detection command to force this and install the updates immediately:

```
wuauclt.exe /detectnow
```

Q: I have set my WSUS Products and Classifications to include Service Packs for both Microsoft Exchange and SQL Server; however, I am not seeing the latest Service Packs in my Updates directory to deploy. Why not?

A: At this time, the current version of WSUS only includes critical- and security-related updates for these products. Service Packs may be available in future releases.

Q: How can I see if any of my WSUS clients successfully installed my recently approved critical updates?

A: You can find these answers in both the *WindowsUpdate.log* and the computers local Event Log under the *Windows Update Agent* source.

Q: I have some WSUS clients that show up in the WSUS console and others that keep disappearing? Am I missing something?

A: You are probably using some type of disk-cloning software to deploy your client machines. WSUS uses the SID of the local computer to create its unique WSUS *ClientID*. When machines are cloned they have the same *ClientID*, causing the WSUS server to replace the "latest" machine that checks in with that *ClientID*. Use a SID regenerator before deploying your cloned machines or to repair those already deployed and affected. Follow these two steps from the WSUS client:

- Delete the following registry keys:
    HKLM\SOFTWARE\Microsoft\Windows\CurrentVersion\WindowsUpdate\ AccountDomainSid
    HKLM\SOFTWARE\Microsoft\Windows\CurrentVersion\WindowsUpdate\ SusClientID
    HKLM\SOFTWARE\Microsoft\Windows\CurrentVersion\WindowsUpdate\ PingID

- Run the following command to reset the local client cookie:

```
wuauclt.exe /resetauthorization /detectnow
```

Q: How can I remotely initiate an AU client detection?

A: You can do this using *Sysinterals*, a free remote execution utility called *psexec.exe*. Run the following command:

```
psexec.exe \\WSUSClient wuauclt.exe /detectnow
```

Chapter 8

Securing WSUS

Solutions in this chapter

- **Configuring Firewalls**
- **Using Secure Sockets Layer (SSL)**
- **Applying WSUS Client Security**

- ☑ **Summary**
- ☑ **Solutions Fast Track**
- ☑ **Frequently Asked Questions**

Introduction

There are a number of simple ways to help secure a Windows Software Update Services (WSUS) platform. This chapter looks at some of the aspects of hardening your WSUS environment while still providing for ease of use.

Configuring Firewalls

In a typical environment, not much has to be done to the firewall configuration in order to allow the WSUS server to download updates from Microsoft. Many environments allow most protocols to go outbound from the inside (trusted) network, but this is not always the case. Some organizations, such as the government and the military, may only allow access via certain protocols and ports, or to a particular list of preapproved sites.

If the restriction within your organization is port-based (limiting the types of Transmission Control Protocol/User Datagram Protocol [TCP/UDP] traffic that is allowed to pass), you won't need to do that much. WSUS only uses port 80 (Hypertext Transfer Protocol [HTTP]) and port 443 (Hypertext Transfer Protocol over SSL [HTTPS]) for accessing the Microsoft update sites. If your organization only allows traffic to pass to specific sites, Microsoft requires that the sites in Table 8.1 be added to the approved list.

Table 8.1 Required Sites for Firewall Access Control Lists

Web Site	Port
windowsupdate.microsoft.com	80
*.windowsupdate.microsoft.com	80
*.windowsupdate.com	80
*.update.microsoft.com	80
download.windowsupdate.com	80
download.microsoft.com	80
*.download.windowsupdate.com	80
wustat.windows.com	80
ntservicepack.microsoft.com	80
*.windowsupdate.microsoft.com	443
*.update.microsoft.com	443

An asterisk (*) represents a wildcard.

SOME INDEPENDENT ADVICE

If you are using a Web filtering service such as Websense (www.websense.com), make sure that it is not blocking access to the Microsoft update site. In a default configuration, Web and uniform resource locator (URL) filters such as Websense will not block the sites listed in Table 8.1. If the URL filter is set to only allow a specific list of approved sites, you will run into the same problem as if your firewall was only allowing limited access to sites.

Once these sites have been granted access through your firewall, you should be able to synchronize with the Windows Update service. If you continue to have problems related to the firewall, you should contact your firewall vendor.

Configuring Firewalls for Inbound Access to WSUS

It is pretty commonplace in today's IT world to have three separate zones configured on your Internet firewall:

- Internal Zone (trusted network)

- External Zone (untrusted network)

- Demilitarized Zone (DMZ) (protected network, typically sits between trusted and untrusted networks)

Servers (and in rare cases, workstations) that live within the DMZ are there because they offer services to the external zone, but still require protection behind a firewall (e.g., Web servers and File Transfer Protocol [FTP] servers). They provide a service to users on the external zone (most commonly the Internet) but should be accessible only by ports 80 or 443 (for Web servers) and ports 20 and 21 (for FTP). Figure 8.1 shows an example of a DMZ.

Figure 8.1 A DMZ

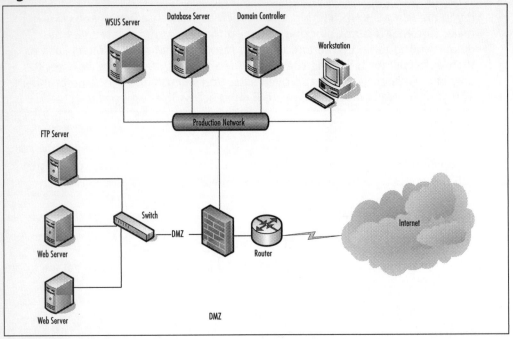

In some cases, you may want the servers in the DMZ to connect to an internal WSUS server for updates. These systems are configured to not initiate an outbound connection via the Internet, to not install another WSUS server in the DMZ, and so forth. Whatever the reason, there are additional configuration changes that must be made on the firewall. The following protocols must be enabled in order for a client machine to be able to access a WSUS server through the firewall:

- HTTP (Port 80)
- HTTPS (Port 443)
- Kerberos-Sec (UDP Port 750)

Kerberos is an authentication protocol that provides secret key cryptography for the purpose of strong authentication. Microsoft has adopted Kerberos for client/server and application authentication. For more information regarding Kerberos, visit http://web.mit.edu/kerberos/www/. For more information regarding the Windows flavor of Kerberos, visit http://support.microsoft.com/default.aspx?scid=kb;en-us;217098.

In order for WSUS clients to communicate with the WSUS server, all three ports must be open in both directions (see Figure 8.2). It is best to configure this in a one-to-one translation, so that if your DMZ is compromised, these ports will be open only between the clients specified and the WSUS server.

Shortcuts...

Group Clients in Your Firewall

Some firewall manufacturers provide for the "grouping" of servers in a firewall rule. These groupings allow you to add individual clients into a single entity for the purpose of limiting the number of rules in the firewall rule base. It is basically the same concept as grouping (and nesting) users and groups within Windows. By using groups, you can reduce the Access Control List, thus making the administrator's life less complicated.

Figure 8.2 Opening Ports for WSUS Access From the DMZ

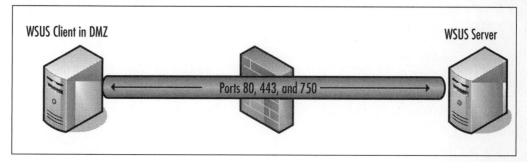

Anytime you "punch a hole" in your firewall, you should understand the full implications of such a change. A good practice is to discuss the implications with the person who "owns the box," to determine if opening these ports or using WSUS on these clients will cause any technical or security issues.

Shortcuts...

Using Microsoft ISA Server 2004

If you use Microsoft Internet Security and Acceleration (ISA) Server as your firewall, visit **http://ww.isaserver.org**. This is the "unofficial" ISA server Web site. There is an article by Steve Moffat that details exactly how to enable an ISA server for use with WSUS. In this article, Mr. Moffat describes how to configure the ISA server to permit itself to be updated, but it can also be used as a guide for allowing other clients to pass through the ISA Server. For more information about ISA Server, we recommend Tom Shinder's book, *Dr. Tom Shinder's Configuring ISA Server 2004* (ISBN: 1-931836-19-1, Syngress Publishing, 2004).

Using SSL

If you are reading this chapter, chances are you understand what SSL, certificates, and certificate authorities are and the purposes they serve. If you are not familiar with these items, chances are you have unknowingly used them dozens of times (e.g., if you purchased this book over the Internet from Syngress Publishing or another online store, you probably used SSL to secure your transaction). SSL provides for the secure transfer of information across a public (and sometimes private) network. Using SSL and digital certificates provides two major benefits:

- Encrypted transfer of private and confidential material (credit card numbers and so on)

- Nonrepudiation (provides proof of data integrity and guarantees data origin)

Although securing security updates may not seem like a high priority, think about it. What if someone "spoofed" the WSUS server and began sending infected "updates" to your clients? Imagine the following scenario:

- You configured group policy to pull updates from a server named MYWSUS.widgets.com, which is responsible for providing updates to 2,000 client computers (see Figure 8.3).

Figure 8.3 A Production Network Using WSUS

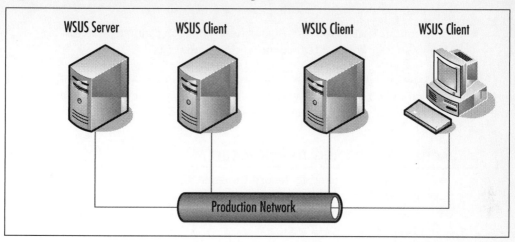

- A would-be hacker has managed to take your WSUS server offline.
- Domain Name Server (DNS) is not configured to allow only secure updates; anyone can register a Fully Qualified Domain Name (FQDN) with it.
- Mr. Hacker brings his "Virus Server" online and registers it with DNS as MYWSUS.widgets.com (see Figure 8.4).

Figure 8.4 A Spoofed WSUS Server

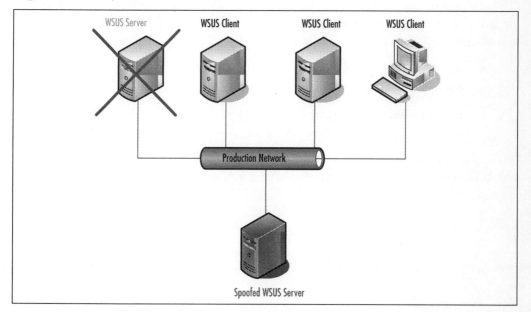

- All your 2,000 WSUS clients begin downloading the infected updates, blissfully unaware that this is not the real MYWSUS server.

- Thirty minutes later, you are in your boss's office explaining why you now have to attempt to fix 2,000 client workstations.

To combat this problem, WSUS is capable of using SSL to secure the transmission of metadata between the server and the clients. The first thing you need to do is prepare the WSUS server to accept SSL instead of the standard HTTP.

BEST PRACTICES ACCORDING TO MICROSOFT

- SSL cannot be used to secure transmission from a remote SQL server to a WSUS server.
- If secure transmissions from SQL to WSUS are required, use Internet Protocol Security (IPSec).
- If IPSec is not an option, consider moving the database onto the WSUS system instead of using remote SQL.
- The Content, ReportWebService, and SelfUpdate virtual directories should not be secured with SSL on the WSUS server. All others can be secured using SSL.

Configuring WSUS for SSL

The first step in using SSL is to obtain a digital certificate for your server. A number of certificate authorities are available on the Internet for this purpose, including the following:

- Verisign (www.verisign.com)
- Thawte (www.thawte.com)
- Digicert (www.digicert.com)

Digital certificate prices vary from vendor to vendor. Each WSUS server in your environment requires its own certificate, so you must plan carefully when deciding if SSL is the way to go. Once you have selected a vendor, you must create a certificate request from the SSL server.

Shortcuts...

Certificates "on the Cheap"

One way to get around the expense of digital certificates is to build your own Certificate Authority (CA) using a Windows 2003 server, which comes packaged with either Windows Server 2003 Standard or Windows Server 2003 Enterprise editions. We will use an internal Windows CA for the remainder of this chapter. For more information on building a Windows 2003 CA, visit http://www.microsoft.com/technet/prodtechnol/windowsserver2003/technologies/security/ws03crtm.mspx. If you have trouble copying that link, go to **http://www.microsoft.com/technet** and type **certificate authority windows 2003** in the Search window. The aforementioned article is titled "Implementing and Administering Certificate Templates in Windows Server 2003."

The following steps guide you through the process of requesting a certificate. This process assumes that you have already installed WSUS on the server.

1. Open the Internet Information Server (IIS) Manager by going to **Start | Administrative Tools | Internet Information Services (IIS Manager)**.

2. Next, select the **Web site that contains the WSUS virtual directories** (for this example, the Default Web Site). To get to the Default Web Site (or any other site), double-click **the name of the server** (in this case, WSUS), and then double-click **Web Sites**. Right-click **Default Web Site** (or the name you chose during installation) and select **Properties**. This opens the properties for the Web site (see Figure 8.5).

Figure 8.5 The Properties Window for the WSUS Web Site

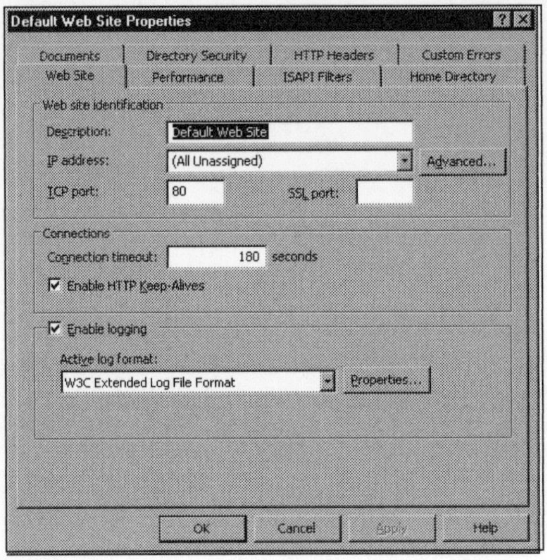

3. From the Properties window, select the **Directory Security** tab.

4. In the Directory Security tab under Secure communications, click the **Server Certificate...** button.

5. The Welcome to the Web Server Certificate Wizard window will open. Read through the welcome screen and click **Next**.

6. Because we need a new certificate, select **Create a new certificate** from the list of methods (see Figure 8.6) and click **Next**.

Figure 8.6 Selecting a Certificate Method

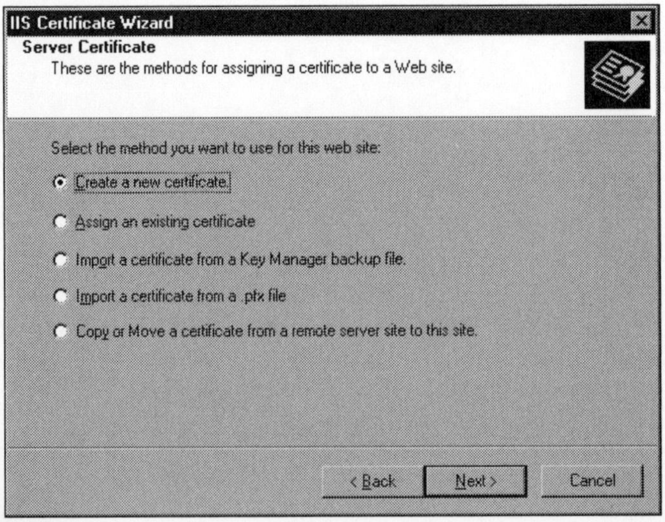

7. When the Delayed or Immediate Request window opens, select the **Prepare the request now send it later** option and click **Next**.

8. Next, enter a name for the new certificate (we use WSUS Certificate). Leave the bit length at 1024. You can increase the bit length, but it will cause a decrease in server performance. Click **Next**.

9. Enter the name of the organization and the organization unit in the Organization Information page (see Figure 8.7). Widgets Inc. and IT are used for this chapter.

Figure 8.7 Entering Organization Information

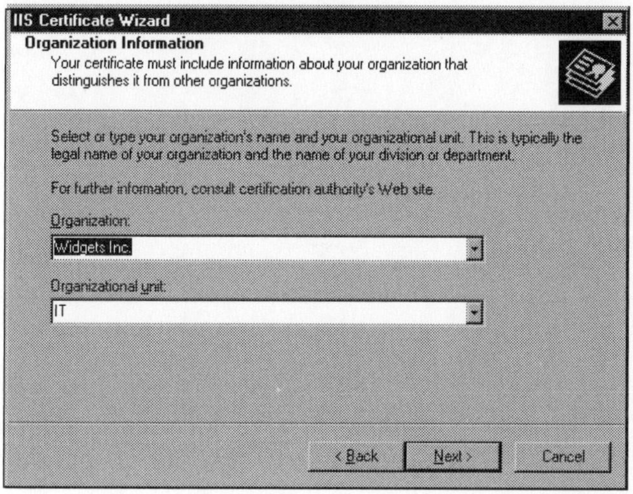

10. Next, determine what the system's common name will be, typically the name of the server that WSUS is running on. In this case, we use wsus. Enter a name for your server and click **Next**.

11. You now need to enter your geographical information. Select a **country**, **state**, and **city** where this server will reside (we use US for the country, Massachusetts for the state, and Boston for the city) (see Figure 8.8). Make sure not to abbreviate. Click **Next** once this step has been completed.

Figure 8.8 Geographical Information

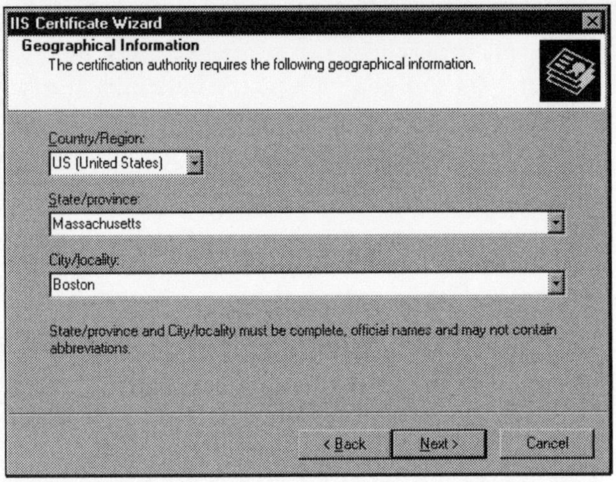

12. Enter a location and filename to save the request information just entered. The default is c:\certreq.txt. Click **Next** to continue.

13. Review the summary of the request. If the information is correct, click **Next** to continue. If you made a mistake, click the **Back** button to go back to the window where you made the mistake and change it.

14. After the request has been generated, click **Finish**.

15. Close the Web site properties.

Now you need to send the request file to your CA. This process (and response time) varies by vendor. If you are using a Windows 2003 CA to generate the ticket, follow the instructions from the Web site provided earlier in the chapter.

Applying the Certificate

Once you have received your certificate from your CA or have generated it yourself, you need to apply it to the WSUS server. To do this, complete the following steps:

1. Open the IIS Manager.

2. Select the Web site containing the WSUS virtual directories (e.g., the Default Web Site). To get to the Default Web Site (or any other site), double-click the **name of the server** (in this case, WSUS), then double-click **Web Sites**. Next, right-click **Default Web Site** (or the name you chose during installation) and select **Properties**. This opens the properties for the Web site.

3. From the Properties window, select the **Directory Security** tab.

4. In the Directory Security tab under Secure communications, click the **Server Certificate...** button.

5. The Welcome to the Web Server Certificate Wizard window will open. Click **Next**.

6. You will notice that the menu has changed since we generated the request (see Figure 8.9). Select **Process the pending request and install the certificate** and click **Next**.

Figure 8.9 Pending Certificate Request

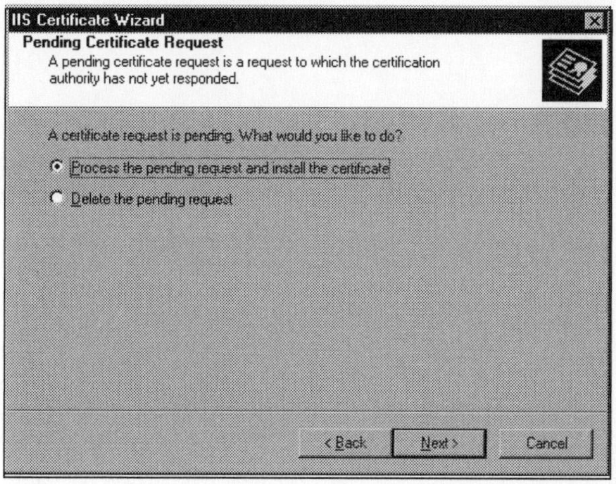

7. Next, browse to the directory where the certificate file you received is stored. Select **the certificate name** and click **Next**.

8. Select an **SSL port** to be used with this Web site. The standard SSL port is 443 (see Figure 8.10). Click **Next** to continue.

Figure 8.10 Setting the SSL Port

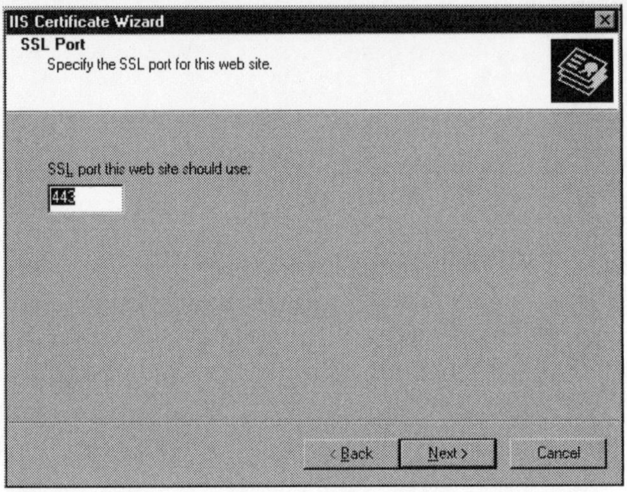

9. Review the certificate summary to verify that the information is correct and click **Next**.

10. Complete the certificate wizard by clicking **Finish**.

Your certificate has been applied to the server. Keep in mind that this process must be completed for each WSUS server you plan to implement in your environment with SSL. A certificate is assigned on a per-server basis, and cannot be used on different servers.

Enabling SSL on the WSUS Virtual Directories

As mentioned earlier in this chapter, there are certain virtual directories that can use SSL; the virtual directories that cannot use SSL would cause the server to fail to provide updates. SSL now needs to be enabled on the following virtual directories:

- ClientWebService
- DSSAuthWebService
- ServerSyncWebService
- SimpleAuthWebService
- WSUSAdmin

The following exercise steps through the process of enabling SSL on the WSUSAdmin virtual directory. Remember to apply this only to the sites listed in the preceding list:

1. Open the IIS Manager.

2. Select the **Web site that contains your WSUS virtual directories** (e.g., the Default Web Site). To get to the Default Web Site (or any other site), double-click the **name of the server** (in this case, WSUS) and then double-click **Web Sites**.

3. Double-click the **Default Web Site**. This displays a list of virtual directories beneath the WSUS Web site (see Figure 8.11).

Figure 8.11 A Listing of Virtual Directories

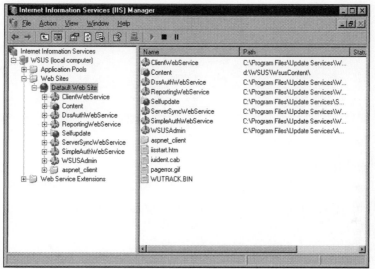

4. Right-click the **WSUSAdmin** virtual directory and click **Properties** from the drop-down list.

5. When the WSUSAdmin Properties dialog box opens, click the **Directory Security** tab.

6. In the Secure communications section of the Directory Security tab, click **Edit...**

7. The Secure Communications window will open (see Figure 8.12). From this window, select **Require secure channel (SSL)**; you can optionally select **Require 128-bit encryption**.

Figure 8.12 The Secure Communications Window

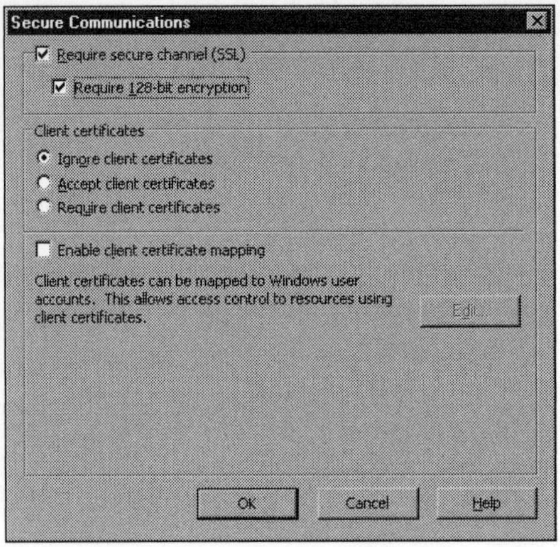

8. Click **OK** to continue.

9. Close the WSUSAdmin properties window by clicking **Apply** and then **OK**.

10. Next, try opening the WSUSAdmin window with HTTP (http://<server-name>/WSUSAdmin). This should fail.

11. Now, try opening the WSUSAdmin window using SSL (https://<server-name>/WSUSAdmin). This should grant access to the WSUSAdmin page. If you are prompted with a security alert, click **OK**.

12. You can verify that the certificate is valid and working by double-clicking the **padlock** in the bottom right of the browser window. Open the Certificate properties window, which provides information about the CA and the certificate itself (see Figure 8.13).

Figure 8.13 The Certificate Properties Window

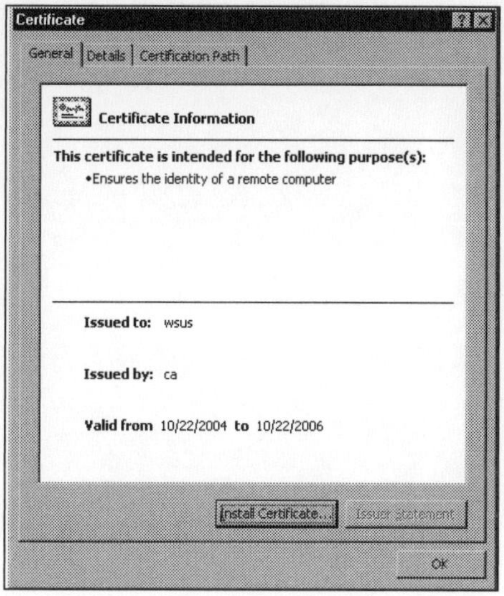

13. Repeat steps 5–12 for the remaining sites.

Applying WSUS Client Security

If you plan to use SSL within your environment, you have to adjust your client configuration so that it knows to use SSL instead of HTTP.

Configuring your clients to use SSL instead of HTTP is fairly simple, but in environments where Group Policy is not used, it can become time-consuming.

Applying WSUS for Clients via Group Policy

If you have already configured a Group Policy Object (GPO) for use with WSUS, then the changes you make will not take very long. From either a Domain Controller, server or workstation with the Administrator tools loaded:

1. Click **Start│Administrative Tools│ Active Directory Users and Computers**.

2. Right-click either the **domain name** (in this case, widgets.ads) or the organizational unit (OU) where you have applied the GPO. Click **Properties**.

3. Select the **Policy where WSUS settings have been applied** (see Figure 8.14) and click **Edit**.

Figure 8.14 Selecting a GPO

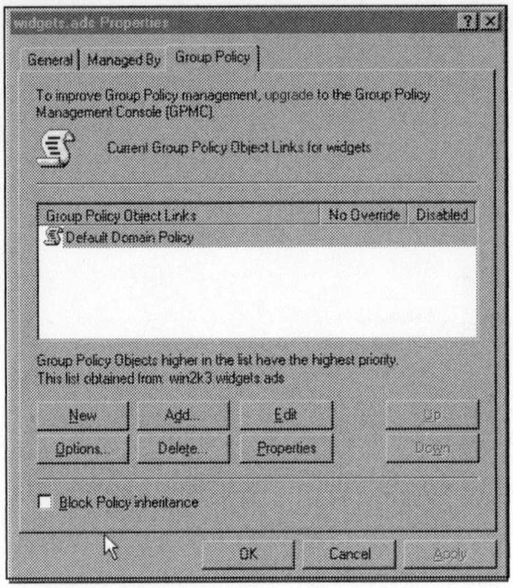

4.   Click **Computer Configuration**.

5.   Click **Administrative Templates**.

6.   Double-click **Windows Components**.

7.   Click **Windows Update**.

8.   In the main window, double-click **Specify intranet Windows update service location**.

9.   When the Specify intranet Windows update service location window opens, change the *Set the intranet update service for detecting updates: and Set the intranet statistics server:* to *https//<servername>* where *<servername>* is the name of your WSUS server (see Figure 8.15).

Figure 8.15 Setting the Update Location

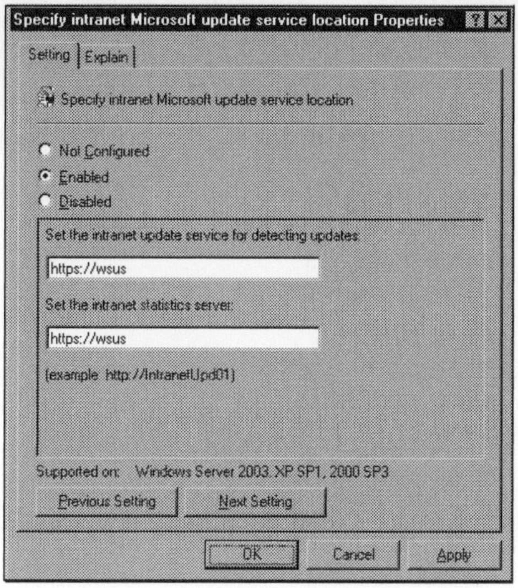

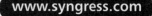

Figure showing dialog: "Specify intranet Microsoft update service location Properties" with Setting and Explain tabs. Options: Not Configured, Enabled (selected), Disabled. "Set the intranet update service for detecting updates:" https://wsus. "Set the intranet statistics server:" https://wsus. "(example: http://IntranetUpd01)". "Supported on: Windows Server 2003, XP SP1, 2000 SP3". Buttons: Previous Setting, Next Setting, OK, Cancel, Apply.

10.   Click **OK**.

11.   Close the Group Policy Editor.

Because this is a change to the group policy, clients either have to wait until their next reboot, or they will have to force a group policy update using *gpupdate* (Windows 2003/XP) or *secedit* (Windows 2000).

Applying WSUS for Clients Manually

The process for applying changes to use SSL manually on clients is not as easy as changing it on a GPO. To address various client types, the following procedure assumes a Windows 2000 client:

1.   Click **Start | Run**.

2.   Next, open the **registry editor**. Type **regedit** in the Run window.

3.   Drill down into the tree to the following subkey:
       HKEY_LOCAL_MACHINE\Software\Policies\Microsoft\Windows\WindowsUpdate.

4.   Double-click
       HKEY_LOCAL_MACHINE\Software\Policies\Microsoft\Windows\WindowsUpdate.

5.   In the main window, the following keys appear: (Default), WUServer, and WUStatusServer (see Figure 8.16).

Figure 8.16 WSUS Registry Keys

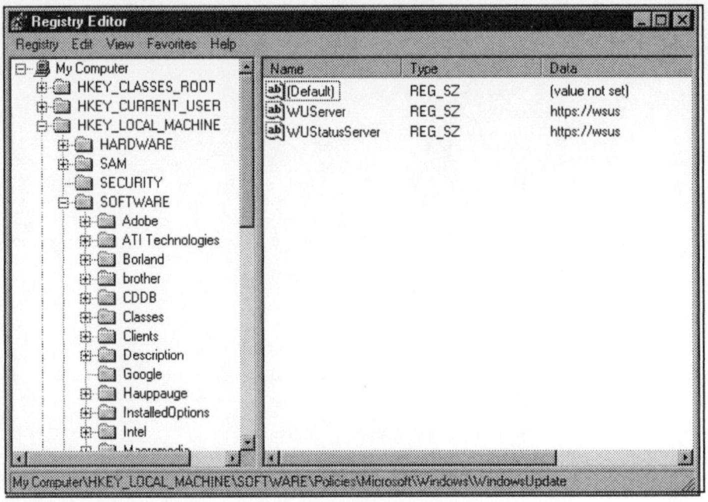

6. Open the **WUServer** and **WUStatusServer** keys one at a time, and change the value to *https://<server>* where *<server>* is the name of your WSUS server.

7. Close the registry editor.

The downside is that you have to perform this on each client. Once the change is made, however, the clients will begin using the SSL site on their next update.

Shortcuts...

Importing a Registry Key

If walking around to each client sounds painful, you can always export the appropriate keys from a sample system and import them into the rest of your clients. You could try e-mailing the key, but most e-mail clients strip registry keys. Alternatively, you could write a simple batch file for importing.

Summary

If security is a key factor in your environment, then taking the necessary steps to secure your WSUS environment only makes sense.

- If you are using restrictive firewall settings, make sure that the appropriate ports and sites are accessible from the WSUS server.

- If you are planning to use WSUS services through a firewall, make sure the appropriate ports are open on the firewall (ports 80, 443, and 750) so that clients can communicate with the WSUS server.

- One of the keys to using SSL is to make sure that you only secure the recommended sites. If you secure all sites, WSUS will fail.

- If the price of a commercial SSL certificate is out of your budget, consider setting up an internal CA with Windows 2003.

- Make sure to adjust GPO or the local security options on all WSUS clients to *https://* so that they can communicate with the WSUS server.

Solutions Fast Track

Configuring Firewalls

- ☑ Make sure your WSUS server has access to the Internet, specifically to the required Microsoft Update sites.

- ☑ Ensure that HTTP, SSL, and Kerberos-sec are all opened on the firewall if you plan on updating clients located on the other side of the firewall.

- ☑ Whenever possible, use groups on your firewall to reduce the number of rules in your firewall's rule base.

Using SSL

- ☑ Make sure not to apply the certificate directly to the Web site—only the specified virtual directories.

- ☑ You must have a certificate for each WSUS server.

- ☑ Only the WSUS metadata is secured. Updates are signed digitally and cannot use SSL for downloading.

Applying WSUS Client Security

- ☑ If you are using GPOs, make sure to change your update site to *https:/<servername>*.

☑ To update the changes on the clients immediately, you need to use *gpupdate* (or *secedit* on Windows 2000).

☑ You can force clients to detect new updates by typing **wuauclt /detectnow** on a command line.

Frequently Asked Questions

The following Frequently Asked Questions, answered by the authors of this book, are designed to both measure your understanding of the concepts presented in this chapter and to assist you with real-life implementation of these concepts. To have your questions about this chapter answered by the author, browse to **www.syngress.com/solutions** and click on the **"Ask the Author"** form.

Q: If we have WSUS running internally, why do we have to make sure that we can access the sites listed?

A: If WSUS is unable to reach these sites, WSUS will continue updating clients, but no new updates will be available. The exception to this is WSUS servers that receive updates from an upstream WSUS server.

Q: You mentioned setting up a CA server internally. How do I do this?

A: Unfortunately, this is beyond the scope of this book. However, there are several resources available on Microsoft's site for setting up a CA.

Q: I have walked through the steps for enabling SSL, but my clients continue to fail whenever they try to get updates. What is going on?

A: Make sure you did not set SSL on the WSUS Web site itself. Also, make sure that you did not set SSL on the virtual directories that cannot support it.

Q: I have set SSL and do not want to wait until my next update period to see if it is working. Is there anything I can do?

A: Yes. From a Windows 2003/XP system, go to a command prompt and type **gpupdate**. Next, type **wuauclt /detectnow**. It should begin updating immediately.

Q: I checked everything in my configuration and am trying to get to my WSUS Administration Web site using HTTPS. It keeps failing. Is there something I am doing wrong?

A: Probably not. Try restarting the IIS service, and also try restarting the Default Web Site (or the WSUS Web site that you built).

Chapter 9

Managing the WSUS Environment

Solutions in this chapter:

- Centralized vs. Distributed Environments
- Synchronization
- Managing Computer Groups
- Producing Reports

- ☑ Summary
- ☑ Solutions Fast Track
- ☑ Frequently Asked Questions

Introduction

Effectively managing your WSUS environment is critical to maintaining a healthy and secure Windows infrastructure. This chapter highlights the two management models available to Windows Software Update Services (WSUS) administrators and the concepts and tasks involved with managing updates and computers. This chapter also discusses the reporting capabilities added to WSUS and the technique for generating status reports for the product updates and computers managed in your WSUS environment.

Centralized vs. Distributed Environments

WSUS deployments are supported in both centralized and distributed environments. Each management model enables you to manage the distribution of updates throughout your organization. The model you choose depends on a variety of factors, including available administrative resources, connectivity, and Active Directory design. You should also consider your organization's cultural and political climate when choosing between the two models. In some cases, it may make more sense to centralize WSUS management; under other conditions, WSUS management should be distributed across different groups of administrators. Furthermore, you are not obliged to commit to only one management model for the entire organization. You can choose to have a centrally managed WSUS environment serving updates to some computers, and one or more autonomous WSUS deployments serving others.

The following sections discuss the differences between the two management models as well as design considerations.

Centralized Management

WSUS servers can be centrally managed using the *replica server* role. When deploying WSUS in the replica server role, you first deploy a single administration server, or master WSUS server. Other WSUS servers are then deployed as subordinate replicas, forming a replica group (see Figure 9.1). You approve updates and create computer groups on the administration server. Those settings are then mirrored by the replica servers to maintain a consistent configuration across the organization.

Figure 9.1 Centralized Management for a WSUS Environment

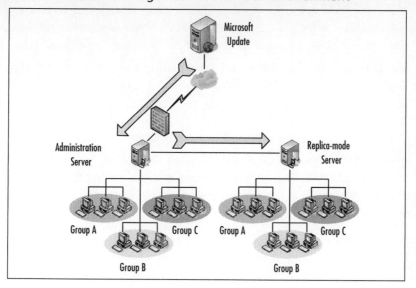

Although centrally managing WSUS helps reduce the complexity and overall administration requirements in larger organizations, there are some caveats. You will only have limited administration capabilities on the WSUS servers running in replica mode. The tasks that can be performed on replica servers include:

- **Assigning Computers That Are Managed By the Replica Server to Computer Groups** Although every computer group created on the administration server will exist on every replica-mode server, you only need to use the computer groups that are appropriate for any particular replica. If computer groups are not needed on a replica server, leave the group empty.

- **Specifying the Update Source** This can be the administration server, some other internal server, or the Microsoft Update servers.

- **Configuring a Synchronization Schedule** Different sites may have unique requirements or bandwidth conditions for synchronization. You can configure a customized synchronization schedule for each replica-mode server that best suits the needs and requirements of that site (e.g., some sites may not be impacted by synchronization during the day). Others may have very little bandwidth between the update source and the replica, requiring you to synchronize during off-hours or at night.

- **Specifying Proxy Server Settings** If you configure these settings, they will be used regardless of what update source you have selected.

- **Viewing Available Updates** You can view available updates and review additional information provided in the metadata content retrieved with each update on any replica server. You can also view the approval status for updates, although approvals can only be changed on the administration server.

- **Monitoring the Update, Synchronization, and Computer Status of the WSUS Server** Each replica-mode server in a replica group has its own unique status for synchronization and targeted computers. You can use the Web-based WSUS console to monitor the status of those items as well as the status of update retrievals through synchronization.

- **Run WSUS Reports** All standard reports are available on replica-mode servers. In addition, you can create custom reports using filters on any replica server, although those reports will only be available on the replica server where they were created.

You can add computers to computer groups on the replica mode servers; however, you cannot create or delete the computer groups themselves. When centrally managing WSUS, all computer groups must be created or deleted on the administration server. Computer groups that have been created or removed will be mirrored by each replica-mode server in the replica group. You may find that some of the sites in your organization do not need all of the computer groups, especially the site managed by the administration server. It is important, however, to create all the computer groups required to satisfy the needs of each site across the organization. Likewise, all update approvals must be configured on the administration server.

Distributed Management

The distributed management model is ideal for situations where site administrators need full control over update approvals and computer groups. In this model, all administration tasks are performed on each replica server, including the creation of computer groups and approvals. Each WSUS server is only configured with the computer groups that the administrator will populate with computers, so you will not have any empty computer groups to clutter up the WSUS configuration (see Figure 9.2). This is the default management mode for WSUS; you do not need to do anything to run WSUS in this model.

Distributed management may satisfy your needs if your organization only has one site or if each site within the organization is autonomously administered. The distributed management model is the only model that satisfies regulatory or political separation of administration (e.g., some countries require companies in the financial industry to be solely responsible for the administration of their computer resources). In this case, your organization may choose to centrally manage the WSUS servers in North America and Europe, but opt for the distributed management model for WSUS servers in Latin America.

You may also choose this model if one or more of your WSUS servers are located on disconnected networks. Although it is possible to centrally manage WSUS servers that cannot communicate with the administration server, there can be a substantial amount of administration overhead incurred to do so in large organizations. A better option may be to have administrators at disconnected sites manage their own independent WSUS server.

Figure 9.2 Distributed Management for a WSUS Environment

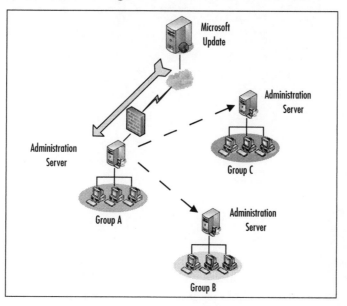

Mixing Centralized and Distributed Management

The optimal management solution for larger organizations seldom uses only one management model. The complexity of such organizations usually creates an administrative nightmare for patch management as servers are spread throughout many geographical locations with various levels of connectivity, language requirements, and administration groups. Figure 9.3 shows a mix of a centralized and distributed management solution.

Figure 9.3 Mixing Both Centralized and Distributed Management

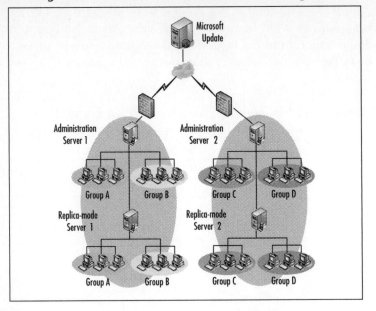

Often the best solution is a mixture of centralized and distributed management (see Figure 9.3). This example shows how groups of well-connected sites can be consolidated into a single replica group, which reduces the number of management points needed to administer the overall WSUS design. Both Administration Server 1 and Administration Server 2 have access to Microsoft Update and serve as the administration server in their respective replica groups. Each WSUS environment has its unique set of computer groups that have been replicated to the replica-mode servers.

Remember that the goal of WSUS is to effectively update your Windows operating systems and other supported Microsoft products while reducing complexity and administrative burden. Administrators should determine whether a single management model or a mixture of models best meets their needs.

BEST PRACTICES ACCORDING TO MICROSOFT

Microsoft recommends testing updates prior to deploying them to production computers. You should have a computer group of test computers that you can target to evaluate the readiness of the updates for your environment. In centrally managed environments, the test computer group is replicated to all replica-mode servers and should have assigned computers that represent the population managed by that server. In distributed environments, you should create a test group manually for each server and assign computers to it where necessary.

SOME INDEPENDENT ADVICE

In some cases, installing and maintaining non-production computers to be used to test updates can be an extensive process requiring a lot of hardware. This is especially true for servers, since they need to have sufficient resources to host the application or service to be tested. A solution to this would be to utilize virtualization software and maintain a group of virtual machines that are grouped together for the purpose of testing updates. The benefits of this solution include rapid provisioning, the ability to restore virtual machines back to a point in time quickly, and a substantial reduction in the number of physical computers that you need on hand to test updates.

Synchronization

Synchronization is the process in which updates are distributed to WSUS servers. WSUS server synchronization follows the parameters that you configure on the Synchronization Options page. The amount of data that is transferred during synchronization is based on updates that have been released since the last time the WSUS server made contact with the update source.

The data that every update contains is composed of two components:

- **Metadata** provides WSUS information particular to the update, including properties of the update, links to Microsoft KB articles, end-user license agreements (EULAs), and whether the update supersedes previous updates for the same product. The metadata is usually much smaller than the actual source file package.

- **Update files** are the actual files needed to update or replace files for software components installed on a client computer.

When your WSUS server synchronizes and receives new updates, the update components are broken down and stored in different locations. Metadata is stored in the SUSDB database. Update files are stored either in the local update source folder or on Microsoft Update servers (depending on how you configured the synchronization options). Metadata is always downloaded during synchronization. If you select a local source folder, WSUS will download both the metadata and the update files for retrieval by the targeted clients. If you configure WSUS to store update files on Microsoft Update servers, only the metadata is downloaded to the WSUS servers. When targeted client computers attempt to install the update, they must retrieve the update files directly from Microsoft Update.

There are pros and cons for both types of updates. Table 9.1 discusses some of these. The recommended choice, however, is to configure the synchronization options to store

update files in a local repository on the WSUS server. The benefits are many, and they
outweigh the disadvantages. The biggest benefit is better control over network bandwidth requirements. Rather than having each client consume precious bandwidth to pull
down its own independent updates across the Internet from Microsoft Update, the
updates are retrieved once and stored locally on the WSUS server(s). Managed clients
then retrieve their update files from the WSUS server rather than from Microsoft
Update.

Table 9.1 Synchronization Method Comparison

Synchronization Method	WSUS Server Impact	Client Impact	Additional Comments
Synchronize metadata only; clients must retrieve update files directly from Microsoft Update.	Low network bandwidth requirements required for WSUS server to synchronize updates. Low storage requirements on WSUS server; only space in database to store new metadata is needed.	High aggregate network traffic and bandwidth requirements because each client independently retrieves update files. Dependency on Internet connectivity for clients to retrieve updates files.	Use of Web-caching servers or appliances will minimize Internet-bound retrieval requests.
Synchronize metadata and all update files	Medium network bandwidth requirements for WSUS servers. First-time synchronization for WSUS servers causes very high network utilization because WSUS must download all existing updates for the selected product categories. High storage requirements. All update files are downloaded, even if not approved.	Clients update quickly on Local Area Networks (LANs) of 100Mb or better. Updates immediately available for clients once approved for install.	This method causes wasted storage resources such as update files for updates that have been declined or otherwise never approved for install reside in the WSUS server's local repository.

Continued

Table 9.1 continued Synchronization Method Comparison

Synchronization Method	WSUS Server Impact	Client Impact	Additional Comments
Synchronize metadata and updates files after being approved for install	Medium network bandwidth requirements for WSUS servers. WSUS servers only retrieve update files for updates that have been approved for install.	Clients update quickly on LANs of 100Mb or better. Clients must wait for approved updates while the WSUS server retrieves update files from Microsoft Update.	Most deployments are configured with this method. Better control over bandwidth needs while maintaining all update files needed in the local WSUS repositories.

Chaining

Compared with simple WSUS deployments, you can also create more complex deployments containing multiple WSUS servers. WSUS gives you the ability to synchronize one WSUS server with another. Chaining WSUS servers allows them to share updates and metadata, thus eliminating the need for each WSUS server to retrieve those files from Microsoft Update.

Two WSUS servers chained together is not the same as the relationship between an administration server and a replica-mode server, as discussed earlier in this chapter. No information regarding computer groups or approvals is shared between chained servers. This type of configuration is useful when WSUS servers have a high-cost connection to the Internet, as found in some countries, or limited connectivity, such as demand-dial connections. This type of configuration is also useful to move updates closer to the clients that need them (e.g., you may choose to put WSUS server in each branch location and configure them to synchronize with a primary WSUS server in the corporate office during the night when users will not be impacted. This will allow those users to receive updates on their local LAN rather than pulling them across the wide area network (WAN) from corporate. Even within the corporate office, chained servers can provide a highly scalable and highly available solution for patching hundreds or thousands of clients (see "Some Independent Advice" for additional details).

There are caveats to take into consideration when chaining WSUS servers. These include:

- **Best Practices Recommend Only Three Levels of Nesting** This means if you need multiple WSUS servers you do not want to chain them all together. Instead, create a hub-and-spoke design.

- **All Members of the Chain Must Use the Same Storage Option** For instance, if you choose the option to maintain updates locally on the master chain server, then all downstream servers will also store their updates locally.

- **All Members of the Chain Must Use the Same Download Options** If the master chain server is configured to only download updates after they have been approved, the downstream servers will also mirror this setting.

- **All Members of the Chain Must Use the Same Product Filtering Options** For instance, if the master chain server is configured to only download updates for Windows and Office (but not Structured Query Language [SQL] Server) then the downstream servers will only have these updates to choose from.

Replicas

Earlier in this chapter, the concept of centrally managed replica groups was discussed. We defined a replica group as a WSUS hierarchy of one administration server and one or more replica-mode servers. When centrally managing WSUS servers, computer group and approval information is shared between all servers in the replica group. Update files and metadata do not fall under this replication scheme.

To maintain consistency in the model used to manage WSUS, you can configure your administration server (which has direct access to the Internet) to serve as the primary source for updates for the replicas. Each replica server would then be configured as a *downstream* update server and obtain its update files and metadata from the *upstream* administration server using the Synchronization Options page.

Disconnected Networks

If your organization includes WSUS servers on disconnected networks, you can follow a two-step export and import process (see Figure 9.4) to update those replica servers. This process requires additional management overhead, but it does guarantee update consistency between all WSUS servers; however, there can be a high degree of lag time for this type of asynchronous synchronization. Good planning will optimize the process and minimize the time it takes to synchronize WSUS servers on disconnected networks.

Figure 9.4 Two-Step Export/Import Process for Disconnected Networks

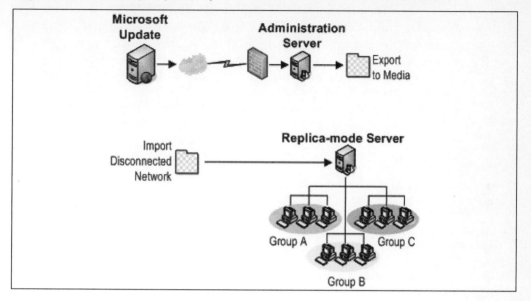

Before attempting to export and import updates between the export server and the disconnected import server, you must first match the advanced synchronization options between the source and destination WSUS servers. This includes the express installation files feature and languages. This ensures that you collect the type of updates you intend to distribute. You do not have to worry about matching settings for schedule, products and classifications, source, or proxy server, because the import steps eliminate the need for these settings. If you are deferring downloads on the export server until updates have been approved, you must approve any pending updates so that they can be downloaded prior to migrating updates to the import server.

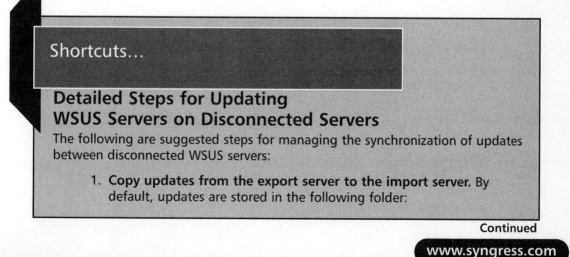

Shortcuts...

Detailed Steps for Updating WSUS Servers on Disconnected Servers

The following are suggested steps for managing the synchronization of updates between disconnected WSUS servers:

1. **Copy updates from the export server to the import server.** By default, updates are stored in the following folder:

Continued

C:\WSUS\WSUSContent. If you specified a different location during the setup process of the export server, use that path instead.

2. **Export update metadata from the database on the export server, and import it into the database on the import server.** You accomplish the metadata import and export by using the command-line utility *WSUSutil.exe*. You must be a member of the local Administrators group on both WSUS servers to export and import metadata. In addition, both operations can only be run from the WSUS servers. Be sure that you are logged on locally onto the export server before performing the export operation, and logged on locally to the import server before attempting to import the metadata.

You can use a file system backup utility to copy update files from the export server to the import server. You should capture and maintain the folder structure for the WSUSContent folder, and the update files should be copied to the local source repository on the import server (this may or may not be the same path as the export server). You can limit how data is copied by making incremental backups rather than full backups of the WSUSContent folder.

BEST PRACTICES ACCORDING TO MICROSOFT

Automatic Updates Configuration for WSUS Servers

If you chain multiple WSUS servers together, Microsoft recommends the following technique to prevent propagating updates with changes that break the protocol for server-to-server communication.

WSUS administrators should point Automatic Updates on all WSUS servers to the deepest downstream WSUS server in the hierarchy. This shields the entire chain from server-to-server protocol-breaking changes, because the downstream WSUS server can be used to update the broken upstream WSUS servers via Automatic Updates.

Export/Import for Disconnected WSUS Servers

Microsoft recommends that you copy updates to the file system of the import server before you import metadata. If WSUS finds metadata for an update that is not in the file system, the WSUS console shows that the update failed to be downloaded. This type of problem can be fixed by copying the update onto the file system of the import server and then again attempting to deploy the update.

SOME INDEPENDENT ADVICE

One of the often overlooked benefits of WSUS versus other patch management products is that WSUS is based on standard Web technology. Updates are distributed via Hypertext Transfer Protocol (HTTP) and Hypertext Transfer Protocol Secure sockets (HTTPS) over ports 80 and 443, respectively. And with Microsoft's Background Intelligent Transfer Server (BITS) technology, WSUS is highly recoverable, allowing interrupted sessions to resume where they left off when connectivity is re-established with WSUS servers. Since BITS uses stateless session with the source Web server, it is possible to develop a highly scalable and highly available solution for WSUS using multiple WSUS servers.

Since Microsoft typically releases there patches on the third Tuesday of the month (commonly referred to as "Patch Tuesday"), a WSUS server managing hundreds or thousands of clients at a single site can become overloaded and perform poorly as clients retrieve their updates. Even worse, if you plan on using WSUS to distribute service packs for Windows or Office, you will quickly find out that just a few WSUS servers is not enough to handle that large of a load.

One solution is to selectively assign clients to specific computer groups managed by different WSUS servers. This type of solution, however, is not very flexible and requires lots of planning to distribute the load evenly between multiple WSUS servers.

Another solution would be to use a common Domain Name Service (DNS) alias with the Internet Protocol (IP) address for each WSUS server. Using round-robin DNS name resolution will balance connecting clients across WSUS servers fairly well; however, clients will be sent to WSUS servers that are offline or otherwise not responding, causing updates to fail.

A more elegant solution to this problem would be to use load-balancing technology. Microsoft's Network Load Balancing (NLB) service or, even better, a network load-balancing appliance or switch provides an effective solution with some intelligent rules to optimize the utilization of your WSUS servers while guaranteeing successful updates for client computers. Switch manufacturers such as Cisco and Nortel produce inexpensive load balancers. Even better, if your WSUS servers are running on blade servers you can provide load-balancing services inside the blade chassis. Both IBM and HP provide Layer 4–7 switches for their chassis, and Dell provides a software-based solution to load-balance functionality to their blades.

Managing Computer Groups

The heart of WSUS management is the capability to target updates to groups of client computers. WSUS provides a mechanism to help you ensure that the right computers get the rights updates at the right time. In fact, computer groups ensure that client computers receive their updates in a consistent manner on an ongoing basis.

Computers will always belong to two groups. Every computer belongs to the All Computers group. However, they will also belong to the Unassigned Computers group until you assign them to your own custom group. A computer can belong to only one group in addition to the All Computers group.

You can assign computers to computer groups using one of two methods. The first method is server-side targeting where you manually move computers from the Unassigned Computers group to a custom computer group. The second method is client-side targeting where you use Group Policy or edited registry settings on client computers. Computers that are configured with client-side targeting automatically add themselves to computer groups on their managing WSUS server. You must choose either server-side or client-side targeting for each WSUS server as a global setting for all managed computers; however, you do not have to configure all your WSUS servers with the same setting. Some can be configured for server-side targeting while others are configured for client-side targeting.

A summary of the computer group targeting methods and their configuration is listed in Table 9.2.

Table 9.2 Computer Group Targeting Method

Targeting Method	Summary	How to Configure
Server-Side Targeting	When configuring server-side targeting, use the WSUS Web-based administration console to create computer groups and then assign client computers to those groups. Server-side targeting is a good choice for organizations that do not have many client computers to update and you want to move client computers into computer groups manually. This method also makes sense for computers that you frequently move between computer groups.	To enable server-side targeting on your WSUS server, click the **Use the Move computers task in Windows Server Update Services** option on the Computers Options page.

Continued

Table 9.2 continued Computer Group Targeting Method

Targeting Method	Summary	How to Configure
Client-Side Targeting	When configuring client-side targeting, you configure client computers to automatically add themselves to the computer groups that you previously created in the WSUS Web-based administration console. You can configure client-side targeting through an Active Directory Group Policy Object (GPO). If client computers are not members of an Active Directory domain, you can automatically assign them to a computer group by editing registry entries for the client computers. This will generate the results as configuration through Group Policy with some additional parameters. When the client computers connect and check-in with their corresponding WSUS server in both cases, they will add themselves into the indicated computer group automatically. Client-side targeting makes sense if you have many client computers and want to automate the process of assigning them to c omputer groups. This is also a good choice when you want to enforce computer group membership without relying on manual intervention of group assignment.	To enable client-side targeting on your WSUS server, click the **Use Group Policy or registry settings on client computers** option on the "Computers Options" page.

Configuring WSUS settings via registry settings can be performed on an individual basis, via login scripts, or through NT 4.0 system policy. Table 9.3 lists the registry entries for the WSUS environment options. These entries can be found under the registry key: *HKEY_LOCAL_MACHINE\Software\Policies\Microsoft\Windows\WindowsUpdate*.

Table 9.3 Registry Entries for Setting WSUS Options

Entry Name	Values	Data Type
ElevateNonAdmins	Possible values: 0 or 1 0: Only users in the Administrators user group can approve or disapprove updates. 1: Users in the Users security group are allowed to approve or disapprove updates.	Reg_DWORD
TargetGroup	Name of the computer group to which the computer belongs. This should be configured for client-side targeting only. **TargetGroupEnabled** should be set along with this policy.	Reg_String
TargetGroupEnabled	Possible values: 0 or 1 0: Do not use client-side targeting. **TargetGroup** should be set along with this policy. 1: Use client-side targeting.	Reg_DWORD
WUServer	The URL of the WSUS server used by Automatic Updates and Application Programming Interface (API) callers. This policy is paired with **WUStatusServer** and should be set along with this policy and should be the same value in order for them to be valid.	Reg_String

Continued

Table 9.3 continued Registry Entries for Setting WSUS Options

Entry Name	Values	Data Type
WUStatusServer	The URL of the server to which reporting information will be sent for client computers that use the WSUS server configured by the **WUServer** key. This policy is paired with **WUServer** and should be set along with this policy and should be set to the same value in order for them to be valid.	Reg_String

Additional configuration of the Automatic Update agent can be also be made via registry settings that can be made on an individual basis, set by login scripts, or through NT 4.0 system policy. Table 9.4 lists the registry entries for the Automatic Update agent options. These entries can be found under the registry key: *HKEY_LOCAL_MACHINE\Software\Policies\Microsoft\Windows\WindowsUpdate\AU*.

Table 9.4 Registry Entries for Automatic Update Agent Configuration

Registry Entry Name	Values	Registry Data Type
AUOptions	Possible values: 2, 3, 4, or 5 2: Notify before download. 3: Automatically download and notify of installation. 4: Automatic download and scheduled installation. This is only valid if values exist for the entries of **ScheduledInstallDay** and **ScheduledInstallTime**. 5: Automatic Updates is required, but end users can configure it.	Reg_DWORD

Continued

Table 9.4 continued Registry Entries for Automatic Update Agent
Configuration

Registry Entry Name	Values	Registry Data Type
AutoInstallMinor Updates	Possible values: 0 or 1 0: Treat minor updates like other updates. 1: Silently install minor updates.	Reg_DWORD
DetectionFrequency	Possible values: time in hours, 1-22. Time between detection cycles.	Reg_DWORD
DetectionFrequency Enabled	Possible values: 0 or 1 0: Disable **Detection Frequency**. 1: Enable **Detection Frequency**.	Reg_DWORD
NoAutoReboot WithLoggedOnUsers	Possible values: 0 or 1 0: Automatic Updates notifies user that the computer will restart in 5 minutes. 1: Logged-on user gets to choose whether or not to restart his or her computer.	Reg_DWORD
NoAutoUpdate	Possible values: 0 or 1 0: Enable Automatic Updates. 1: Disable Automatic Updates.	Reg_DWORD
RebootRelaunch Timeout	Possible values: time in minutes, 1–1440. Time between prompting again for a scheduled restart.	Reg_DWORD
RebootRelaunch TimeoutEnabled	Possible values: 0 or 1 0: Disable **Reboot RelaunchTimeout**. 1: Enable **Reboot RelaunchTimeout**.	Reg_DWORD

Continued

Table 9.4 continued Registry Entries for Automatic Update Agent Configuration

Registry Entry Name	Values	Registry Data Type
RebootWarning Timeout	Possible values: time in minutes, 1-30. Length, in minutes, of the restart warning countdown after installing updates with a deadline or scheduled updates.	Reg_DWORD
RebootWarning TimeoutEnabled	Possible values: 0 or 1 0: Disable custom **RebootWarningTimeout** (use the default value of 5 minutes). 1: Enable **Reboot WarningTimeout**.	Reg_DWORD
RescheduleWaitTime	Possible values: time in minutes, 1–60. Time, in minutes, that Automatic Updates should wait at startup before applying updates from a missed scheduled installation time. Note that this policy applies only to scheduled installations, not deadlines. Updates whose deadlines have expired should always be installed as soon as possible.	Reg_DWORD
RescheduleWait TimeEnabled	Possible values: 0 or 1 0: Disable **Reschedule WaitTime**. 1: Enable **RescheduleWait Time**	Reg_DWORD

Continued

Table 9.4 continued Registry Entries for Automatic Update Agent
Configuration

Registry Entry Name	Values	Registry Data Type
ScheduledInstallDay	Possible values: 0-7 0: Every day. 1 through 7: The days of the week from Sunday (1) to Saturday (7). This policy is only valid if AUOptions equals 4.	Reg_DWORD
ScheduledInstall Time	Possible values: time of day in 24-hour format, 0–23.	Reg_DWORD
UseWUServer	The WUServer value is not respected unless this key is set.	Reg_DWORD

BEST PRACTICES ACCORDING TO MICROSOFT

If your organization has an Active Directory domain, configure multiple computers using GPOs. Microsoft recommends that you create a new GPO that contains only WSUS settings. Link the new WSUS GPO to the appropriate Organizational Units (OUs) within the Active Directory domain(s) being managed by WSUS. Create as many GPOs as needed to cover the variations in client configuration in your deployment.

SOME INDEPENDENT ADVICE

Managing WSUS through GPOs is effective and simple. If you want advanced control of WSUS, however, or if the computers you want to manage are not members of an Active Directory domain, Microsoft provides a software development kit (SDK) available for download on its site. The SDK exposes a Component Object Model (COM)-based API for managing both client computers and WSUS servers. If you are familiar with scripting against COM objects or have development experience with VisualBasic.NET, the SDK provides a powerful and extremely granular interface to manage your WSUS environment.

The WSUS SDK includes some samples that demonstrate the flexibility of the API, and can be downloaded from *www.microsoft.com/windowsserversystem/ updateservices/downloads/default.mspx*.

Producing Reports

One of features that the original SUS product lacked was reporting capabilities. With the introduction of WSUS, Microsoft now provides administrators the ability to produce status reports without having to use a third-party reporting product to do so.

The standard reports built into WSUS include reports for update, synchronization, and computer status as well as an overall summary of the WSUS deployment. These reports are available directly from the Web-based WSUS console. Each report can have filters applied to only produce the information that you need. The following is a list and description of each of the standard reports available:

- **Status of Updates** This report returns the status of all approved updates by computer group and computer.

- **Status of Computers** This report provides the status of client computers and the status of updates on those computers. Among the data available in this report is a summary of updates that have been installed or are needed for a particular computer or group of computers.

- **Synchronization Results** You can use this report to view a list of new updates, update revisions, and errors that occurred during synchronization.

- **Settings Summary** This is a summary report of the settings configured through the Options page.

You can quickly access any of these reports on the Reports page. Once you select the particular reports that you wish to view, you can apply additional filters as needed. You can also obtain a print-ready version of the report that opens up in another browser window. Print-ready is also available from the Updates and Computers pages. Although you can only produce a report for a specific update or specific computer, this is a quick way to get a report for any single targeted item.

Status of Updates Report

The Status of Updates report delivers a view of the status for all of your approved updates. This report only provides information about updates that are of approval type *installed* or *detect only*. You can narrow the results by selecting the status to be used as filter criteria. By default, the report displays an alphabetical list of approved updates. You can filter the display by approval action and computer group by making appropriate selections that achieve the desired result under **View** and then clicking **Apply**. Your filter is reset to the default list of all updates when you close the Status of Updates report.

The information displayed in the report is based on data stored in the WSUS database. This data reflects the most recent status of client computers the last time they contacted the WSUS server. There is some inherent latency between the time that you change the approvals for one or more updates and the time when that status is updated in the database. By default, client computers contact their managing WSUS server every 22 hours. This interval is configurable through Group Policy or by editing registry settings.

The data the report returns can be presented in three different views: the status of an update at a high level, by computer group, or by computer. The Update Summary view is the default view that appears when you run a Status of Updates report. The information displayed in the update summary view consists of:

- **Title** This is the name of the update, usually including the Microsoft Knowledge Base article number supporting the update. To view the properties for an update, click an update in this column. The update properties box provides general information about the update, status information for the update by computer group, and any available information about changes to the update. This is also the same information displayed in the computer group view. You can also expand this view into computer view by expanding a computer group.

- **Installed** The number of computers on which the update has been successfully installed.

- **Needed** The number of client computers that have detected an available update for software products on the computer, but have not successfully installed the update. Only a detect-only action has been performed for the update. If an update requires a restart, then a computer that has installed the update will continue to appear in the Needed column until it is restarted.

- **Failed** The number of computers that last reported a failed download, installation, or removal of an update.

- **Last updated** The last time any action for the update occurred.

The computer group view displays the status of an update by computer group. To use this view, expand any update that is listed in update summary view. In addition to status count information (similar to the update summary view), the information displayed in the computer group view also contains:

- **Computer Group** The name of the computer group to which the update has been targeted.

- **Approval** The action that this update has been approved for, specific to the group.

- **Deadline** The deadline for the action, if you have set a deadline.

The computer view displays the status of each computer in a computer group. To use the computer view, expand a computer group.

Shortcuts...

Producing Update Compliance Reports

The audience for your reports can range from the IT security officer and senior management to auditors evaluating your level of compliance to documented policies and processes. WSUS can help you produce reports as part of your overall compliance strategy. You can view or print two types of compliance status reports, one for individual computers and one for individual updates.

To run a computer compliance status report:

1. On the WSUS console toolbar, click **Computers,** and then click the computer for which you want to produce the compliance status report.

2. Click **Print status report**.

3. If you want more information about a specific update under Update Status, you can select **the title of an individual update** or click the **status for the update**.

4. To print the report, press the **File** menu, and then press **Print**.

To run an Update Compliance status report:

1. On the WSUS console toolbar, select **Updates,** and then click the update for which you want to produce the compliance report.

2. Click **Print status report**.

3. To print the report, click the **File**, and then click **Print**.

Status of Computers Report

The Status of Computers report provides both a cumulative and individual update status summary for computers in the computer group and for the update status results you select in the view criteria. The following table provides more information about the status provided for each update.

To display additional information about a specific computer, you can expand the computer (click the **+** sign next to the computer) to view the status of individual updates for the computer. In addition, you can see the properties of an individual update by clicking the title of the update. To view more information about the specific status result of an update, click the **status for the update**.

Synchronization Results Report

The Synchronization Results report enables you to see synchronization information for your WSUS server. This report includes any errors generated during schedule synchronization runs as well as a list of any new updates that have been released.

The report has four items:

- **Last Synchronization** Displays information about the last time the WSUS server synchronized with Microsoft Update or another WSUS server, and if it was a successful synchronization.

- **Synchronization Summary** Displays summary information about new updates and errors that occurred during synchronization.

- **Errors** For each error, displays the date of the error, a description of the error, and the update ID associated with the error.

- **New Updates** Displays the updates that have been synchronized to the WSUS server for the given time period.

Settings Summary Report

The Settings Summary report enables you to view and print a summary of all of the settings that can be specified on the Options page.

BEST PRACTICES ACCORDING TO MICROSOFT

You can use a command-line tool on client computers that are running the WSUS client software (Automatic Updates) to initiate contact between the client computer and WSUS server. This can be useful if you want to get immediate update status for a particular computer; you can run this tool to force connection and then generate a Status of Updates report.

To manually invoke contact from the client computer to the WSUS server, run the following from a command prompt: *wuauclt.exe /detectnow*

When you require multiple computers to contact their respective WSUS servers, you can write a script that will force the Update Detection from Automatic Update Client to check for updates.

Copy and paste the following code into a text file and name it *AUForceUpdate.cmd*. You can then execute the script remotely against the particular computer(s):

```
@echo off
Echo This batch file will Force the Update Detection from the AU
client:
Echo 1. Stops the Automatic Updates Service (wuauserv)
Echo 2. Deletes the LastWaitTimeout registry key (if it exists)
```

```
    Echo 3. Deletes the DetectionStartTime registry key (if it
exists)
    Echo 4. Deletes the NextDetectionTime registry key (if it
exists)
    Echo 5. Restart the Automatic Updates Service (wuauserv)
    Echo 6. Force the detection
    Pause@echo on
    net stop wuauserv
    REG DELETE
"HKLM\Software\Microsoft\Windows\CurrentVersion\WindowsUpdate\Auto
Update" /v LastWaitTimeout /f
    REG DELETE
"HKLM\Software\Microsoft\Windows\CurrentVersion\WindowsUpdate\Auto
Update" /v DetectionStartTime /f
Reg Delete
"HKLM\Software\Microsoft\Windows\CurrentVersion\WindowsUpdate\Auto
Update" /v NextDetectionTime /f
    net start wuauserv
    wuauclt /detectnow
    @echo off
    Echo This AU client will now check for the Updates on the Local
WSUS Server.
Pause
```

SOME INDEPENDENT ADVICE

One of the challenges for environments with multiple downstream replica WSUS servers is to provide a consolidate report of update and computer status. Since each WSUS server has its own database, the needed data is distributed across the organization rather than stored in a single data source. Fortunately, Microsoft has provided a way to develop tools to retrieve and centralize the data. You can download a sample of such a tool from Microsoft's download site (*http://download.microsoft.com*). This tool uses the WSUS application programming interface (API) to demonstrate centralized monitoring and reporting for WSUS. It creates a single report of update and computer status from the WSUS servers in your WSUS environment. The sample package also contains sample source files to customize or extend the tool functionality of the tool to meet specific needs.

Summary

One of the biggest enhancements found in WSUS is the management capabilities. You can now efficiently and effectively manage software updates and computers, regardless of the size of your organization. The WSUS management capabilities consist of the following features:

- You can manage WSUS centrally with a single administrator or distribute management tasks to multiple administrators responsible for their own segment of the infrastructure.

- WSUS gives you better control over update approvals and the distribution of those updates through a new Web-based administration console, Active Directory GPOs or registry settings, and powerful command-line utilities and APIs.

- A new WSUS reporting feature in the Web-based administration console provides an interface where you can also check the status of the updates and your computers throughout your WSUS environment.

Solutions Fast Track

Centralized vs. Distributed Environments

☑ When designing your WSUS environment, you should consider your organization's administrative resources, connectivity, and Active Directory design. You should consider corporate culture and political factors as well.

☑ The centralized management model provides the highest level of configuration control while ensuring consistency through your organization. In a WSUS replica group, the subordinate replica-mode servers receive most of their configuration settings from the administration, or master, server.

☑ The distributed management model allows you to establish more than one administration server with or without subordinate replicas. This model gives different areas independent control over their portion of the infrastructure. In return, it has higher administration requirements as the WSUS servers are autonomously administered.

☑ In some cases, it is not possible to purely manage your WSUS environment centrally or in a distributed fashion. A hybrid solution can be developed that will satisfy all the needs of your organization and combine the best of both management models.

Synchronization

☑ Synchronizing the metadata and update files for available software updates is managed separately from WSUS configuration.

☑ Each WSUS server must be configured with an update source from where it synchronizes software updates. At least one of these servers must retrieve software updates directly from Microsoft Update.

☑ When chaining WSUS servers, the first server in the chain is the definitive reference for which updates are available for your organization. If a specific update is not available on the first WSUS server in the chain, it will not be available to other downstream WSUS servers, regardless of approval status.

☑ When deciding on a synchronization method, consider the impact the method has to the WSUS servers and client computers. Factors such as network bandwidth and lag-time to distribute updates fully vary between each method.

☑ WSUS provides an mechanism to export software updates that can be imported onto WSUS server located on disconnected networks. This method has the risk of having the longest lag-time when distributing updates. This must be managed carefully to ensure that update files are available to client computers when updates are approved.

Managing Computer Groups

☑ Server-side targeting gives you very granular control over individual computers. This is an ideal targeting method for small organizations with a small number of clients to update. In larger environments, server-side targeting becomes very difficult to manage.

☑ Client-side targeting is better suited to large environments where individual group assignment is not feasible. Clients can be assigned to the appropriate WSUS server and computer group through GPOs or registry settings.

☑ Only client-side targeting provides a way to automate the configuration of the Windows Update client configuration.

☑ When using GPOs, enter the Windows Update administrative template into the group policy editor before you can configure these settings.

Producing Reports

☑ Standard WSUS reports provide administrators insight into the organization's update and computer status.

☑ The data in the report is based on the status of the client computers when they last contacted their assigned WSUS server. In order to reflect the most up-to-date information in your reports, use the *wuauclt.exe* utility to force server contact.

☑ The system overview report is a great tool to document the configuration of your WSUS environment.

Frequently Asked Questions

The following Frequently Asked Questions, answered by the authors of this book, are designed to both measure your understanding of the concepts presented in this chapter and to assist you with real-life implementation of these concepts. To have your questions about this chapter answered by the author, browse to **www.syngress.com/solutions** and click on the **"Ask the Author"** form.

Q: Which management model is best for deploying WSUS to a single site?

A: For small and medium-sized organizations with only one site, you can effectively manage client computers with a single WSUS server. If you only deploy one server, there is no difference between deploying WSUS server in a centralized management model or a distributed management model.

Q: We have chosen to manage our WSUS client computers with GPOs. Where can I find the *wuau.adm* file that includes all the new WSUS options?

A: There are several places to find this file. It is available on every computer Windows XP running Service Pack 2 in the *windows\inf* folder. Additionally, you can find this file on the WSUS server itself. Browse to the *%ProgramFiles%\Update Services\Selfupdate\au\x86* folder and locate the *wucltui.cab* file under your language folder. In that cabinet file, you will find the updated *wuau.adm* file.

Q: I want to simplify my distributed environment by centrally managing my WSUS servers under a single administration server. Is this possible?

A: You cannot reconfigure a WSUS server as a replica-mode server after installation. If you want the server to be a replica, you must uninstall and reinstall WSUS. Make sure you select the **This server should inherit the settings from the following server** option on the Mirror Update Settings step of the setup wizard.

Q: Is the database on the "master" or upstream WSUS server meant to be the database for all downstream servers, or will a SQL Server database need to be set up individually for each downstream server?

A: Each WSUS server requires its own Microsoft SQL Desktop Edition (MSDE) or SQL Server database.

Q: Can I centrally manage WSUS servers that are on disconnected networks?

A: No. You can synchronize servers that are on disconnected networks using the two-step import and export process; however, this only moves metadata and update files from the export server to the disconnected import server. Computer groups and update approval status are not shared between the export and import servers. Consequently, you must create computer groups and approve synchronized updates independently on disconnected servers.

Q: Some of my replica servers do not have direct access to the Internet. Can I import metadata and update files from an export server?

A: No. You cannot import updates to servers that are being centrally managed. The replicas only synchronize computer groups and approvals with the administration server. You can also configure the synchronization options on the replica-mode servers to retrieve updates from the administration server, Microsoft Update, or some other source.

Q: If you have a group set up in WSUS as detect-only and you change the options to install, do the updates that are set as detect-only ever get installed after the change or do those updates need to be changed manually?

A: Yes, they do get installed after the change. This is only after Automatic Update Client completes the next detection cycle. The update detection interval can be configured for Automatic Update agents using the registry entry settings mentioned in this chapter.

Q: Our company just extended its operations to a country that runs Microsoft software in another language. I want to manage those computers with the same WSUS environment that is already deployed. What issues can arise if I change the language options on the administration server? How can I work around those issues?

A: If you change language options on a centrally managed server, you can create a situation where the number of updates approved on a parent upstream server does not match the number of approved updates on a replica server. Microsoft recommends that you manually synchronize them between the centrally managed WSUS server and its replica servers.

Q: Are there any issues with me allowing my WSUS environment to update software for another organization?

A: Yes. Although WSUS is a free offering from Microsoft, users must follow the guidelines and requirements outlined in the EULA. The EULA for WSUS prohibits an organization to manage updates for computers that are not under its complete control. In other words, you can only update computers that belong to your organization.

Chapter 10

Using WSUS on a Disconnected Network

Solutions in this chapter:

- **Disconnected Networks**
- **Configuring WSUS**

☑ **Summary**

☑ **Solutions Fast Track**

☑ **Frequently Asked Questions**

Introduction

By the end of this chapter, you will understand some disconnected network scenarios and learn how to address their individual concerns. This chapter walks you through the steps for exporting settings and data from a "connected" network, and then importing it into a "disconnected" network.

Disconnected Networks

A disconnected network is a set of computers that have been either physically or logically separated from the production environment. There are many reasons for using a disconnected network in a business enterprise (e.g., a government organization needs a disconnected network to separate certain systems from the general public in order to address government-wide security requirements, or test labs where IT departments need a disconnected network to ensure that data cannot cross between two networks except via removable data.

You may be asking yourself, "If a network is completely disconnected, why do I have to worry about updating machines on that network?" When a network is isolated, it can still be susceptible to viruses. Computers and media that are infected with a virus can still be easily introduced into an isolated network.

SOME INDEPENDENT ADVICE

There are many ways to isolate a network to the point where no removable media can be introduced into it. However, you still have to address things such as someone introducing a wireless access point into the network. By simply plugging in a $50.00 device from the local office supply store, your disconnected network is now accessible to the whole world. On the other hand, when securing a network you need to be careful not to secure it to the point that it becomes unusable. If you are interested in learning more about network security, obtain a copy of *Hack Proofing Your Network, Second Edition*, published by Syngress (ISBN 1928994709).

Sample Disconnected Networks

The following sections discuss three different disconnected network scenarios—remote office, a demilitarized zone (DMZ), and a lab environment.

Disconnected Remote Office

One common disconnected network is a remote office (see Figure 10.1). Some businesses must have a presence in remote locations of the world because they need to have a physical address in that location in order to do business (e.g., an insurance company needs to have an office on a tropical island in order to do business there); however, it may not be financially sensible to provide those users with Internet or wide area network (WAN) access back to the home office.

Figure 10.1 A Remote Office Disconnected from the Outside World

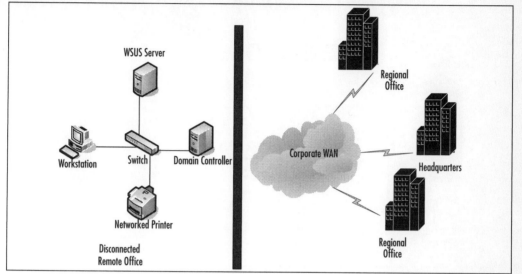

Although the network is completely isolated from the outside world, a traveling representative or executive could easily transport a virus into the network. Typically, these types of offices do not have a dedicated IT person. This is where a Windows Server Update Services (WSUS) server is extremely useful.

Disconnected DMZ

By definition, a DMZ is not disconnected; it is typically *connected* to the outside world, but isolated from the public by a firewall. However, when working with WSUS server and Active Directory, it is considered disconnected, because it typically is not part of the same Windows Active Directory Services (ADS) structure of the production network. In Figure 10.2, the DMZ allows only inbound requests to the Web servers. Consequently, the Web servers would not be able to use Windows Update services directly from Microsoft.

Because of this, WSUS servers residing in a DMZ must be treated as a WSUS server that lives in a remote office. You would still need to perform the same update and configuration process to keep the WSUS server up-to-date.

Figure 10.2 A DMZ Disconnected from the Production Network

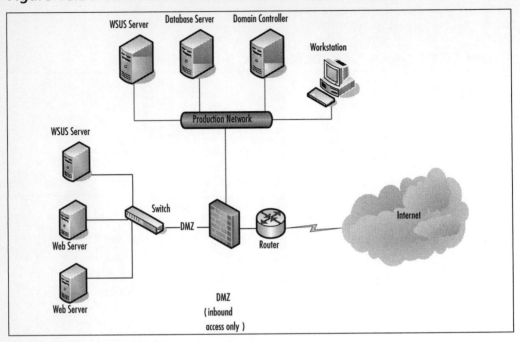

Disconnected Lab

A lab is another example of a common disconnected network (see Figure 10.3). Because a lab is typically used for testing new equipment or software, most administrators do not want anyone to be able to touch the production domain in any way. In many instances, they also do not want it to be accessible via the Internet. The extent to which a lab is disconnected depends on the business needs of the organization or to the IT security requirements.

Configuring WSUS

The previous section was intended to get you thinking about some of the places where you need to address servers and workstations in disconnected areas. This section discusses how to configure and update WSUS servers in those areas.

Microsoft has simplified the process of updating disconnected WSUS servers to three steps:

1. Match the advanced server options.
2. Copy the WSUS updates.
3. Copy the WSUS metadata.

Figure 10.3 A Lab Disconnected from the Outside World

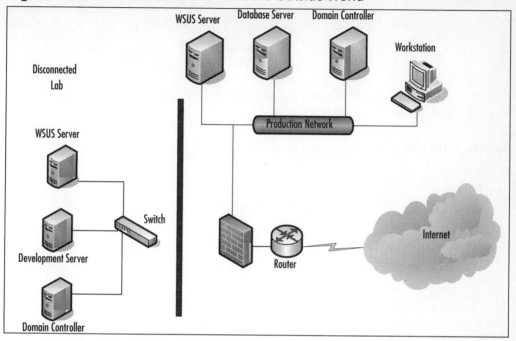

The first thing you need to do is configure the WSUS server. Once the server has been built and WSUS has been installed, check the Advanced Synchronization Options of the export server to make sure it matches the settings on the import server.

Setting the Advanced Synchronization Options

The Advanced Synchronization Options of a WSUS server cover two items:

- **Location of Update Files** Allows you to determine if updates will be downloaded and stored locally on the server, or if WSUS will redirect users to the Microsoft Update Web site.

- **Languages** Allows the administrator to specify which languages WSUS will download updates for.

As mentioned, the Advanced Synchronization Options must mirror each other exactly in order for the import on the disconnected server to work. To make sure that the Advanced Synchronization Options match on both servers:

1. From the WSUS Home page of the export server, click the **Options** button (see Figure 10.4).

Figure 10.4 The Options Button on the WSUS Home Page

2. When the Option window opens, click on the **Synchronization Options** button (see Figure 10.5).

Figure 10.5 The Synchronization Options Button

3. When the Synchronization Options window opens, scroll to the bottom and click the **Advanced** button under the section titled Update Files and Languages.

4. You may receive a warning about changing advanced settings. Read through the message and then click **OK.**

5. Open the same window on the Import (disconnected) server and verify that the settings in the Advanced Synchronization Options window match (see Figure 10.6).

Figure 10.6 The Advanced Synchronization Options Window

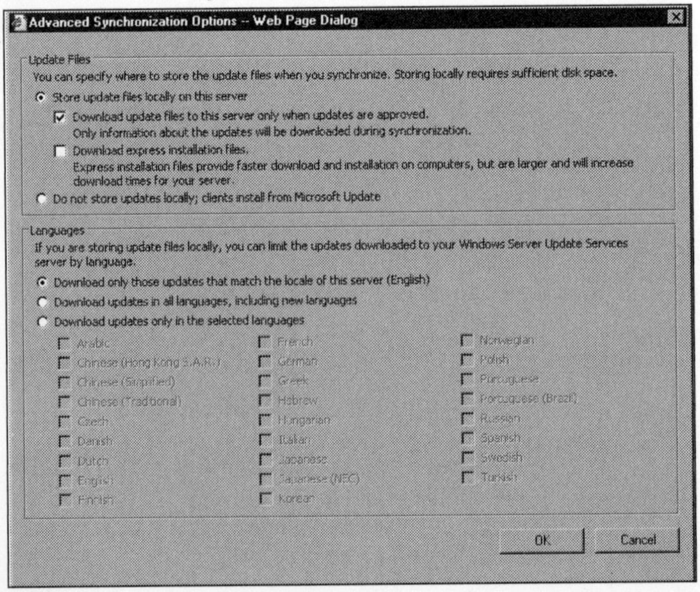

6.   Once you have verified the settings, click **OK**.

Copying Updates

Now you need to copy the updates that were previously downloaded on the export server to the import server. Basically, you need to perform a backup of the data that has been stored in the /*WSUSContent* directory. You may use any back-up software to perform this task; however, to stay Microsoft-centric, we use the native NTBackup software provided with Windows 2003:

1.   From the WSUS export server, click **Start** | **All Programs** | **Accessories** | **System Tools** | **Backup**.

2.   If the Backup or Restore Wizard opens, click **Advanced Mode** (see Figure 10.7).

Figure 10.7 The Backup or Restore Wizard

3.   When the backup utility opens, click on the **Backup** tab.

4.   Locate the *WSUSContent* and place a checkmark in the box next to the WSUSContent folder.

5.   In the Backup media or file name window, choose a local drive with sufficient space, and name your file *WSUSContent.bkf* (see Figure 10.8).

Figure 10.8 Selecting the WSUS Content and Setting the Backup File Name

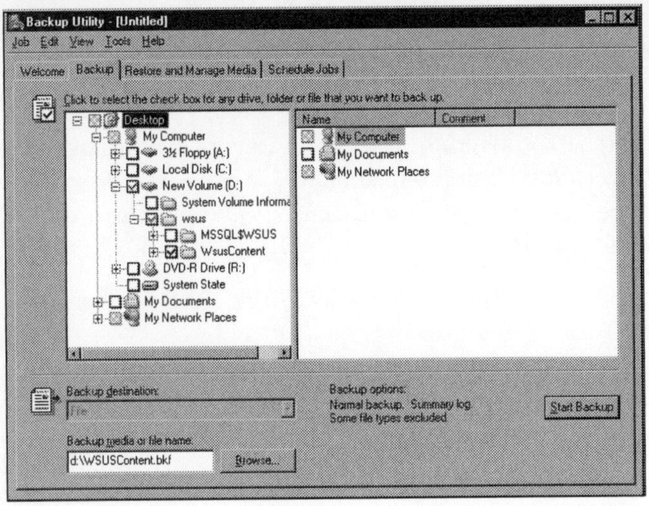

6. Click **Start Backup** to continue.

7. When the Backup Job Information window opens, enter a description for the backup job and click **Start Backup** (see Figure 10.9).

Figure 10.9 Starting the Backup Job

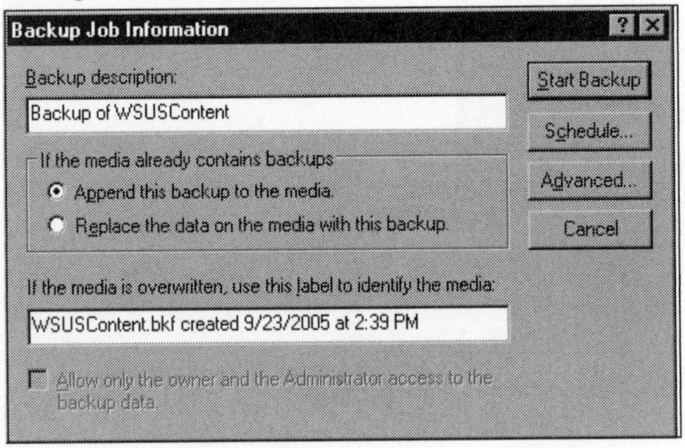

8. The backup job proceeds. Once it is complete, click **Close**.

Shortcuts…

Scheduling the Backup

If you want to save some time, effort, and hard drive space when creating the backup file, you should consider scheduling the backup job using the **Schedule** button (see Figure 10.9). You can also conserve hard drive space using incremental backups. This way, when you re-run the backup job at a later date, the only thing you will be backing up is new content.

Now you need to find a way to move WSUSContent to the other server. You can use any type of media, as long as the import server can read it—for example, CD-RW (if the file is small enough), a DVD-RW, a Universal Serial Bus (USB) drive, or several floppy disks.

Once the media has been delivered to the location where the disconnected server is, perform the following steps:

1. Copy the *.bkf* file from the removable media to a local hard drive.

2. From the WSUS export server, click **Start | All Programs | Accessories | System Tools | Backup**.

3. If the Backup or Restore Wizard opens, click **Advanced Mode**.

4. Click the **Restore and Manage Media** window.

5. Click on **Tools | Catalog** a backup file.

6. Enter the location of the backup file in the **Open:** box (see Figure 10.10) and click **OK**. The backup file will be cataloged and available for restore.

Figure 10.10 Cataloging the Backup File

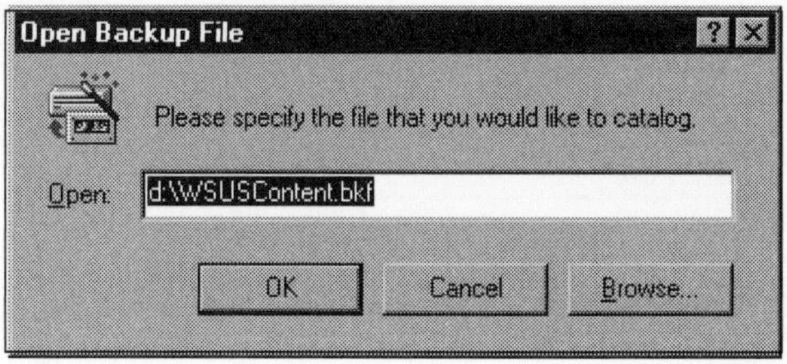

7. Select the backup file by highlighting it.

8. Under Restore files to:, select **Alternate Location** from the drop-down menu.

9. Under Alternate location, browse to the folder that holds *WSUSContent* on the import location (see Figure 10.11).

Figure 10.11 The Restore and Manage Media Window

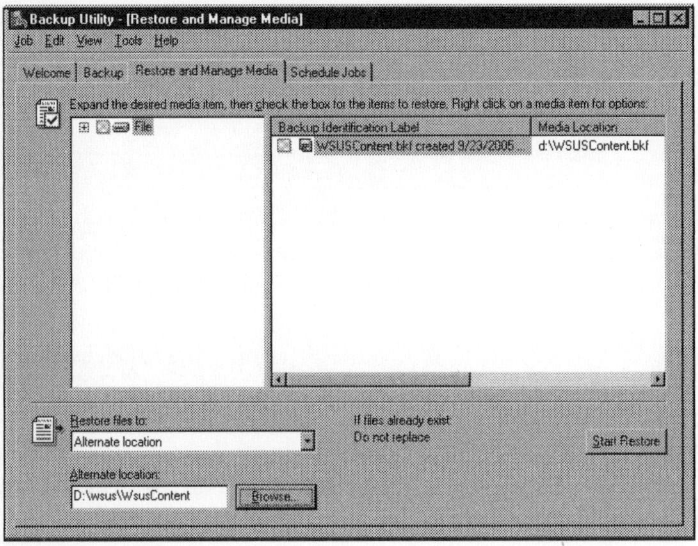

10. Click **Start Restore**.

11. Confirm the restore by clicking **OK** (see Figure 10.12).

Figure 10.12 Confirming the Restore

12. When the restore is complete, click **Close**. The restore of the WSUS content to the import server is complete.

Copying the WSUS Metadata

The last step in configuring a disconnected WSUS server is to copy the WSUS metadata from the export server to the import server. Unfortunately, there is neither a wizard nor a graphical user interface (GUI)-based means of exporting and importing the metadata. However, Microsoft has provided a command line utility for performing this task. By default, the utility is installed into the */Program Files/Update Services/Tools* directory. In the final section of this chapter, we walk through moving over the metadata.

1. From the export server, click **Start** | **Run** and type *cmd.exe.*

2. Change to the directories where the WSUS program files were copied. (In our example, this is located at *c://Program Files/Update Services/Tools.*)

3. Next, export the metadata using the following command: *wsusutil export wsusex.cab wsusex.log.* This specifies the cabinet file and log file that the WSUS utility will create for import onto the other server (see Figure 10.13). Press **Enter** to begin the export.

Figure 10.13 Exporting the WSUS Metadata

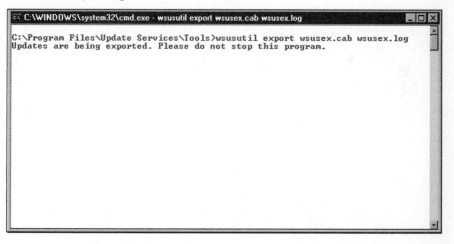

```
C:\WINDOWS\system32\cmd.exe - wsusutil export wsusex.cab wsusex.log

C:\Program Files\Update Services\Tools>wsusutil export wsusex.cab wsusex.log
Updates are being exported. Please do not stop this program.
```

4. Once the export is complete, copy the *.cab* and *.log* files to removable media.

Once the removable media arrives at the location where the import server exists, follow these steps:

1. From the export server, go to a command prompt. Click **Start** | **Run** and type *cmd.exe.*

2. Change to the directory where the WSUS program files were copied. (In our example, this is located at *c://Program Files/Update Services/Tools.*)

3. Next, import the metadata using the following command: *wsusutil import wsusex.cab wsusex.log*. This specifies the cabinet file and log file that the WSUS utility will import into the server (see Figure 10.14). Press **Enter** to begin the export. Do not be surprised if the import takes a considerable amount of time.

Figure 10.14 Importing the WSUS Metadata

4. Once the import is complete, open the WSUS Administration window to verify that the import was successful. To verify, check to see if any new updates exist.

Summary

Even if you never have to configure a disconnected WSUS server in your environment, you have still learned an easy way to prepare a "hot spare" WSUS server for your environment. Because WSUS does not necessarily need to run on a dedicated server, this is a great way to offer some redundancy into your environment. For those who may have to configure a disconnected WSUS server, the discussions in this chapter will help ease the pain of remotely administering a domain of Windows systems. Let's recap some of the finer points of a disconnected server configuration:

- Disconnected servers can take on a variety of flavors. Take a look at your environment to see if you can apply this method to your enterprise.

- Exporting and importing from one server to another is a fairly simple process.

- Plan your media appropriately when planning to move the data from one server to another.

Solutions Fast Track

Disconnected Networks

☑ A disconnected network has no means of receiving updates from any outside source.

☑ A disconnected network does not mean that a virus or security breach cannot be introduced.

☑ A WSUS server can exist in a disconnected network without the need for connectivity to the outside world.

Configuring WSUS

☑ Make sure your Advanced Synchronization Options match.

☑ Use a reliable backup software and removable media for transporting the WSUS data.

☑ The WSUS command line utility creates a .cab (cabinet) and .log file, which contain the necessary WSUS metadata.

Frequently Asked Questions

The following Frequently Asked Questions, answered by the authors of this book, are designed to both measure your understanding of the concepts presented in this chapter and to assist you with real-life implementation of these concepts. To have your questions about this chapter answered by the author, browse to **www.syngress.com/solutions** and click on the **"Ask the Author"** form.

Q: If I have a WSUS server in a DMZ that is connected to the Internet, why not just grant outbound requests through the firewall to download updates?

A: You could certainly do that, but you will need to check with your IT security officer to make sure that it does not breach any security requirements.

Q: I do not have any technical people in my remote office. Can I somehow schedule the imports?

A: Sure. You can use the Windows scheduler to schedule the restore and to run a Disk Operating System (DOS) script to import the metadata; however, someone will still need to be there to insert the media containing the update.

Q: My import seems to take excessively long. Why is that?

A: Microsoft states that it can take up to four hours to validate the data being imported.

Q: Speaking of the amount of data, it took me two DVD-RWs to save my WSUSContent. Why so much data?

A: Chances are, you are downloading updates in multiple languages. Consider removing any updates in languages you do not need.

Chapter 11

Troubleshooting WSUS

Solutions in this chapter:

- **Installation Issues**
- **Administration Issues**
- **WSUS Client Software Issues**

☑ **Summary**

☑ **Solutions Fast Track**

☑ **Frequently Asked Questions**

Introduction

To believe that WSUS will always deploy perfectly, operate flawlessly, and work forever is overly optimistic. For the most part, Windows Server Update Services (WSUS) is reliable; however, this chapter discusses several areas where problems and issues can arise and suggests different ways to resolve those problems.

Installation Issues

There are a few issues that you must address to ensure a trouble-free WSUS installation:

- Make sure that the server is enabled and running when you launch WSUS setup. If you choose to use Windows Microsoft SQL Server 2000 Desktop Engine (WMSDE) as the supporting database, and the server is not running on the computer where you intend to install WSUS, the WSUS installation fails. To install WMSDE, the server must be running.

- Make sure you have met all of the installation requirements for the computer on which you are installing WSUS. It should have a relatively beefy central processing unit (CPU), a fast network connection with plenty of available memory, and so on.

- Make sure you are running the latest, updated versions of Windows 2000 Server or Windows Server 2003, and that you have enough free disk space on the partition or drive on which you would like to install WSUS.

If you are upgrading to a newer release of WSUS, take precautions against an upgrade failure during the actual setup process by backing up your existing configuration before starting. There are some weaker points to the process, particularly the Microsoft SQL Desktop Edition (MSDE) installation and *asp.net* setups, and if an error crops up during one of those stages, it is possible that you could lose the configurations and settings you painstakingly created. (See Chapter 6 for information on backing up your WSUS configuration.)

There is also extra work required if you want to uninstall WSUS from a machine that used a Structured Query Language (SQL) server as the supporting database. WSUS Setup creates local SQL Server accounts—the Network Service and *asp.net* accounts—that are not deleted by the WSUS uninstall component. This is done to make sure that other applications or databases that might be using these accounts do not fail. If you know that another application is not using those accounts, you can manually remove them from the SQL Server machine.

BEST PRACTICES ACCORDING TO MICROSOFT

- Always back up your existing configurations before doing anything.
- If you are deploying an enterprise-class WSUS configuration, seriously consider using SQL Server over MSDE.

Administration Issues

During the day-to-day operation of the server end of your WSUS deployment, you may run into issues with synchronization, console access, approving updates, and update storage. The hints, tips, and suggestions in this section will help you troubleshoot any problems that arise.

Synchronization

If you are having problems with the synchronization of updates, look at the some of the following rough patches for some assistance:

- Check proxy server settings from the WSUS console. If your proxy server supports authentication, make sure you have the correct user name, password, and domain. Also be aware that by using basic authentication, you are sending your credential information in plaintext over the wire.

- Verify the name of the upstream WSUS server. This must be spelled exactly. If you suspect other communication or name resolution problems, try pinging the upstream server from the downstream WSUS server that is having the problems. Just make sure when pinging that you are using the same naming convention used in the WSUS console.

- Check the update storage options you have configured. If you are using a chain of WSUS servers together in a hierarchy, the entire hierarchy must use the same update storage option; otherwise, the synchronizations fail. Consequently, if the upstream server stores content locally, each of the downstream WSUS servers must store content locally as well. Make sure that each WSUS server in the chain uses the same option for update storage.

- Verify permissions on the update storage directory. Check to see that the folder where you download update files has "Read" permissions for NETWORK SERVICE and for Authenticated Users, whether or not the server you download the update files to is an upstream or downstream machine. The directory is c:\Update Services\UScontent. (See Figure 11.1)

Figure 11.1 Verifying Permissions

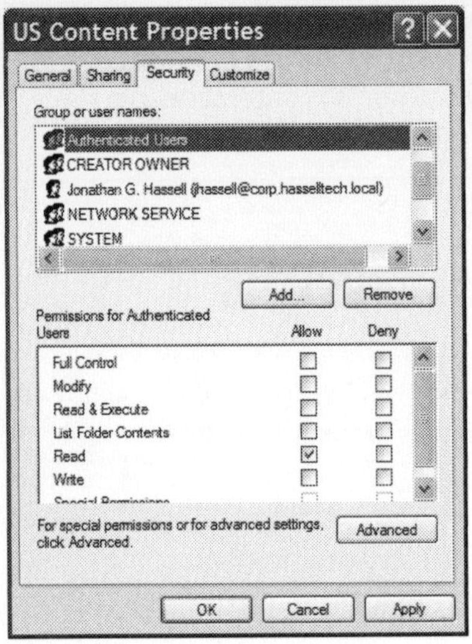

- Make sure the upstream WSUS server actually has updates available. There are a couple of scenarios where there might be a mismatch in update availability. In the first scenario, an upstream server is reinstalled; thus, the list of classifications and updates that the administrator selects changes. A future synchronization will fail when a downstream server asks for updates that do not exist on the upstream server. In the second scenario, you might configure a downstream server to retrieve updates from a different upstream server with another set of products and classifications selected. Either of these scenarios would result in mismatched update numbers. There are a few ways to fix this: (1.) Specify the missing updates on the upstream server and then synchronize from the update source; (2.) make sure you cancel the updates that are not on the upstream server and decline the old updates on the downstream server; or (3.) if the missing updates are available on the upstream server, then the error is transient, and things will eventually fix themselves.

- Try restarting the Background Intelligent Transfer Service (BITS) service. You can do this from the Services Microsoft Management Console (MMC) under Administrative Tools in the Start menu (see Figure 11.2).

Figure 11.2 Restarting BITS

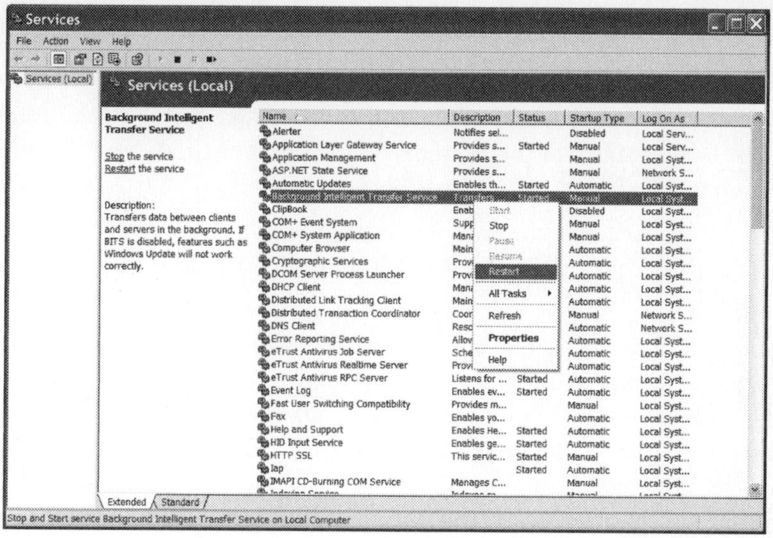

- Try restarting the WSUS service. Again, this can be done from the Services MMC console under Administrative Tools in the Start menu. Try to synchronize again.

- Make sure your environment supports Hypertext Transfer Protocol (HTTP) v1.1. If you are receiving errors regarding the Range protocol being unsupported, you must change a setting from the command line. Stop the WSUS service and issue the following command: **"%programfiles%\Update Services\tools\osql\osql.exe" -S** *SQL_InstanceName* **-E -b -n –Q "USE SUSDB update tbConfigurationC set BitsDownloadPriorityForeground=1".** Replace the *SQL_instanceName* as appropriate. Then, restart the WSUS service and perform the synchronization again.

Some Independent Advice

We have found that a lot of WSUS problems are solved by the timeless Windows fix: *reboot*. If you do not want to take down the whole machine, just restart the BITS service and the WSUS service and try again.

Console Access Issues

If you are getting errors or otherwise having trouble opening or accessing the WSUS console, consider the following scenarios:

- Make sure the appropriate users have been granted access to the console. Users must be a member of the Administrators group or the WSUS Administrators group on the server on which WSUS is installed.

- Do not try to access the console via an Internet Protocol (IP) address when you are working with a proxy server. Instead, use a domain name to access the console.

- You encounter a timeout message when trying to retrieve the console. Timeout messages are typical indicators of a busy CPU on the WSUS server. It is probably close to, if not directly at, maximum utilization, which makes accessing the database time out. A quick fix is to make sure that antivirus software is not installed on the WSUS server, because it can overload the CPU during synchronization. If you want antivirus software on that server, configure the antivirus software to ignore the areas where WSUS content is stored.

- You cannot access the console on a Windows 2000 Server domain controller. This is probably because the IWAM account cannot read the assembly directory for support of *asp.net* functions and operations. Granting read access for the IWAM account to *%windir%\assembly* should solve the problem (see Figure 11.3).

Figure 11.3 Granting Permissions for an IWAM Account

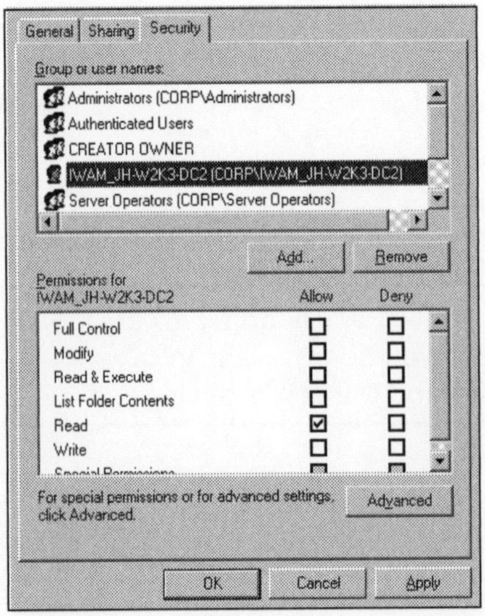

- After promoting the WSUS server machine to a domain controller, you are having trouble accessing the console. If Internet Information Server (IIS) 6.0 and *asp.net* are installed on the server before the server is promoted to a DC, the Network Service group does not have sufficient permissions to access the temporary *asp.net* files folder. You can either make sure that you promote the WSUS server to a domain controller before you install IIS 6.0 and *asp.net*, or manually grant the appropriate permissions for the Network Service group by issuing the following command from the command line: *c:\windows\microsoft .net\framework\v1.1.4322\aspnet_regiis −i.*

SOME INDEPENDENT ADVICE

Deploy WSUS on a freshly installed machine and, if at all possible, avoid using a domain controller as your WSUS server, which adds a layer of complexity that sometimes introduces problems.

Update Approvals

Are some of your approvals going awry? The following is a list of places you can look for hints on how to fix those problems.

- Give your approvals up to one minute to take effect. According to Microsoft, "if you approve an update on the WSUS console and there are client computers running detection at that exact moment, those computers might not get the approved update until they go through another detection cycle. The WSUS server requires approximately one minute before offering newly approved updates to client computers." Do not panic if things do not happen instantaneously.

- If you are using IIS Lockdown, make sure to allow *.exe* files to come through; otherwise, you will lose most of your updates. To enable *.exe* files to be passed, open the *urlscan.ini* file and remove *.exe* from the [*DenyExtensions*] section. While you have the file open, make sure that the GET, HEAD, POST, and OPTIONS entries appear in the [AllowVerbs] section.

- You might find that the number of approved updates on a parent upstream server does not match the number of approved updates on a replica server. This might happen if you reconfigured your language settings after your first synchronized the machines.

Storage

The main problem of update storage is when the updates listed within the WSUS console do not match those that are actually contained within the update storage folder on the local machine. If updates are stored on a disk separate from the WSUS application itself, and you replace the disk with a blank disk (because of a failure or upgrade or similar circumstances), the WSUS application still shows all of the updates as downloaded.

This is fairly easy to fix; just issue *wsusutil.exe* reset from the command line. Be aware that this can make WSUS unresponsive to client requests and console access for up to five minutes; therefore, do not panic if it looks like everything has frozen.

WSUS Client Software Issues

This section looks at some of the different problems you can have on the client, from self-updating and download problems, to client-side targeting issues where computers do not appear in the correct groups in the WSUS console.

Client Self-Update Problems

If you are having problems directly on the client with the Automatic Updates software, look at the following suggestions and procedures:

- Verify that your clients are pointed to the WSUS server. (See Chapter 7 for detailed instructions on configuring this option through the Registry or Group Policy.)

- Make sure the *selfupdate* tree exists on the WSUS server. This virtual directory holds the latest WSUS client. To ensure that the self-update tree is working properly, issue the following at the command prompt of the WSUS server: *cscript c:\program files\microsoft windows server update services\setup\InstallSelfupdateOnPort80.vbs.*

- Look at IIS logs 404 (file not found), 401/403 (authentication/access), and 500 (Internal server error) errors, which may give a clue about where things are going wrong. Then, look in the IIS documentation for an explanation of any problems found in the IIS logs.

- Make sure that Windows SharePoint Services (WSS) and WSUS do not collide. WSS likes to use port 80 whenever it is the first Web application installed on a newly minted IIS machine. You may need to exclude certain requests from automatically being absorbed by the Internet Server Application Programming Interface (ISAPI) dynamic link library (DLL) that WSS uses. To do so:

1. Open the WSS Central Administration site.

2. Click **Virtual Server Configuration** and then click **Configure Virtual Server Settings**.

3. Click **Default Web Site ? Virtual Server Management** and then click **Define managed paths**.

4. In the Add a new path box, set the type to excluded path. Under Path, type the following: **/iuident.cab /wutrack.bin /clientwebservice /Selfupdate**.

- Ensure that the client computers have good, reliable network access. Try browsing to a Web page hosted on the same server as the WSUS software. Make sure the client has a valid IP address and can browse outside of the network Try performing a traceroute to see if you have a malfunctioning router along the path those packets would travel to and from the WSUS server.

Client-Side Targeting Issues

You might find that there are some difficulties when using client-side targeting to assign computers to groups for use with WSUS. Here are some points to check if you are having trouble in this area:

- Make sure that your clients are configured to use client-side targeting (see Figure 11.4). (See Chapter 5 for how to configure the console for such activity.)

Figure 11.4 Configuring Clients for Client-Side Targeting

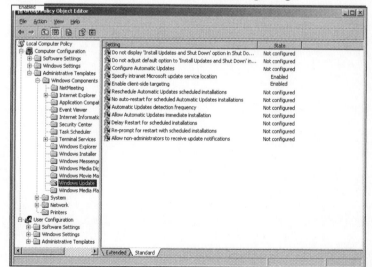

- Check to ensure that the target group names on the client match the target group names on the server. Look at the Group Policy Object (GPO) or the registry setting where you enabled client-side targeting and verify that there are no differences between the name of the computer group used in Group Policy and the name of the group used on the server. WSUS loads the computer into the Unassigned Computers group if it cannot find a matching server-side group.

- Give changes at least one hour to take effect. When you make a change to group membership using client-side targeting and the machine has already pinged the WSUS server for the first time, it takes about an hour for the server to change the computer's group membership, because WSUS uses cookies that are set to expire after 60 minutes to manage client-side group membership.

Summary

You have deployed WSUS in this book, but it is also important to have information at hand in case something goes wrong. This chapter examined several areas where problems and issues can creep in (including trouble spots on both the client and the server) and discussed solutions for problems with synchronization, approvals, console access, storage, self-updating, and targeting.

Solutions Fast Track

Installation Issues

- ☑ Back up your current configuration before upgrading to a future release of WSUS in case something goes awry.

- ☑ Make sure the Server is enabled and running when you launch WSUS setup.

- ☑ Ensure all of WSUS' hardware requirements and software prerequisites are met.

Administration Issues

- ☑ If you are having problems with synchronization, check the proxy server issues and the permissions on the update storage directory, and try restarting both the BITS and core WSUS services.

- ☑ If you are having console access issues, make sure all users that need access to the console are members of the Administrators or WSUS Administrators groups.

- ☑ If you are having trouble with update approvals, try re-synchronizing your updates, give changes an hour or so to take effect, and make sure you have not locked Internet Explorer too tightly with URLScan.

WSUS Client Software Issues

- ☑ If your clients are not automatically self-updating to the latest software, make sure they are pointed to the WSUS server, have no network connectivity problems, and are correctly configured to use a proxy server.

- ☑ If client-side targeting does not seem to be working, make sure that the group names on the clients match the group names configured in the WSUS console. Give changes about an hour to take effect.

Frequently Asked Questions

The following Frequently Asked Questions, answered by the authors of this book, are designed to both measure your understanding of the concepts presented in this chapter and to assist you with real-life implementation of these concepts. To have your questions about this chapter answered by the author, browse to **www.syngress.com/solutions** and click on the **"Ask the Author"** form.

Q: What happens if client computers are pointed to a SUS server instead of a WSUS server?

A: If you have the Automatic Updates client installed but the client computer is pointed to a SUS server, the Automatic Updates software reverts to "legacy" mode. When you point Automatic Updates away from the SUS server, it automatically comes out of legacy mode and the new client user interface appears.

Q: Is there any way I can make sure that the latest bits for the Automatic Updates client software actually exist on my WSUS server?

A: Yes. In a browser, head to http://WSUSServerName/iuident.cab and see if you are asked to download something. If you are, cancel out—it is not possible to actually do anything with that file, but it does show what AU uses for self-updating.

Q: What are some quick error entries to look for in the Event Log?

A: The most common errors to look for include 404 (file not found), 401/403 (authentication/access), and 500 (Internal server error) errors.

Q: Why am I getting timeout messages when I try to load the WSUS console?

A: This is usually caused by AV software running on the WSUS server. Configure the antivirus software to ignore where WSUS content is store, or do not install it on the server in the first place.

Index

A

D

Syngress: *The Definition of a Serious Security Library*

Syn·gress (sin-gres): *noun, sing.* Freedom from risk or danger; safety. See *security*.